James Leslie Mitchell

First published in Great Britain, 2003
by the Association for Scottish Literary Studies
Department of Scottish History
9 University Gardens
University of Glasgow
Glasgow G12 8QH

British Library Cataloguing in Publication Data
A CIP record for this book is available from the
British Library

ISBN 0 948877 54 5

The Association for Scottish Literary Studies acknowledges
the support of the Scottish Arts Council towards the
publication of this book.

Typeset by Roger Booth Associates, Hassocks, West Sussex
Printed by Ritchie (UK) Ltd, Kilmarnock

A FLAME IN THE MEARNS

LEWIS GRASSIC GIBBON
A CENTENARY CELEBRATION

Edited by

Margery Palmer McCulloch
and
Sarah M. Dunnigan

This man set the flame
of his native genius
under the cumbering whin
of the untilled field;
Lit a fire in the Mearns
to illumine Scotland,
clearing the sullen soil
for a richer yield.

Arbuthnott Churchyard,
23rd February 1935
Helen Cruickshank

Association for Scottish Literary Studies
Occasional Papers: Number 13

THE ASSOCIATION FOR SCOTTISH LITERARY STUDIES aims to promote the study, teaching and writing of Scottish literature, and to further the study of the languages of Scotland.

To these ends, the ASLS publishes works of Scottish literature; literary criticism and in-depth reviews of Scottish books in *Scottish Studies Review*; short articles, features and news in *ScotLit*; and scholarly studies of language in *Scottish Language*. It also publishes *New Writing Scotland*, an annual anthology of new poetry, drama and short fiction, in Scots, English and Gaelic. ASLS has also prepared a range of teaching materials covering Scottish language and literature for use in schools.

All the above publications are available as a single 'package', in return for an annual subscription. Enquiries should be sent to:

ASLS
Department of Scottish History
9 University Gardens
University of Glasgow
Glasgow G12 8QH.

Telephone/fax: +44 (0)141 330 5309
e-mail: office@asls.org.uk
or visit our website at **www.asls.org.uk**

Contents

Acknowledgements

The editors would like to thank Rhea Martin for permission to quote from the works of Lewis Grassic Gibbon (J. Leslie Mitchell) and to reproduce the photographs in the collection. Acknowledgement is also made to the Estate of Helen Cruickshank for the quotation from 'Spring in the Mearns' from the collection *Sea Buckthorn*. We are very much indebted to Isabella Williamson and the Grassic Gibbon Centre at Arbuthnott, both for the financial help the Centre has given towards the collection and for the advice and help Isabella Williamson has personally given us. Duncan Jones of the Association for Scottish Literary Studies has assisted us with good advice through his understanding of the publishing process, and has sorted out many problems which seemed insuperable. The project itself would not have been possible without the enthusiasm of David Hewitt and his colleagues at the University of Aberdeen who undertook the task of organising the Centenary Conference in Aberdeen in the summer of 2001. This collection of essays has flowed from that beginning. Finally, we would like to thank all the present contributors and all those enthusiastic readers and writers in the past who have kept alive the life and work of Lewis Grassic Gibbon.

Abbreviations and Frequently Cited Sources

Since frequent reference is made in the following essays to the books of *A Scots Quair* trilogy: *Sunset Song* (1932); *Cloud Howe* (1933) and *Grey Granite* (1934), for convenience we have used the Canongate Classics edition of the trilogy (1995), edited and introduced by Tom Crawford, as our source for quotations. Page numbers are given in the text, preceded by the relevant title abbreviation. Similarly, quotations from Gibbon's essays in *Scottish Scene or the Intelligent Man's Guide to Albyn*, the book published jointly with Hugh MacDiarmid in 1934, are for convenience of access referenced in the text from *Smeddum: A Lewis Grassic Gibbon Anthology*, edited by Valentina Bold and published in the Canongate Classics series in 2001. Sources of quotations from other texts are as stated in the individual essays.

Abbreviations

CH   *Cloud Howe*

GG   *Grey Granite*

IS   *Image and Superscription*

Sm   *Smeddum: A Grassic Gibbon Anthology*

Sp   *Spartacus*

SR   *Stained Radiance*

SS   *Sunset Song*

Preface

Duncan McLean has an interesting comment on the work of Lewis Grassic Gibbon: it depicted 'a place I knew', whereas Kelman depicted 'the place I lived in right now'[1]. The comment highlights some of the strengths of Lewis Grassic Gibbon (James Leslie Mitchell [1901-35]) and also some of the reasons why it has taken several decades since his sudden death for his work to receive the kind of critical attention it obviously deserves. Shortly after McLean's words were published, national newspapers carried the results of reader polls nominating the authors most popular in Scotland, and Lewis Grassic Gibbon's name ran like a refrain through the replies. More remarkably, bookshops carry his work which sells well, and he is now read far beyond the ranks of the enthusiasts (who have always been to the fore since its first publication) and the school children who in the 1970s and 1980s were often enthusiastic, but sometimes unwilling, consumers, particularly of *Sunset Song*.

This is the first important point which any assessment or re-assessment faces. For *Sunset Song* is easily the author's most popular work, to the extent that its long shadow has tended to obscure its status as the first part of a trilogy. The author knew that its popularity would outstrip that of *Cloud Howe*; indeed he predicted that readers would not like the ending of *Grey Granite*; and publication of the trilogy in single volumes amply confirmed that the first part outsold the others by a wide margin. Happily, most people now buy the trilogy complete, and it is up to the author to carry the readers beyond the war memorial and the lament of the pipes in Kinraddie to face up to the changing Scotland which was his subject in the remainder of the trilogy. For taking Gibbon seriously as a serious author involves taking his social criticism seriously;[2] and now that his essays and short stories are widely available – in *The Speak of the Mearns* and in the recent *Smeddum* anthology – it is possible to pinpoint the criticisms being developed in *Cloud Howe* and *Grey Granite*: the imposition of factory-style labour on a working class more accustomed to the rhythms of rural life, the degradation of the living conditions in town and city, the implacable financial pressure of an international depression which bore hard on Scotland in the 1930s and impoverished whole cities the size of Aberdeen and Glasgow. Gibbon's essays are as angry as the essays MacDiarmid contributed to *Scottish Scene* (1934)[3], which they published together, but they are all the more effective for their development in fiction, particularly in the second half of *Grey Granite* where memories of Aberdeen – admittedly over a decade out of date – allowed Gibbon to bring to life a stratum of Scottish existence which had had scant attention in popular fiction. Significantly, the work 'stuck' on him in the South: he had to come to Scotland, indeed to his birthplace at Echt, to find the words to finish *Grey Granite*, not with any ringing declaration or call to arms, but with an enigma which cruelly anticipated his disappearance from the scene shortly after and before he could live to see the rise of fascism, the prospect of which already alarmed him in the early 1930s.

A second reason for Gibbon's rise in critical esteem lies in the recognition he now has for serious and important experiments in language – again, experiments which can be followed easily now that 'Literary Lights' and his other essays are readily available. For Gibbon's literary style, less formally challenging than the Synthetic Scots formulations of MacDiarmid's lyrics, less daunting than many of the modern phonetic spellings of urban or rural Scots in poetry and prose, lends itself to ready comprehension; or if not complete comprehension, to sufficient comprehension to enable his fiction to be appreciated without interference. Amply confirmed in a variety of settings – schoolroom, university lecture hall, television and radio serialisation, Prime Productions' successful tours – Grassic Gibbon's Scots conveys its language through phonetic tricks (including the printing of a similar word in English) and through masterful command of cadence and vocabulary, trying 'to mould the English language into the rhythms and cadences of Scots spoken speech, and to inject into the English vocabulary such minimum number of words from Braid Scots as that remodelling requires', as he describes it in 'Literary Lights'. The technique works: it is also one, it has been suggested, that he used to familiarise the reader with the rhythms and cadences of spoken Latin and other tongues in his non-Scottish fiction, the demotic English-Greek of the Cairo novels, the Latin-moulded sentences of the English commentary in *Spartacus*.[4]

Mention of *Spartacus* raises the third, perhaps the most spectacular reason for Gibbon's new critical visibility: his work's availability in modern reprints, a process begun in the 1960s with inexpensive editions of *A Scots Quair* and unevenly pursued since by Jarrolds (later Hutchinson) with editions of the *Quair* and a collection called *A Scots Hairst* and a regrettably short-lived *Spartacus*. Pan, Penguin and Longman at various times reprinted the *Quair* or single novels from it, and there were brief reprints of some of the other fiction, notably a full edition of *Spartacus* from the Association for Scottish Literary Studies. *Scottish Scene* was available for a time in a library reprint from Portway and there have been translations of some of the novels[5].

Slowly, the materials for studying Gibbon have been gathering. The National Library of Scotland has an impressive collection, largely the gift of Gibbon's family and now available to interested scholars who have in consequence access to the author's extraordinary correspondence.[6] Edinburgh University Library has the author's private collection of books, save a few still in family hands; other libraries (some in far-flung places) have single letters, and again some remain in private hands. Three major impulses to study have come to fruition. Firstly, the Canongate editions of the *Quair*, now happily available in one volume to encourage people to take the whole trilogy seriously, are in print with Tom Crawford's excellent introductions. With *Smeddum: A Lewis Grassic Gibbon Anthology*, Canongate added Valentina Bold's reprint of much of the difficult-to-find early and minor work, the short stories, and many essays. Secondly, the Grassic Gibbon Centre in Arbuthnott has opened and has grown steadily, with exhibition space, archives, photographic archives, a programme of publication, and a steady outreach to the communities and above all the schools. *Sunset Song* has been memorably performed by Prime Productions in the Centre.[7] And thirdly, Polygon Books launched a magnificent enterprise to bring back into print the whole range of Grassic Gibbon's hectic output during his writing years, in paperback and priced for general reader use, student use and school use. With the sale of Polygon Books to Birlinn Books, the series is to be continued and several of the volumes have sold well enough already to merit reprinting.

Duncan McLean's comment about Grassic Gibbon's novels being about places we know is an interesting one. One of Gibbon's achievements was to transform Scotland into a place 'we' do know – from first hand or not, present or past. Gibbon's extraordinary sales overseas (including the USA, a market he attacked with great professionalism) illustrate the success of a technique which draws the reader imaginatively in to the remembered life of Arbuthnott: smells, sounds, festivals, sights, pains. Small wonder Chris Guthrie loved and hated it in a breath; small wonder that at her own wedding feast she should hear arguments about a dying Scots language, should sing songs about Flodden and the past – and that the author should try to persuade the readers that her generation were *the last of the Peasants, the last of the Old Scots Folk*. To have persuaded an enormous readership that they 'know' this Scotland is no mean achievement: to persuade them further that there is a new Scotland coming after, with new challenges and a new society arising from the collapse of a depression-haunted city is his major achievement in the *Quair*.

It is for this reason that in the new decade we need, and at last we are within reach of, the rest of his work, the science-fiction novellas, the English and Oriental short stories, the autobiographical novels in London and in Scotland, the non-fiction works about exploration and about the spread of the 'civilisation' that Gibbon so despised, and identified as the root of his generation's malaise. We need to measure Gibbon up against the challenges of the new critical approaches which have transformed Scottish literary writing: to use the insights of feminism, cultural study, political analysis, linguistic theory – to ask seriously where the limits of success are in his dazzling range of styles, how far the self-evident speed at which some of the work was composed compromises its quality. We need to give him credit for the magnificent creation of Chris, even as we need to acknowledge the irritation we feel with some of his other characters. We need to acknowledge the fascination he manages to convey, to share, for the Roman civilisation which spawned the Spartacist rebellion, for Spartacus himself. The years he spent in Egypt obviously gave him material for imaginatively splendid fiction. We need to measure it against modern ideas of post-modernity[8] and post-colonialism, and we need to look at the stylistics of much of his neglected 'English' fiction.

In short, there could hardly be a better time to ask why Gibbon writes of a place we know – and ask whether we still know it, or will continue to know it, as the pace of Gibbon criticism and republication mounts. This new collection of essays is an important step in that process.

Ian Campbell
University of Edinburgh

Notes

1. Quoted by Cristie L. March, *Rewriting Scotland* (Manchester: Manchester University Press, 2002), p. 40.
2. A minimal bibliography would include D. F. Young, *Beyond the Sunset* (Aberdeen: Impulse, 1973), W. K. Malcolm, *A Blasphemer and Reformer* (Aberdeen: Aberdeen University Press, 1984), and Uwe Zagratzki, *Libertäre und utopische Tendenzen im Erzählwerk James Leslie Mitchells (Lewis Grassic Gibbons)* (Frankfurt am Main: Peter Lang, 1991).
3. For more details of the relationship between the two contributors, see Ian Campbell, 'Gibbon and MacDiarmid at Play: The Evolution of *Scottish Scene*', *The Bibliotheck* 13:2 (1986), pp. 44-52.

4. See, for instance, Ian Campbell, 'The Grassic Gibbon Style' in *Studies in Scottish Fiction: Twentieth Century* (Scottish Studies no. 10), ed. by J. Schwend and H.W. Drescher (Frankfurt and Bern: Peter Lang, 1990), pp. 271-87; and the Polygon reprint of *Spartacus* (Edinburgh: Polygon, 2001), pp. xviii-xxi.

5. There is now an excellent collection of reprints in Arbuthnott.

6. See Ian Campbell, 'Lewis Grassic Gibbon Correspondence: A Background and Checklist', *The Bibliotheck* 12:2 (1984), pp. 46-57 and subsequent addenda and amplifications, notably by William K. Malcolm.

7. Grassic Gibbon Centre, Arbuthnott Parish Hall, Arbuthnott, Laurencekirk AB30 1YB 01561-361668 (Isabella Williamson, director) fax 01561 361742

8. Jeremy Idle has an important essay, introducing selected short stories set in Egypt and the East, in the 1994 Polygon version (not the earlier 1982 Ramsay Head version) of Lewis Grassic Gibbon, *The Speak of the Mearns: With Selected Short Stories and Essays* ed. by Ian Campbell and Jeremy Idle (Edinburgh: Polygon, 1994).

Introduction

Margery Palmer McCulloch and
Sarah M. Dunnigan

Leslie Mitchell and the Scottish Renaissance

From the perspective of the early twenty-first century, J. Leslie Mitchell –
or Lewis Grassic Gibbon, the pseudonym by which he is best known – is
regarded as a central figure in the interwar Scottish literary revival of the
previous century. What is less often remembered, or realised, is the
relatively late stage at which he came to be associated with the revival and
the age difference between him and the major writers who initiated it.

Like their non-Scottish contemporaries T. S. Eliot, D. H. Lawrence and
James Joyce, Hugh MacDiarmid, Edwin Muir and Neil Gunn were born
in the late 1880s or early 1890s, as were others such as James Bridie and
Compton Mackenzie. The influence of late Romanticism and the several
cultural and philosophical crises of the Victorian age are therefore to be
found in their work alongside the experimentation and uncertainties of
modernism. Leslie Mitchell, on the other hand, was born in 1901, and
while ten or twelve years may not seem sufficient to call a generational
difference, these years came at a critical point in regard to the experiences
which shaped him as adolescent and young adult.

MacDiarmid, for example, served in Salonika with the Royal Army
Medical Corps during World War One and for him, as for others of his
generation, the war was an event which shattered the continuity of past and
present. As Edwin Muir describes it in his *Autobiography*: 'The generation to
which I belong has survived an age, and the part of our life which is still
immobilized there is like a sentence broken off before it could be completed;
the future in which it would have written its last word was snatched away
and a raw new present abruptly substituted.'[1] Leslie Mitchell was a boy aged
thirteen at the outbreak of hostilities and the war therefore impacted upon
his life in a more everyday, localised way. Hypocrisy, jingoism, profiteering

and injustice are the indictments against the war found in his later fiction and essays, not the philosophical awareness of a cataclysmic break with the past given expression in much art of the modernist period.

In addition, the Russian Revolution of 1917 was an event of immediate, formative significance for Mitchell. In 1918, as a young newspaper reporter, he attended the foundation meeting of an Aberdeen Soviet, even becoming elected (temporarily) to the Soviet Council; and in 1919 he became involved with communist sympathisers in Glasgow. In contrast, while Marxism was to become a major theme for MacDiarmid in his poems to Lenin in the fashionably political thirties, in the years immediately following the end of World War One, it was the regeneration of Scotland and a revolution in Scottish literary culture that preoccupied him, not Marxist politics. And while the teenage Mitchell was becoming actively involved in left-wing politics in Glasgow in 1919, Edwin Muir was leaving that city for the literary metropolis of London after the success of his first book *We Moderns*.

One experience Mitchell did share with Muir and MacDiarmid was that of self-education. Both these older writers achieved their 'higher education' through the pages of the influential and Europe-oriented *New Age* periodical, edited by A.R. Orage, and both eventually became contributors themselves. For Mitchell, post-school education was achieved through travel abroad and voracious reading during his periods of service in the British forces. In Mitchell and MacDiarmid in particular, this self-education often produced an idiosyncratic mixture of influences and antagonisms in their writing, a disinclination to take account of opposing or preceding viewpoints. At its best, however, it produced a vitality of argument and the capacity to topple false idols from long-occupied pedestals. In the case of both writers, 'shouting too loudly' was a vigorous tool of regeneration.

A Scots Quair, written under the pen-name of Lewis Grassic Gibbon, is now in retrospect seen to be Mitchell's outstanding literary achievement, a significant contribution to British interwar literature as well as to the Scottish literary renaissance of the period. Yet at his untimely death in 1935 this was not so clear, especially, it would seem, to the author himself, whose plans for future writing involved the continuation of the Mitchell imprint. Nevertheless, his comments about the nature of Scottish writing in the essay 'Literary Lights' and the language and narrative experiments he conducted in *Sunset Song*, his Scottish short stories and the two later books of the *Scots Quair* trilogy, all demonstrate how acutely he must have thought about how to capture 'Scottishness' in literature; how to allow his home culture 'equality of dialogue', to borrow a phrase from the later, and related, James Kelman's narrative methodology.

One mystery which time has not satisfactorily uncovered in relation to his Scottish work, is what eventually led Mitchell to attempt both a Scottish subject and a relevant narrative form and so translate himself into Lewis Grassic Gibbon: a mystery which has interesting similarities with that behind C. M. Grieve's transformation of himself into Hugh MacDiarmid through the writing of 'The Watergaw' ten years previously, despite his simultaneous battle with the London Burns Club over its attempt to promote the Scots language. In his biography of Mitchell/Gibbon, Ian Munro comments that Mitchell knew MacDiarmid's 'remarkable Scottish poetic work, *A Drunk Man Looks at the Thistle*, [...] admired it greatly and had been enthusiastic about the early MacDiarmid lyrics long before he met the author'.[2] Munro gives no firm evidence to support these comments and it is therefore uncertain just when Mitchell became aware of MacDiarmid's work, although, being the omnivorous reader that he was and being knowledgeable about Scottish affairs, despite his exile abroad or in the south of England, it seems unlikely that he would not have heard of the cultural revolution being attempted north of the border. Isobel Murray in the present volume, and in previous essays on the *Quair*, suggests that Chris Guthrie's creator may well have owed a debt to female characterisations in fiction by Nan Shepherd and Willa Muir. A discovery of Leslie Mitchell's reading list would indeed be a prize! Without this, however, one can only speculate as to the extent of his knowledge of contemporary Scottish writers and their work before the publication of *Sunset Song* in 1932.

Mitchell himself said that he first met MacDiarmid in London 'when we tried to form a section of the Revolutionary Writers of the World: He had just finished writing the "Second Hymn to Lenin" [and] founding a new English weekly'.[3] This information would place the meeting most probably in 1932, before MacDiarmid's retreat to Scotland (and eventually Whalsay) in August of that year, and thus before the appearance of *Sunset Song* in the late summer. A closer relationship between the two writers was established in 1934, when Mitchell, now Gibbon, proposed that MacDiarmid should collaborate with him in the writing of *Scottish Scene.*

Although 'Lewis Grassic Gibbon' was therefore a late entrant to the Scottish literary revival, he was instantly welcomed by those already involved. As a reviewer, George Malcolm Thomson had read *Sunset Song* before its official publication date of 2 September 1932 and wrote to Helen Cruickshank on 24 August:

> If you have not already done so, get hold of a novel *Sunset Song* by L.G. Gibbon, whoever he or she may be. It seems to me the pioneer of

something new and very interesting in Scottish letters. Perhaps the first really Scottish novel.

Cruickshank herself wrote of her response:

> I was especially interested, because the novel was set in the Howe of the Mearns, where my paternal grandfather had been a land worker on just such a farm as Blawearie. Now, in 'Sunset Song' it seemed to me that the inarticulate land of my forefathers had at last found an authentic voice.[4]

Cruickshank's elderly but determined mother became a fan of the book also and instructed Helen to write to its author, giving an invitation to visit. A friendship developed and 'in the course of the next two and a half years, he stayed at my home on, I think, four occasions, usually on his way to or from the north. I visited his home in Welwyn just before his boy Daryll was born in 1934'.[5]

Other Scottish writers were equally quick to praise the book. Donald Carswell wrote from Hampstead:

> You have written a damn good book – the best Scotch book since Galt. I started on 'Sunset Song' with a violent prejudice. 'Oh, another of the bloody awful Scottish renascence abortions – frightfully stylised'. But I soon changed my tune. There's no doubt you have got the essential Scotland.[6]

Compton Mackenzie, reviewing it in the *Daily Mail*, called it 'the richest novel about Scottish life written for many years'.[7] Neil Gunn, who in 1926 had himself been praised by MacDiarmid as 'the only Scottish prose-writer of promise [...] something new, and big in Scottish literature', wrote in 1933 after the publication of *Cloud Howe*: 'I read *Cloud Howe* hardly hoping I may say, that the splendid levels of *Sunset Song* would be reached and maintained. [...] but sure and clear as ever you have once more come into your own realm and rule as a king.'[8]

In his turn, Mitchell, for a newcomer, showed a surprisingly wide awareness of contemporary Scottish writing in his 'Literary Lights' essay in *Scottish Scene* – what he described, according to Helen Cruickshank, as 'a perfect haggis of a book'.[9] The tone of the essay is ironical throughout, taking several swipes at writers from 'Scotshire' who claim to be making a *Scottish* renaissance through writing in *English*. Behind the playful mockery, however, there is a thorough awareness of a wide range of work by writers including Bridie, Mitchison, Gunn, Blake, Willa Muir, Catherine Carswell,

Buchan, Cronin, Linklater; and poets such as MacDiarmid and Lewis Spence ('the two solitary literary lights in modern Scots literature'). Of Muriel Stuart, an English poet whom MacDiarmid mistakenly claimed as one of the female flagships of his renaissance, Mitchell comments: 'she is as little Scots as Dante' (thus showing more acuity than the several critics and anthologists who have unquestioningly followed MacDiarmid's lead since the 1920s).[10] Mitchell's sure grasp of the range and nature of the new Scottish literary scene in this essay seems to me circumstantial evidence for his interest in and awareness of it in the years before *Sunset Song* made him part of the revival. To have read and digested such a range of work between 1932 and 1934, in addition to his own writing commitments as both Mitchell and Gibbon, does not seem a possible feat, even for such a reader and workaholic as Gibbon showed himself to be. Whatever his previous awareness might have been, however, once *Sunset Song* was in the public domain, he quickly became a central member of the literary revival, even if, like Edwin Muir, he was sceptical about a nationalist route to regeneration.

Mitchell's untimely death in February 1935 at the age of thirty-four was marked by a lamentation the scale of which patterned the outbreak of praise which had greeted his first Scottish novel. MacDiarmid wrote from Whalsay: 'We are extremely sorry and have been able to think of little else since. [...] Leslie's death is a serious blow to Scottish literature.' Neil Gunn, too, was one of many writers who wrote of both personal loss and loss to literature: 'I cannot tell you how deeply distressed I was at the sad news. [...] Of all our writers he is just the man we could least afford to lose.'[11] Helen Cruickshank tells how Nan Shepherd and Eric Linklater, fellow members of Scottish PEN, came down from Aberdeen to join her at the burial of his ashes in Arbuthnott churchyard:

> It was just such a day as Leslie described so well: a lovely day of sunshine and blue skies, with white cumulus clouds scudding over the Grampians, smoke blowing over the furrows from burning whins, and drifts of snow-drops blooming in the Churchyard by the side of Bervie water.[12]

The poem she wrote for him on that day (the last stanza of which we have quoted on our title page) focuses not on the sadness of his loss, but on what he achieved 'to illumine Scotland' in his short life.

Changing Critical Perspectives

Gibbon is a writer whose place within the Scottish literary canon and within the heart of 'the common [Scottish] reader' is secure. On World Book Day,

March 2003, *Sunset Song* was voted by readers of BBC Radio 4 as the book which most epitomised Scotland. And yet, as the bibliographical checklist of Gibbon's writing compiled by Hamish Whyte testifies, *Sunset Song*, and the *Quair* trilogy, is only one part of a prodigious output. It is an incomplete, and therefore imperfect, view of Gibbon which endures and which the present collection attempts to redress. This is the first volume of essays on Gibbon's work to be published; plans for a Festschrift were made immediately after Gibbon's death by Helen Cruickshank and others but were abandoned; as Ian Campbell notes, 'delay and recrimination and a curiously half-hearted commitment by the Scottish and English literati seems to have sunk the project without trace.'[13] The essays in this volume are testament to change and diversity within critical responses to James Leslie Mitchell/ Lewis Grassic Gibbon's work. Several of the contributors highlight overlooked continuities and contrasts between his non-fictional prose and the novels; and return our attention to the relatively neglected English novels such as *Spartacus* and *Image and Superscription*. And if Gibbon the fiction-writer and prose polemicist are already known, then Gibbon the poet is newly discovered in Valentina Bold's exploration of the poetry, first collected in her anthology, *Smeddum* (2001). Though many of these essays return to the *Quair* trilogy and the well-known short fiction, they do so by bringing fresh perspectives to enduring preoccupations. By introducing new critical or theoretical concerns to Gibbon's work, its contemporary significance is amply demonstrated.

And yet, with the exception of Peter Whitfield's *Grassic Gibbon and his World* (1994), there has not been a book-length study of Gibbon's writing since the fruitful critical period of the 1980s. On the surface, it might seem as though this most prolific, diverse, and iconoclastic of modern Scottish writers had fallen out of favour. It is ironic that Gibbon, who mistrusted and was suspicious of the Scottish propensity for historical and cultural 'icon-minting', as Gerard Carruthers puts it in his essay on Gibbon's ambiguous Enlightenment inheritance, has himself become a Scottish icon; but one, as Keith Dixon contends in his essay, which travesties rather than does justice to the political radicalism and uncompromising nature of Gibbon's political and artistic beliefs. For Dixon, the dubious 'canonisation' of Gibbon within the Scottish educational and critical establishment has led to 'the erasure of his politics'. Once the political radicalism is excised, then so too is the richness and difficulty of the range of his writings. Dixon blames the prevalence of what he calls 'nationalist and accommodative readings' imposed upon a writer who could be bitterly sceptical of 'small nation' nationalism. In Dixon's opinion, Scotland's contemporary 'cultural radicals' have no cause to feel estranged from Gibbon. This is illustrated by David Borthwick's essay which fosters dialogue between the politics and fictional practice of Gibbon and Irvine Welsh, and opens up a space which illuminates Gibbon's links with other writers such as James Kelman. Many of these essays, such as Carruthers' which examines the interesting and contradictory entanglement of Gibbon with eighteenth-century Scottish cultural and literary history, highlight the nature of the peculiar silences or elisions of Scottish criticism with respect to a writer so well known and yet still unknown.

Several essays attest a renewed interest in the artistic and ideological representation of women in Gibbon's work; from the redoubtable fierceness and enduring spirit of Meg Menzies in 'Smeddum' to the Magdalene of 'Forsaken'. From the etherealised female figures of the poetry to the suffering, pregnant Thea Mayven of *Stained Radiance*, Gibbon's female portraits are diverse and provocative. It is Chris Guthrie, of course, who has engendered most debate. Isobel Murray's essay, 'Gibbon's Chris: a celebration with some reservations', is a candid and witty look at a character who has inspired different emotions in both female and male readers. She points out that for some critics Chris appears as an 'authentic' and 'real' representation of womanhood. To others such 'veracity' is invalidated by the fact that she is the creation of a male author. 'Chris Caledonia' is also burdened by the weight of national and natural symbolism which Gibbon imposes on her. Murray compares this to the depictions of female subjectivity in the writings of Gibbon's female contemporaries such as Nan Shepherd and Willa Muir. She suggests that such women writers resist the voyeuristic objectification of Gibbon's Chris, persistently fixed by the narrative gaze when contemplating her own mirror-image: 'Below the tilt of her left breast was a dimple, she saw it and bent to look at it and the moonlight ran down her back, so queer the moonlight she felt the running of that beam along her back.'[14] Such eroticism, however, can be contrasted with the disturbingly violent, sometimes misogynistic portrayals of sexuality, and of female and male sexual desires elsewhere in his fiction; 'its cruelty and its shame', as Thea puts it in *Stained Radiance*,[15] renders it a destructive power. Yet, as Murray's essay concedes and others in this volume demonstrate, Gibbon's representation of female experience is complex. The Marxist, materialist analyses to which his fiction so obviously responds reveal how it portrays the social and political oppression of women; at the same time, his female protagonists rarely seem to discover the opportunity to resist or transform their position of social and cultural quiescence. Alison Lumsden's essay, 'Women's Time: reading the *Quair* as a feminist text', suggests an interesting new avenue of exploration by considering Chris's representation in the light of poststructuralist feminist theory. She reinterprets the nature of Chris's 'divided selves' in the context of Julia Kristeva's theories of subjectivity. The fluidity of Chris's identities throughout the *Quair* can be conceived as a modernist and feminist illustration of Kristeva's 'subject-in-process', a subversion of traditional notions of the autonomous unified (masculine) subject. The persistent imaginative desire of Gibbon and his protagonist to 'live existence all time in eternity' as he put it in *Scottish Scene* (*Sm*, 89), mirrored in the *Quair*'s litany that 'nothing endures', is compared by Lumsden to the 'cyclical' and 'monumental' nature of 'women's time', opposed to the onward, linear processes of history. For Lumsden, this sheds new light on the relationships of Gibbon's female characters to politics, religion and history. Chris's enigmatic fate at the Quair's end, 'sitting here quiet' and contemplating that 'Change whose face she'd once feared to see',[16] acquires new resonances.

The nature of Gibbon's political passions are explored in essays by Bill Malcolm, Keith Dixon, and David Borthwick. Gibbon's credo for a revolutionary socialism was fiercely argued in *Scottish Scene* and, as Dixon rightly observes, his writing is sometimes imbued with an 'apocalyptic tone'. The denunciations of obscene poverty in the 'Glasgow' essay, and elegies for the successive decay and decline of 'civilisation', embodied in the Diffusionist ideas for which Gibbon is well-known, both arise out of what William Malcolm eloquently terms Gibbon's 'emotional humanism' in his 'Shouting Too Loudly: Leslie Mitchell, Humanism and the Art of Excess': a 'passionate interest in all peoples'. Gibbon's radical left-wing political ideology is shot through with fierce compassion and intense alertness to suffering and pain (whether inflicted by poverty, hardship, or political oppression). It is Gibbon's unflinching depiction of physical and emotional pain that makes much of his work, such as *Spartacus* (discussed by both Malcolm and John Corbett), 'difficult' and 'uncomfortable' reading. As Corbett notes, the reader is often compelled to assume the position of horrified voyeur. And, as Bill Malcolm suggests, the incorporation of such unexpectedly shocking and spectacular scenes is comparable to the Russian film director, Sergei Mikhailovich Eisenstein's cinematic and theatrical technique of montage. Yet, as Malcolm argues, depictions of extreme violence and pain in the novels *Image and Superscription* and *Spartacus* have coherent aesthetic and moral purpose. For Malcolm, Gibbon's writing can be considered an exemplary instance of *littérature engagée*: a literature which is driven by the moral obligation to improve the condition of society and humankind. As Carruthers observes, Gibbon is wary of being judged an 'intellectual'; the famous assertion of the 'Glasgow' essay, '[t]here is nothing in culture or art that is worth the life and elementary happiness of one of those thousands who rot in the Glasgow slums' (*Sm*, 102) damningly delimits the role of art. And yet one can imagine that Gibbon would have had sympathy with Marxist literary criticism, and with the idea that literature can powerfully subvert prevailing ideologies. David Borthwick in his essay, 'From *Grey Granite* to Urban Grit: a revolution in perspectives', compellingly analyses Gibbon's portrayal of class politics and social injustice in the third novel of the trilogy. He emphasises the nature of urban alienation and economic and class conflict in Gibbon's Duncairn by comparison with the dispossessed protagonists of Irvine Welsh's fiction. In the opening essay, 'Modernism and Marxism in *A Scots Quair*', Margery Palmer McCulloch touches on Gibbon's Marxist exploration of contemporary and historical forces in the *Quair* in her analysis of Gibbon's literary modernism. She proposes that the question of 'correct' or 'progressivist' political ideology is left open at the ending of the trilogy, as is the nature of Chris's own fate. 'Life-giving' humanity, rather than 'impersonal ideology', is seen to endure. Gibbon's writing is inescapably political (Valentina Bold alludes to the 'politicised spirituality' of Gibbon's poetry) but in diverse ways.

New intellectual contexts for Gibbon are discovered in this collection. Gerard Carruthers's essay, 'Lewis Grassic Gibbon and the Scottish Enlightenment', explores his paradoxical attitude to the nature and legacy of eighteenth-century Scottish culture and thought. He demonstrates that Gibbon can be considered an 'Enlightenment' man. His is a post-Enlightenment voice, whether acknowledged or not: Gibbon's concerns with the nature of individual identity and perception, the relationship of an individual to 'modernity' or 'civilisation' are preoccupations of the *Quair* which are strongly rooted in Scottish Enlightenment ideas about environmental and psychological influence. Carruthers forges a connection between Chris Guthrie's mystical communion with landscape and ancestral memory at the standing stones with the quest for alterity or 'otherness' found in James Macpherson's *Ossian*.

Interest in the intellectual, cultural, and political nature of Gibbon's writing in this collection is balanced by essays which analyse Gibbon's literary artistry. John Corbett's essay, 'Ecstasy Controlled: the prose styles of Lewis Grassic Gibbon and James Leslie Mitchell', examines the way in which Gibbon's prose style in the *Quair* and elsewhere can be considered as the 'literary construction of Scots speech', rather than an authentic recreation of north-east spoken Scots. Corbett demonstrates the ways in which Gibbon's prose style reproduces features of orality, the most important of these being rhythmic quality. Offering a detailed analysis of the prose style of Gibbon's novel, *Spartacus,* Corbett illustrates how Gibbon's writing calls attention to its 'translated quality': the deliberate foregrounding of its Latinate constructions. He perceives this 'foreignising strategy' in the *Quair* also; apparently dissimilar texts are linked by the way in which they construct a 'half-elided other', whether Latinisms or Scots terms, behind the English prose. For Alison Lumsden, Gibbon's use of Scots in his fiction mirrors what contemporary theorists conceive as the disrupting or 'shattering' strategies of poetic language. These articulate the conventionally repressed and marginal.

Gibbon's narrative subversions are not only linguistic or 'poetic'. Catriona Low's essay, 'The Rendering of Community Voices in the short stories of Lewis Grassic Gibbon', explores the carefully crafted diversity of the narrative voice in 'Smeddum', 'Greenden', 'Clay' and 'Sim'; in particular the shifting and ironic 'community' voice which allows various manipulations of perspective and judgement. Margery Palmer McCulloch relates Gibbon's practice of diverse narrative focalisation to modernist experimentations in narrative form. Though Gibbon's political opinions naturally incline him to favour a form of socialist realist narrative (which Malcolm's essay explores), his narrative styles persistently avoid 'objectivity' and encompass arrestingly imagistic depictions: 'it has the most unique of tangs, this season haunted by the laplaplap of the peesie's wings, by great moons that come nowhere as in Scotland, unending moons when the harvesting carts plod through great thickets of fir-shadow to the cornyards deep in glaur' (*Sm*, 94). His famously lyrical depictions of the Mearns landscape, in his fiction and non-fiction, can, as McCulloch observes, be considered a Scottish Fauve landscape. Such painterly techniques help to cement his relationship with the literary aesthetics of modernism.

In the opening of his essay, 'The Land', Gibbon muses on the 'idle task of voyaging with a pen' (*Sm*, 81). Valentina Bold's essay on Gibbon's poetry, 'From Exile: the poetry of Lewis Grassic Gibbon', suggests that Gibbon's conceit is realised in the different states which his poetry articulates: 'literal, political, spiritual, and emotional displacements.' Bold suggests that Gibbon's poetry, more than his prose, can be considered a witness to his 'emotional states'. The poems are interesting for the ways in which they speak of his love for Rhea, experiences of exile, and loss. But it is difficult not to speculate on the degree to which Gibbon's own traumatic experiences 'haunt' his writing, such as the loss of his child, Ray, within six days of her birth. While literary theory may disavow the importance of 'the author' in the understanding of her or his art, the 'life' lived by James Leslie Mitchell/Lewis Grassic Gibbon is too compelling to elide. This essay collection offers the reader insights into both the art and the life. Gibbon's enduring power is demonstrated by the success and vitality of the Lewis Grassic Gibbon Centre at Arbuthnott, founded in 1992 and now managed by Isabella Williamson. The process by which the Centre came into existence, its transformation into a 'community business', a centre of local employment, and a unique educational and archival resource, is told here by Isabella Williamson herself in 'The Kindness of Friends: The Grassic Gibbon Centre'. Williamson's creativity and vision, and the energy and commitment of those who work with her, are appropriately 'celebrated' in this volume.

These essays collectively demonstrate a new vitality and energy in Gibbon studies which will open up his work to new and continuing reader-ships. Though the volume is only a representative selection of the current state of Gibbon scholarship, it should also reveal new areas for consideration (novels such as *Stained Radiance,* and his Eastern science fiction, for example), and to suggest further critical explorations of the kind which Ian Campbell outlines in his Preface. The title of this centenary volume is inspired by the final stanza of Helen Cruickshank's poem, 'Spring in the Mearns: In Memoriam, Lewis Grassic Gibbon', given in the title page. Cruickshank's illuminating flame captures the idea of the passionate radical from the North East which this book celebrates.

Notes

1. Edwin Muir, *An Autobiography* (London: Hogarth Press, 1954), p. 194.
2. Ian S. Munro, *Leslie Mitchell:Lewis Grassic Gibbon* (Edinburgh: Oliver & Boyd, 1966), p. 151.
3. James Leslie Mitchell, 'Grieve – Scotsman', *Free Man* 2, 9 September 1933, p. 7. Also quoted by MacDiarmid in *Lucky Poet* (London: Methuen, 1943), p. 72.
4. Helen Cruickshank, quotation from letter from George Malcolm Thomson and comment on her response, 'Notes on Lewis Grassic Gibbon', Helen B. Cruickshank Papers, MS2, Folder 7, A1, University of Stirling Library.
5. Ibid, A2.
6. Letter from Donald Carswell 17 August 1932, quoted by Ian Munro, *Leslie Mitchell:Lewis Grassic Gibbon*, p. 74.
7. Compton Mackenzie, *Daily Mail*, 13 September 1932.

8. Hugh MacDiarmid, *Contemporary Scottish Studies* (London: Parsons, 1926), pp.268-69; Neil M. Gunn, Letter to J. Leslie Mitchell 17 July 1933, quoted by Munro, p.118.

9. Helen Cruickshank Papers, University of Stirling Library, MS2 Folder 7, A4.

10. Lewis Grassic Gibbon and Hugh MacDiarmid, *Scottish Scene or the Intelligent Man's Guide to Albion* (London: Jarrolds, 1934), p.203. For Muriel Stuart, see Margery [Palmer] McCulloch, 'A Cuckoo in the Nest of Singing Birds?', *Scottish Literary Journal* 16:1 (1989), pp.51-58.

11. Hugh MacDiarmid, Letter of Saturday [10 February 1935] to Rhea Mitchell, *The Letters of Hugh MacDiarmid* ed. by Alan Bold (Athens: University of Georgia Press, 1984), p.559; Neil M. Gunn, Letter to Rhea Mitchell, 15 February 1935, quoted in Munro, p.208.

12. Helen B. Cruickshank Papers, University of Stirling Library, MS2, Folder 7, C2.

13. Ian Campbell, 'A Tribute that Never Was: The Plan for A Lewis Grassic Gibbon Festchrift', *Studies in Scottish Literature*, 20 (1985), p.227.

14. *A Scots Quair* ed. by Tom Crawford (Edinburgh: Canongate, 1995), p.71.

15. *Stained Radiance* (Edinburgh: Polygon, 1993), p.103.

16. *Quair*, p.203.

Modernism and Marxism in *A Scots Quair*

Margery Palmer McCulloch

Despite its dialectical title, my essay is as much concerned with narrative form as it is with ideology. What interests me about *A Scots Quair* is the way in which this text of the later modernist period dramatises and interrogates the politics and social history of its time through formal devices of characterisation, setting and voice; and through the presentation of the responses of its fictional characters to the events which overtake them and which some of them try actively to shape. Leslie Mitchell — or Lewis Grassic Gibbon as I will call him in relation to *A Scots Quair* — was himself a young man still in the process of intellectual formation in the early 1930s, absorbing and responding to influences. He had also recently lived through or, in the case of *Grey Granite*, was actually living through some of the events and political responses presented in the fictional world of the *Quair*. The dynamic of his trilogy is therefore inherently related to the dynamic of political events in the contemporaneous 'real-life' world.

In regard to the modernistic narrative devices employed in the trilogy, it is frustrating that there is so little written specifically about literary matters in Gibbon's essays and letters. The principal literary essay is, of course, 'Literary Lights' from *Scottish Scene*,[1] in which he insists that few of the writers of the literary revival movement have qualities to justify their consideration as Scottish writers, as opposed to English writers from the county of Scotshire. His criterion for judgement here is language, whether Scots or Gaelic, and it is interesting that, like MacDiarmid and Muir in their unnecessary quarrel over Muir's *Scott and Scotland*, Gibbon in this essay ignores the fact that Scottish English, even in the 1930s, was the medium of communication for a large number of Scots for everyday discourse as well as for creative writing. The more significant section of the 'Literary Lights' essay, however, is where Gibbon discusses his own attempts to develop a specifically Scottish medium for his narrative in the books of the *Scots Quair* trilogy. He comments:

The technique of Lewis Grassic Gibbon in his trilogy *A Scots Quair* – of which only Parts I and II, *Sunset Song* and *Cloud Howe*, have yet been published – is to mould the English language into the rhythms and cadences of Scots spoken speech, and to inject into the English vocabulary such minimum number of words from Braid Scots as that remodelling requires. His scene so far has been a comparatively uncrowded and simple one – the countryside and village of modern Scotland. Whether his technique is adequate to compass and express the life of an industrialized Scots town in all its complexity is yet to be demonstrated; whether his peculiar style may not become either intolerably mannered or degenerate, in the fashion of Joyce, into the unfortunate unintelligibilities of a literary second childhood, is also in question. (*Sm*, 135)

The apparently derogatory reference to Joyce is intriguing in relation to what would now be seen as the *modernist* as well as the *Scottish* technique of the *Quair*. For the free indirect style of the *Sunset Song* narrative, the blurring of the distinction between the voices of narrator and characters, has much in common with Joyce's experimentation, as it has also with Virginia Woolf's approach in a novel such as *Mrs Dalloway*. The comments Gibbon makes about Joyce's work must apply in this instance to *Ulysses*, for *Finnegans Wake*, usually cited as Joyce's descent into incomprehensibility, was not published until 1939, four years after Gibbon's death. And in *Ulysses*, Joyce carries out his narrative experimentation in the city context of Dublin. With Gibbon, however, one can never be sure that any such negative views are not in fact presented ironically, used to forestall criticism of his own experimentation; other references to Joyce in 'Literary Lights' suggest a more positive evaluation. At the beginning of the essay, for example, Joyce is linked to Proust in a speculation that among the many unread published books, there may well have been overlooked 'a Scots Joyce, a Scots Proust'; while later Gibbon plays with the idea of a possible future 'Scots James Joyce' who will 'electrify' the Scottish scene, this time in company with a 'Scots Virginia Woolf' who will 'astound' it (*Sm*, 124, 127). Such pointing to three of the most experimental fiction writers of the early twentieth century fits with the comments in his essay 'The Land' about the pleasure he himself finds in the '*manipulation of words* on a blank page' (*Sm*, 84; my italics); not, one notices, the manipulation of *ideas*. These references and comments, although few in number, when brought together with the innovative narrative methodology in all three books of the *Quair*, provide strong circumstantial evidence in my view for Gibbon's interest in literary form as well as political ideology, and, especially, for his interest in the experimental fiction of the modernist period. What is so significant about *A Scots Quair* itself is the way in which he has succeeded in marrying a modernistic fictional form with a Marxist exploration of contemporary and historical forces, an exploration more often conducted in fiction through socialist-realist methodology.

The opening of 'Ploughing' in *Sunset Song* offers a fine example of Gibbon's innovative narrative approach, which includes also a bringing together of the oral and the literary. Beginning, apparently, with the voice of a traditional third-person narrator, the narrative quickly modulates into the generic 'you' and then into the voice of Chris Guthrie herself: 'Folk said there hadn't been such a drought since eighty-three and Long Rob of the Mill said you couldn't blame *this* one on Gladstone, anyway, and everybody laughed except father, God knows why.' (*SS*, 25)[2] One senses immediately that this will be a story of lives told from the inside, where the reader will also be encouraged to 'belong' as opposed to observing from a distance. The passage is compelling rhythmically and in its linguistic vibrancy and colour. What we have personified here is a Scottish Fauve landscape:

> Below and around where Chris Guthrie lay the June moors whispered and rustled and shook their cloaks, yellow with broom and powdered faintly with purple, that was the heather but not the full passion of its colour yet. And in the east against the cobalt blue of the sky lay the shimmer of the North Sea that was by Bervie (*SS*, 25)

Each word chosen communicates in its distinctive way a countryside throbbing with life: the wind 'shook and played in the moors and went dandering up the sleeping Grampians, the rushes pecked and quivered about the loch when its hand was upon them'; the everyday and the erotic mingle in the imagery of the parks which lie like a mythical earth-goddess 'fair parched, sucked dry, the red clay soil of Blawearie gaping open for the rain that seemed never-coming'. And then, at the end of this introductory descriptive passage there is the alien technological image of the motor-car 'shooming through them [the roads] like kettles under steam' (*SS*, 25) – a motor-car which intrudes into the life of the community and almost knocks down Chae Strachan's son: a narrative detail which, with hindsight, points imagistically towards the technology which is even then beginning to undermine traditional ways of farming, and which, in the form of the armaments of war, brings the final disintegration of the community at the end of the novel. Through this small, almost unnoticed imagistic detail and the economic characterisations of Chae Strachan and Long Rob in their responses to the motorist and Chae's court appearance,

Gibbon unobtrusively introduces the ideological context of the novel
alongside its modernistic descriptive prose and focalisation. This is very
clever writing which has to be read in its entirety to be fully appreciated.

   The section which follows this imagistic opening moves anachronistically to the story of Chris's parents and is even more important, at this
early stage of the narrative, for an understanding of the way in which
ideological discourse is communicated through voice and characterisation.
This section begins with the voice of Chris remembering her mother and
then modulates into the voice of the mother herself, into her own memories
as she had perhaps told them to her daughter:

> [B]ut fine she'd liked it, she'd never forget the singing of the winds in
> those fields when she was young or the daft crying of the lambs she herded
> or the feel of the earth below her toes. *Oh, Chris, my lass, there are better
> things than your books or studies or loving or bedding, there's the countryside your
> own, you its, in the days when you're neither bairn nor woman.* (SS, 27)

This is followed by a meeting between the mother and John Guthrie at a
ploughing match in which it is clear that the 'brave young childe with a
red head and the swackest legs you ever saw' would carry off the prize. And
Guthrie carries off more than the ploughing prize: 'For as he rode from the
park on one horse he patted the back of the other and cried to Jean
Murdoch with a glint from his dour, sharp eye *Jump up if you like.* And she
cried back *I like fine!* and caught the horse by its mane and swung herself
there till Guthrie's hand caught her and set her steady on the back of the
beast.' (SS, 28)

   What is captured here is the immediate attraction between two young
people, the flexible movement of Gibbon's prose communicating their
impetuosity and willingness to risk putting their lives together. From an
ideological perspective, the ensuing narrative shows, economically but
forcibly, how this early joy in each other becomes warped and destroyed by
external forces they are unable to control: the struggle to farm unrewarding
land, repeated pregnancies, physically difficult for the mother, the
continuing extra mouths to feed. It demonstrates through *showing* as
opposed to *telling* the way in which our lives can be determined not only by
factors outwith our control, but also by our own unwillingness to open our
minds to change, by our refusal to question dominant ideologies. In his
poem 'London', William Blake speaks of 'mind-forg'd manacles':

In every cry of every Man,
In every Infant's cry of fear,
In every voice, in every ban,
The mind-forg'd manacles I hear:[3]

and Gibbon's narrative shows how we can put these manacles on our own minds, as well as have them imposed upon us. John Guthrie, for example, refuses to question his Old Testament religion. His blind sexual cruelty to his wife – '*We'll have what God in His mercy may send to us, woman. See you to that.*' – is patterned in his violent behaviour towards his young son who calls to the new horse '*Come over, Jehovah*': a name whose wonderful sound seems to the child to match the wonder the animal holds for him, but a use which Guthrie can interpret only as blasphemous (*SS*, 28, 30). John Guthrie is to a large extent portrayed negatively in his relations with his family and might easily be dismissed as a cruel, authoritarian husband and father. Yet that brief capturing of the early attraction between two young people remains in the mind as a touchstone of what might have been and it conditions us to think about why he has become the man he has. This portrayal of the Guthrie marriage is paralleled in a passage from Gibbon's essay 'The Land' in which he talks of the cyclical struggle of marriage and breeding and endless work, and adds:

> [I]t was a perfect Spenglerian cycle. Yet it was waste effort, it was as foolish as the plod of an ass in a treadmill, innumerable generations of asses. If the clumsy fumblements of contraception have done no more than break the wheel and play of that ancient cycle they have done much. (*Sm*, 93)

Marx's view of the historical process was two-fold: on the one hand, he saw it as deterministic, sweeping human beings along with it; on the other, he believed that human beings should be active in helping to shape that historical process. Gibbon, too, in his essay 'Religion' stresses that 'men are not merely the victims, the hapless leaves storm-blown, of historic forces, but may guide if they cannot generate that storm' (*Sm*, 166). The conflict played out in the three books of *A Scots Quair* is that between those who attempt to guide or shape events and those who refuse to question, who obstinately or apathetically hold to old ways of thinking and behaviour. In *Sunset Song*, for example, Chris is notable for the way she makes choices with regard to her own life. She chooses to stay on the land, to put aside the 'English Chris'; she asks Ewan to share her life and the farm with her; she learns how to control her fertility, so that she will not follow on her mother's road; and she never loses her sense of *self*-possession, even in the darkest days of the ironically named 'harvest' section of the book. As has often been noted, *Sunset Song* is both the song of a young woman growing to adulthood and simultaneously the end of an old song for a rural way of life that is dying. Gibbon's insight in the book is that although the historical process was working against that way of life, it did not need to work to its end as it did. People could have responded to events in a way that would have shaped them less harshly.

The harshest major event in the narrative is the intrusion of the Great War into the life of the community. In Gibbon's presentation, we find the hypocrisy, self-seeking and readiness to adhere unthinkingly to religious and political propaganda characteristic of many contemporaneous accounts of the home front in that war, and found also in Gibbon's comments about the war in his essays. Chris and Long Rob are branded as pro-German because they dare question gossip and newspaper stories; Chae Strachan emotionally thrusts aside his socialist principles and rushes off to fight, behaviour which patterns Gibbon's comment in *Scottish Scene* about H.G. Wells: 'That unique internationalist, Mr H.G. Wells, erupted like an urgent geyser – "every sword drawn against Germany is a sword drawn for peace!"' (*Sm*, 145). Ewan, who is not a thinker like his wife, also submits to the hysteria, enlists and is eventually shot as a deserter. Even Long Rob, imprisoned for his pacificism in the early years of the war, eventually complies with the authorities and is killed fighting in France. All the horror of the war is brought alive by its enactment through these characters we have come to know, and by our realisation that, although the war itself was beyond their control, in the areas of life where they did have choice and the opportunity to use their minds to question and evaluate, the inhabitants of Kinraddie mostly did not use that choice, or, as in the case of the home-front profiteers, they used choice to their own advantage by cutting down for short-term profit the trees which sheltered the farming lands, thus hastening the demise of farming after the war.

Sunset Song is heartbreaking in the tragedy of its ending, but that ending also leaves open the possibility of something positive coming out of the disaster with its intimation of the forthcoming marriage of Chris to the new Christian Socialist minister Robert Colquohoun, who has himself been gassed in the war and has come home with a mission to make Christ's gospel relevant to the everyday lives of people here on earth: a mission interrogated in the second book of the trilogy.

Cloud Howe is probably the least discussed book in the *Quair*. Edwin Muir called it 'an unusually bad novel' in the *Listener* of 9 August 1933: an extreme view which was not supported by other Scottish Renaissance writers such as Neil Gunn, George Blake and Naomi Mitchison, for example.[4] *Cloud Howe* is certainly not so immediately striking as either the first or final book, and with Chris no longer at the centre of events, her perspective cannot be as pervasive as in *Sunset Song*. Nevertheless, while the formal, modernistic attributes of this second book may be less significant, what is of much interest is its dynamic presentation of religion and politics.

In his *Scottish Scene* essay and in *Sunset Song*, Gibbon's presentation of religion is a negative one. In *Sunset Song*, religion and its Kinraddie minister are brought to us like E. M. Forster's 'flat'[5] characters and very often in the guise of stereotypical music-hall Scotch comics. Kinraddie's minister is always pompous, ludicrous, lecherous, gluttonous and self-serving, while the religion he preaches is the harsh creed that has warped unthinking adherents such as John Guthrie. In *Cloud Howe*, on the other hand, it is as if Gibbon is giving religion, in the form of Christian Socialism, a second chance to prove itself as an ideology which can help shape a new society. Religion is brought to the foreground of the narrative and the portrayal of Robert's attempt to make it meaningful to the lives of the inhabitants of Segget is sympathetic, his own characterisation rounded.[6] Yet while Robert may seem to have taken over from Chris as the dominant presence in many parts of the novel, Chris's perspective is still important, even if communicated obliquely. At the end of the 'Cirrus' chapter, for example, we find Chris on the hillside at the Kaimes ruins, thinking of Robert and his dream of a new age. She wonders, was his

> dream just a dream? Was there a new time coming to the earth, when nowhere a bairn would cry in the night, or a woman go bowed as her mother had done, or a man turn into a tormented beast, as her father, or into a bullet-torn corpse, as had Ewan? A time when those folk down there in Segget might be what Robert said all might be, companions with God on a terrible adventure?

Then, breaking into her thoughts:

> Suddenly, far down and beyond the toun there came a screech as the morning grew, a screech like an hungered beast in pain. The hooters were blowing in the Segget Mills. (*CH*, 34)

This harsh interruption to Chris's uncertain questioning – reminding the reader, perhaps, of Dickens's 'melancholy, mad elephants'[7] in the Coketown factories of *Hard Times* – suggests through its imagery of 'screeching' and 'hungered beast in pain' that Robert's dream may well be illusory, as indeed it proves to be. For the Segget people are divided among themselves, between the gentry and the incomers, the spinners. Robert is trusted by neither group and attacked by the more conservative because he identifies with the workers and tries to improve their conditions. Ironically, these uneducated workers don't trust him either, because this is not the traditional role they expect of a churchman. Their contempt, as portrayed in the narrative, may well derive from Gibbon's own contempt for institutionalised religion and his view that 'religion is no more fundamental to the human character than cancer is fundamental to the human brain' (*Sm*, 152). One could argue, therefore, that the failure of Robert's dream is as much predetermined by his author's views on religion as it is by the fictional conflicts of Segget, for even at its most sympathetic with regard to Robert, the narrative, through Gibbon's characterisation of Chris's response, is negatively directed, as can be seen in the following passage:

> Then he started talking of the Miners, of Labour, of the coming struggle
> in the month of May, he hoped and believed that that was beginning of
> the era of Man made free at last, Man who was God, Man splendid again.
> Christ meant and intended no more when He said he was the Son of Man,
> when He preached the Kingdom of Heaven – He meant it on Earth.
> Christ was no godlet, but a leader and hero –

And as Robert continues to talk out his dream:

> He forgot Chris, striding up and down the slope; excitement kindled in
> his harsh, kind eyes. And Chris watched him, standing, her stick behind
> her, her arms looped about it, saying nothing to him but hearing and
> seeing, him and the hills and the song that both made. And suddenly she
> felt quite feared. (*CH*, 143)

The 'Stratus' chapter is the political heart of *Cloud Howe* and its presentation of the failure of the General Strike is reminiscent of the scenario played out in the symbolic 'Ballad of the Crucified Rose' (or 'Ballad of the General Strike') section of MacDiarmid's *A Drunk Man Looks at the Thistle*. In Gibbon's novel, the failure marks both the end of Robert's dream and the betrayal of the workers, partly through their own in-fighting, but also betrayal by their leaders and politicians. As in MacDiarmid's ballad:

> The vices that defeat the dream
> Are in the plant itsel',
> And till they're purged its virtues maun
> In pain and misery dwell.[8]

Politics and political factions are the stereotypical 'flat characters' in *Cloud Howe*, as religion had previously been in *Sunset Song*, and the prejudice-ridden nature of the characters depicted points once again to the importance of interrogating existing ideologies and attitudes, of being prepared to cast the manacles from our own minds as well as fighting against external oppression. There are no ideological positives in this book. All conventional political parties are scorned, religion is seen ultimately as providing no answers, nationalism is rejected. We are left with the continuing personal self-possession of Chris: 'She had found in the moors and the sun and the sea her surety unshaken, lost maybe herself, but she followed no cloud, be it named or unnamed' (*CH*, 173). We are also left with the impersonal rationality of her son Ewan, and his is the philosophy which takes us into *Grey Granite* and into the interrogation of yet another possible way forward. This time the hard, impersonal ideology of Marxism patterns the flint and granite images associated with the characterisation of Ewan who takes up work in a city metal foundry after the untimely death of his stepfather. In contrast to the epilogue and prologue which separates the first two books in the trilogy, the second and third books flow into each other without obstruction, a structural narrative device which emphasises the connectedness of their ideological discourse.

Despite the fears he expressed in 'Literary Lights', Gibbon seems to me remarkably successful in his creation of an urban setting in *Grey Granite* and in the translation of his modernistic narrative voice from rural to urban context. As in the earlier books, it is Chris's perspective which opens the *Grey Granite* scene as she pauses for breath, not this time at the Standing Stones above Blawearie or the Kaimes ruins above Segget, but at a turn in the steep steps which lead up to Windmill Place in the city of Duncairn. Immediately we feel we are in a new environment with the quicker pulse of the city, its damp, dirty fog and swish of traffic, its expansive yet fragmented setting where there is no possibility of a cohesive community, not even of the limited kind there was in Segget. In Duncairn there is the impersonality of city streets, the perception of a variety of occupations and classes with separate interests, of townspeople who are unlikely ever to meet up with one another, of areas of the city outwith their experience. Despite the continuing modernistic elements in Gibbon's narrative form, this is not the modernist city of alienated but fascinated intellectuals and artists found at the beginning of the century, not the 'unreal city' of Eliot's *The Waste Land*.[9] This is a proletarian city of slums and class warfare, of economic injustice and protest; the kind of city which provided a setting for the real-life socialist and Marxist debates and action of the interwar period. Ewan and

Chris are considered 'toffs' (*GG*, 21, 23) in this new world, despite the fact that Chris has to work long hours in her boarding-house and Ewan has chosen to enter a factory. Chris does not recognise the word 'keelie' (*GG*, 26) used by Ewan of his fellow workers, although she understands his dismissive intonation – something she thinks should not be used towards working people, of whom she considers herself one. For the workers at Gowans and Gloag's, however, the independence of mind shown by Ewan and Chris and their conscious sense of self marks them out as different. In the exchanges between Ewan and his fellow apprentices, we are shown the narrow perspectives of the workers, their petty enmities and rivalries, their unwillingness to unite in the attempt to better their situation. The employers seem firmly in control here and, as in James Kelman's later *The Bus Conductor Hines*, we are given an insight into how generations of industrial working, poor living conditions and lack of education can sap initiative, so that there remains little belief in the possibility of escape from what seems a predestined place in life.

Gibbon is successful also in bringing us the diverse voices of his socially fragmented city. After its Chris-centred opening, focalisation in this last book moves from one particular group to another and between characters within groups. Thus we have perspectives from the foundry workers, sometimes given through an anonymous yet individualised industrial worker's voice; sometimes there is a kind of insider 'group' voice, reminding one of the Kinraddie community voice, yet representative only of a section of the townspeople here; sometimes the maid Meg is the focaliser, sometimes Ewan's girlfriend and co-socialist worker Ellen. Perspectives come also from Chris and Ewan and from a whole range of minor one-dimensional characters such as the boarding-house inmates, the provost and labour leader, the chief of police, the minister and his housekeeper. Undeveloped as they are, these characters speak to us for and by themselves, as opposed to being spoken about by a conventional omniscient narrative voice. This is an unusual and important step forward in portraying a fragmented urban environment, anticipating in many ways the later urban narratives of Kelman. The language used also anticipates Kelman's practice. It is still the remodelling of English into the rhythms and cadences of spoken Scots as Gibbon described it in 'Literary Lights', but these are now urban rhythms and the lexis includes words such as 'keelie' which Chris does not understand.

Gibbon's methodology can be seen to good effect in passages such as the Paldy Parish narrative in the early stages of the novel and the later socialist march to the Town Hall (*GG*, 19, 53). In the evocation of a June night in the Paldy Parish slum, with its smells and heat and lack of privacy, focalisation moves from a man to his wife to his daughter, each of them expressing their awareness of the privations of their present situation. The parents' despairing memories and the determination of their daughter to escape their fate are brought alive by synaesthetic imagery and the rhythms of their unspoken thoughts. The terrible irony of their situation is communicated later in the plot when the girl Meg becomes pregnant by her boyfriend, so that the cycle of entrapment is set to continue. The presentation of the socialist march is equally powerful. The main focaliser here is an anonymous man on the march, but his perspective is also a group perspective for the class of workers to which he belongs. In addition, included within his voice is the perspective of his wife – and of all the wives. As he remembers what *she* thinks of protest activity, he remembers also his comrades, the ones who emigrated and the ones who were killed in the war; he remembers the war itself; and while we are privy to his thoughts and memories, the narrative is simultaneously bringing to us the crowds lining the streets, the noise of the drum and the singing and the traffic. And then, there is the slowing of the march, the disbelief when it begins to be diverted away from the Town Hall, the angry breaking of the line and the charge of the police horses. This is a wonderful passage of narrative which demands to be read aloud (*GG*, 53-6).

The socialist march to the Town Hall transfers the struggle to find a new order of society from *Cloud Howe*'s religious search to the political context, but the interrogation of political systems in this final book is hardly more optimistic than the blind antagonisms which destroyed Robert in its predecessor. As we have seen, a recurring theme in all three books of the *Quair* is that we imprison ourselves by our unwillingness to examine dominant ideologies and conventional responses. In Duncairn, the workers reject parties and policies which are attempting to bring about change, something we see also in the Paldy Parish view of the danger of the 'Communionists' (*GG*, 20). There is hatred of the upper classes and the better off, yet, paradoxically, the workers give their votes to the very people to whose advantage it is to maintain the *status quo*. Ewan is at the heart of the struggle with his adherence to communism, but his presentation is such that it does not encourage the reader to believe that the resolution of social ills lies with his impersonal ideology and its rejection of human needs and commitments. He seems a *willed* character, as if his author had decided that he wanted to depict someone free from the emotions which so often hinder the making of objective decisions, someone who would put the fight for a new order of society first. This characterisation is reminiscent of

MacDiarmid's *First Hymn to Lenin* of 1931 which brushes humanity aside
with its 'What maitters't wha we kill/To lessen that foulest murder that
deprives/Maist men o' real lives?'[10]

As in *Cloud Howe* in relation to Robert's Christian Socialist dreams, I
believe Chris's perspective is important both in any assessment of Ewan's
commitment to the new Marxist religion and of his author's commitment
to Ewan. As they have supper together for the last time before Ewan leaves
on the Hunger March and Chris returns to the croft at Cairndhu where she
was born, Chris responds to her son's teasing questions by saying she was
thinking

> *Of Robert and this faith of yours. The world's sought faiths for thousands of years
> and found only death or unease in them. Yours is just another dark cloud to me
> – or a great rock you're trying to push up a hill.*

Ewan's response, communicated through Chris's perspective, is that 'it was
the rock was pushing him; and sat dreaming again, who had called Robert
dreamer'. The passage ends with Ewan's enigmatic words:

> *There will always be you and I, I think, Mother. It's the old fight that maybe will
> never have a finish, whatever the names we give to it – the fight in the end between
> FREEDOM and GOD.* (GG, 202)

Gibbon is not helpful here. Are we to understand that Ewan is suggesting
that he and Chris are together in the fight for freedom against those who
hold, like Robert, to a supernatural creed? Or is he pointing to the
separation – only too obvious to the reader – between his fight for a new
society and his mother's holding to the old commitment to the land and
history and human values? Although many readers and critics see Gibbon
as endorsing Ewan and his commitment to a Marxist way forward, it seems
to me that, however we interpret the words quoted above, the author is at
this point positioning Chris so that she offers an alternative, even sceptical
perspective on Ewan's ideological commitments as she had done previously
in relation to Robert's. If we accept Chris's perspective as continuing to be
valid, we have then to accept the book's ending as an open one, with the
story of Ewan still in process, as many of the ideas and ideologies in the
trilogy have been ideas in process; the author himself an experiencing
human being responding to the changing times in which he lived.

Chris's own fate at the end of the trilogy has also aroused contrary
interpretations. Angus Calder, for example, suggests that her return to
Cairndhu is a defeat and that 'her peasant values drag her into regression,

stasis, and death'.[11] This does not seem to me to be a credible reading in the light of Gibbon's previous characterisation of Chris. As we have experienced, her touchstones have not been religion or any social or political ideology, but a sense of at-one-ness with the land and an awareness of change and of the countless human beings who have lived, loved, suffered and worked the land before her. Her chief quality is her self-possessedness, her capacity to consider, to withdraw into herself at moments of crisis and to draw strength from her sense of self. Throughout the trilogy, women are the ones who hold true to *human* values, and although Chris appears to go with the flow of history, yet we see that she acts to shape her life where she can, choosing what is life-giving as opposed to what is imprisoning. In *Grey Granite*, Ellen, too, opts for the life-giving as opposed to the impersonal ideology of Ewan.

For me, then, this focus on humanity is the principal 'meaning' or 'message' of the trilogy, not the endorsement of any particular ideology; a humanity communicated so variously and vitally by Gibbon's modernistic narrative method, something quite new in Scottish fiction.

Notes

1. Lewis Grassic Gibbon and Hugh MacDiarmid, *Scottish Scene or The Intelligent Man's Guide to Albyn* (London: Jarrolds, 1934). Quotations from Gibbon's essays will be referenced from the recent reprint in *Smeddum: A Lewis Grassic Gibbon Anthology*, ed. by Valentina Bold (Edinburgh: Canongate, 2001), with page numbers given in the text, preceded by *Sm*.

2. Lewis Grassic Gibbon, *Sunset Song* (London: Jarrolds, 1932). Quotations will be referenced from the 1995 Canongate Classics edition of *A Scots Quair*, ed. with an introd. by Tom Crawford and incorporating his previous eds. of the three books (*SS*, 1988, *CH*, 1989 and *GG*, 1990).

3. William Blake, *Selected Poems*, ed. by P.H. Butter (London: Dent, 1982), p.36.

4. See Ian S. Munro, *Leslie Mitchell: Lewis Grassic Gibbon* (Edinburgh: Oliver & Boyd, 1966), pp.117-21 for information about contemporaneous responses to *Cloud Howe*. Muir's review is on p.222 of the *Listener* of 9 August 1933.

5. See E.M. Forster, *Aspects of the Novel* (1927), reprinted. (Harmondsworth: Penguin Books, 1962), pp.75-89.

6. Helen Cruickshank reports a conversation between Gibbon and her mother who, unlike Helen herself, was strongly appreciative of the characterisation of Colquohoun: 'Eh, what a fine character ye've made o' the minister, Robert Colquohoun, he's the best in the book'. He 'clappit her kindly on the shoulder' and replied: 'I agree with you, Mrs Cruickshank. You and I are the only people who appreciate Robert. And, of course, *we're* right'. (Helen Cruickshank papers, Stirling University Library, MS2, folder 7, C1.)

7. See Charles Dickens, *Hard Times* (1854) reprinted (Harmondsworth: Penguin Books, 1969), pp. 107, 146.

8. Hugh MacDiarmid, *A Drunk Man Looks at the Thistle* (1926) in *Hugh MacDiarmid: Selected Poems*, ed. by Alan Riach and Michael Grieve (Harmondsworth: Penguin Books, 1994), p. 66.

9. T. S. Eliot, *The Waste Land* (1922) in *Collected Poems 1909-1962* (London: Faber and Faber, 1974), p. 65.

10. Hugh MacDiarmid, *Selected Poems*, p. 140.

11. Angus Calder, 'A Mania for Self-Reliance: Grassic Gibbon's *Scots Quair*' in *The Uses of Fiction*, ed. by Douglas Jefferson and Graham Martin (Milton Keynes: The Open University Press, 1982), p. 112.

'Women's Time':
Reading the *Quair* as a Feminist Text

Alison Lumsden

Women critics, and particularly those writing within overtly feminist frameworks, have often ignored Lewis Grassic Gibbon's *A Scots Quair*, leading Keith Dixon to conclude that its 'libertarian, feminist representation of women' is one of the 'rough edges' that has been rubbed off the trilogy to make it acceptable to the Scottish education system.[1] For some women readers the *Quair* is regarded as a worrying appropriation of female experience by a male author. Others, such as Isobel Murray, suggest that while there may be much positive analysis of women's experience in the novels, their central character Chris, and particularly Gibbon's treatment of her in his conclusion, remains problematic.[2]

These criticisms of the *Quair* are based on what is essentially an Anglo-American feminist reading model which seeks to find in texts either positive representations of female experience or, unfortunately what is rather more common, negative portrayals of women at the hands of patriarchy. It is possible, however, to find much that is positive within the *Quair* using this critical paradigm. Keith Dixon himself argues for a 'feminist representation of women' in Gibbon's work and concludes:

> Grassic Gibbon's representation of women in his fictional writing is undoubtedly subversive, in that it breaks radically with dominant literary stereotypes, revealing not only the realities of women's oppression but also insisting on the positive dimensions of their reactions to their condition. He develops neither a paternalistic nor a miserabilist vision of women and femininity.[3]

Sandra Hunter, similarly, argues that Gibbon was 'interested in the role of women and concerned with the unfairness meted out to them in a paternalistic society' and concludes that '[t]hroughout his writings he

portrayed a sympathetic attitude towards women – a radical departure
from the stereotypes in much contemporary literature.'[4] Carol Anderson,
in one of the most sustained feminist readings of the *Quair*, also identifies
much positive analysis of women's experience in the trilogy. A notable
feature of it, she suggests, 'is a new and self-conscious interest in the role
of women in society' by which 'the unjustness of society in its treatment
of women is exposed and explored, and the struggles of women are made
a central concern'.[5]

However, while the Anglo-American feminist critical model may
recognise much that is positive in relation to feminine experience in the
Quair, by concentrating on 'images of women' criticism and on the
character of Chris herself, it repeatedly reaches an impasse which renders
the trilogy problematic for the feminist reader. Ultimately, even
Anderson, in spite of her attempt to read the novels sympathetically, must
conclude that Gibbon still presents 'stereotypic ideas of "femininity" by
associating women with organicism and a relationship with nature, and by
representing women repeatedly in terms of private rather than "public"
commitment, and "passivity" rather than action'.[6] She remains troubled,
too, by the *Quair*'s conclusion, suggesting that Chris's withdrawal can only
be read in terms of defeat, an understandable response to the protagonist's
experience. 'Society' she concludes, 'has been in the broadest sense
destructive for Chris – for the woman', and the novel's ending must
therefore be read as a kind of symbolic martyrdom wherein Gibbon relies
on a 'view of female nature that is ultimately somewhat conservative'.[7]

The Anglo-American 'images of women' model of feminist criticism
offers only one way of approaching the trilogy, however, and an alternative
may be found in continental European feminist thought. This approach
has, it seems, yet to be applied to Gibbon's work but it may provide an
interesting paradigm by which we might approach *A Scots Quair* as a
feminist text or, perhaps even as what we may guardedly call an example of
écriture féminine.

Continental feminism in the latter part of the twentieth century
concerned itself less with searching for images of women in texts than with
analysing the inherent problematics of femininity in relation to an
essentially patriarchal social order. Critics such as Hélène Cixous and Julia
Kristeva concentrate less on issues such as social equality – rendering their
work somewhat problematic for many practical feminists – and more on
theoretical issues of the difference or otherness of the feminine and the
consequent tensions involved in its collusion with, and exclusion from,
patriarchal structures. For Cixous, one provisional response to this tension,

and a methodology by which the feminine might assert itself in relation to patriarchal systems, lies in the concept of *écriture féminine*. Broadly speaking, this notion draws on poststructuralist thought to define a model of literary production which, by a variety of internal strategies, seeks to challenge the totalities of masculine discourse, although, perhaps paradoxically, it can be created by both male and female writers. It makes this challenge, it is suggested, by launching an assault on homogeneity, by disrupting models based on binary opposition, and by revelling in *différance* through its repeated resistance to closure. By such strategies *écriture féminine*, or 'radical writing', to use Julia Kristeva's more inclusive term, arguably allows the feminine to erupt into the text, thus continually disrupting patriarchal, totalising impulses within it.[8] While such theories may seem far removed from Gibbon's *A Scots Quair* they may, nevertheless, provide useful strategies for re-reading the novels as a so called 'feminist' text. Three aspects of the *Quair* are particularly fruitful for exploration within these models: the representation of Chris's concept of subjectivity; the ways in which the trilogy deals with time and history, particularly in relation to its conclusion; and, finally, the novel's linguistic and poetic strategies.

Chris's almost obsessional concern with the divided nature of her own subjectivity is manifested, of course, in her awareness of her initially divided self – the English Chris and the Scots Chris, the Guthrie and the Murdoch; in her repeated objectification of herself in regarding her mirror image; and, perhaps, most interesting of all, in her growing awareness that she is not one Chris or even two, but indeed many. While her quest in the trilogy may seem to be that of finding a unified identity – 'that third and last Chris' (*SS*, 71) to be found through sexual love, or that next and seemingly real Chris discovered through pregnancy and motherhood – this search for a 'You' that is not overtaken by other selves is repeatedly defeated by the recognition that her subjectivity consists, in fact, of several selves co-existing within the one:

> Were she sure of herself as Ewan of himself, she might go her own way and not heed to any, have men to lie with her when she desired them (and faith, that would sure be seldom enough!), do and say all the things that came crying her to do, go hide long days in the haughs of the Mounth – up in the silence and the hill-bird's cry, no soul to vex, and to watch the clouds sailing and passing out over the Howe, unending over the Howe of the World; that – or sing and be glad by a fire; or wash and toil and be tired with her toil as once she had been in her days on a croft – a million things, Chris-alone, Chris-herself, with Chris Guthrie, Chris Tavendale, Chris Colquohoun dead! (*CH*, 166)

For the female Chris, to be 'You' is to be 'a million things': schoolgirl, wife, mother, lover, Chris Guthrie, Chris Tavendale, Chris Colquohoun, Chris Ogilvie.

In the post-Freudian, post-Lacanian world which we as readers inhabit, an awareness of the lack of any unified subjectivity is, perhaps, inescapable for everyone, but feminist critics have argued that it has been a particularly predominant preoccupation of women's writing throughout the twentieth century. Deirdre Burton draws attention to this preoccupation in the *Quair,* suggesting that it is one of the features of it which meant that '[r]eading Lewis Grassic Gibbon's famous trilogy in the early 1980s', she had to remind herself continually that she 'was *not* reading a work by a modern female writer, who wrote from women's cultural experience, and with a strong political commitment to specifically feminist perspectives on major socialist issues'.[9] She suggests that in 'both poetry and prose by women' and 'certainly in explicitly feminist work'

> such features and devices are absolutely commonplace – almost an identifying characteristic of women's writing in this century. What is surprising, and impressive, here is Gibbon's sympathetic sense of the massive centrality of the dilemma of contradictory subject positions in female experience. It is seldom far from Chris's consciousness – or ours.[10]

Interestingly, a similar alignment of a multiplistic subjectivity with the feminine is also at play within the *Quair,* for while Gibbon repeatedly foregrounds an acute awareness of it in relation to Chris, it is an aspect of social identity which is not extended to the male characters in the trilogy. On the contrary, in the case of young Ewan, for example, we are repeatedly told that he is 'sure of himself', so certain that his lineage, his ancestry is irrelevant to his own sense of self, that he can say: *'that's nothing to do with me, has it? I'm neither you nor my father: I'm myself.'* (*GG*, 26) While Ewan may glimpse alternative selves in his relationship with Ellen or at the hands of police brutality he is not haunted by them, as his mother is, but quickly reasserts his own, sure sense of identity.

For many modern women writers an insistence on the multiplistic nature of subjectivity is one of the strategies employed to counteract patriarchy – a means of avoiding its binary of either/or, to use Cixous's terms. By foregrounding and even celebrating the evasiveness and fluidity of feminine subjectivity writers seek to launch an attack on the totalising impulses within patriarchal discourse and its repeated desires for the homogeneity embodied in the unified subject. For poststructuralists in general, and for many continental feminists, this desire to disrupt or unsettle homogeneity has its origin in the fact that such totalising impulses within discourse are frequently associated with 'death'. They argue that only by silencing or 'killing off' those other voices, those alternative selves, can the dominant discourse, often associated with patriarchy, retain control and present itself as 'total' or 'complete'. Suggestively, in the *Quair* too, it is only by imagining 'Chris Guthrie, Chris Tavendale, Chris Colquohoun dead' (*CH*, 166) that Chris can imagine 'Chris-alone, Chris-herself' and, finally, she realises that it is, in fact, only through death that the unified subject can, indeed, exist: 'Face thinner and straighter and stranger than once, as though it were shedding mask on mask down to one last reality – the skull, she supposed, that final reality.' (*GG*, 2) It is, this seems to suggest, only in death, the skull, the 'final reality' that the unified subject, one without 'masks' or alternative personae, can be achieved.

By foregrounding an interest in the divided nature of subjectivity, then, and in aligning this with the feminine, the *Quair* manifests surprisingly modern interests and lends itself to analysis within the frameworks of late twentieth-century feminist theory. Gibbon's trilogy, consequently, emerges as a text that sets up a radical dynamic, positing a multivalent, elusive and essentially feminine model alongside the apparent impulse towards homogeneity inscribed within patriarchal experience. This dynamic, which involves the juxtaposition of the characters of young Ewan and Chris, also informs another aspect of the trilogy, which, while it has already been given significant attention, also lends itself to a feminist reading: the treatment of history, politics and time.

In her essay 'Women's Time',[11] Julia Kristeva suggests that there are different ways to consider time. She describes the time of history as *linear* time; time as 'project, teleology, [...] departure, progression and arrival'[12] while 'women's time' is linked both to *cyclical* time (repetition) and to what she calls *monumental* time, described as 'eternity':

> As for time, female subjectivity would seem to provide a specific measure that essentially retains *repetition* and *eternity* from among the multiple modalities of time known through the history of civilizations. On the one hand, there are cycles, gestation, the eternal recurrence of a biological rhythm which conforms to that of nature and imposes a temporality whose stereotyping may shock, but whose regularity and unison with what is experienced as extra-subjective time, cosmic time, occasion vertiginous visions and unnameable *jouissance*. On the other hand, and perhaps as a consequence, there is the massive presence of a monumental temporality, without cleavage or escape, which has so little to do with linear time (which passes) that the very word 'temporality' hardly fits.[13]

The problem which vexes second-stage feminism, she argues, is how to give voice to those experiences of time 'left mute by culture in the past' and which, in particular, because they draw attention to the difference of the feminine, have been rendered 'non-existent' by socialism and Marxism.[14]

It does not take a great deal of imagination to see how Kristeva's concepts of time can be employed to provide a fruitful reading of some of the dynamics at work within *A Scots Quair*. In fact, in his essay 'The Land' (1934), Gibbon himself draws a not dissimilar distinction between the linear time of history and what he calls 'spiral' time, a time linked to Eternity: 'It is strange to think that, if events never die (as some of the wise have supposed), but live existence all time in Eternity, back through the time-spirals, still alive and aware in that world seven thousand years ago, the hunters are *now* lying down their first night in Scotland, with their tall, deep-bosomed sinewy mates and their children, tired from trek.' (*Sm*, 89) This concept of time also seems to haunt *A Scots Quair*, and the problematics which are embodied within the trilogy regarding time, change and politics may be seen as particularly resonant for a feminist discussion when considered alongside Kristeva's concerns with the relationship of women's time to the linear time of history.

Certainly, if the *Quair* is a 'subversive' feminist text, it explores 'the unfairness meted out to' women at the hands of patriarchy not in terms of their straightforward equality with men but in the surprisingly contemporary terms of their differences. As in Kristeva's work, such differences are often defined in terms of apparent biological imperatives. Clearly, at a practical level at least, the novel repeatedly explores a tension between the horrors, and the often unspoken joys, of a woman's biological condition. Chris's mother's suicide, her own mixed responses to pregnancy, and the numerous unwanted pregnancies in the trilogy all reflect the negative side of a woman's reproductive capacity, and an increasing knowledge of birth control described in the novels suggests a growing possibility for freedom and choice for women. However, Gibbon also suggests the crucial position of such biological imperatives in the construction of a feminine subjectivity. For Ma Cleghorn, as for many women in these novels, the very sight of a spinster makes her 'mad to go tearing out and grab the first soss that you met in breeks' (*GG*, 10), and she also suggests that a woman beyond child-bearing age, or without children, has lost a crucial part of her female identity. While Ma's opinions may be idiosyncratic, her thoughts nevertheless affect Chris, causing her to question her own femininity and sense of self: 'And somehow Ma's daft words bade in her mind, those about a woman having finished with things when she finished having bairns, just an empty drum, an old fruit squeezed and rotting away, useless, unkenned, unstirred by the agonies of bearing a bairn, heeding it, feeding it, watching it grow – was she now no more than that herself?' (*GG*, 76). Kristeva supports her thesis on time by suggesting that 'we have seen in the past few years an increasing number of women who not only consider their maternity compatible with their professional life or their feminist involvement [...] but also find it indispensable to their discovery, not of the plenitude, but of the complexity of the female experience, with all that this complexity comprises in joy and pain'.[15]

If the *Quair* foregrounds a comparable difference between men and women in biological terms it, like Kristeva, seems also to propose a similar, and perhaps inseparable, dynamic at work in their relationships to politics, religion and history, arguably the concerns of linear time, as opposed to those of women's biologically related experience of temporality. Chris's own detachment from the political and religious concerns of the men in the trilogy has been well documented; it is what Anderson recognises as a 'private' rather than a 'public' commitment, 'passivity' rather than 'action'. However, Anderson also hints that Chris's method of proceeding may well represent the 'third way', 'a *female* "way" which might prove the salvation of this society, but which is never allowed to succeed'.[16] Certainly Chris's relationship to history and politics is not simply rejected in the text, but is part of a complex attempt to reconcile the perpetual 'change' of linear time with her own desire for that which is enduring. It is, indeed, time in its linear form which repeatedly disrupts Chris's search for happiness and, indeed, her desire for a unified self. Repeatedly, time is evoked as the force which destroys and brings change; in *Cloud Howe* '[Time haunts] their tracks with unstaying feet' (*CH*, 13), and a cold and mechanical look at the clock marks change as Ma Cleghorn dies in *Grey Granite* (*GG*, 104). It is against such change that Chris repeatedly pits herself, recognising that it is at odds with some other eternal or monumental version of herself, again, suggestively, linked to her biological potential:

> Strange that his [Ewan's] body had once come from yours in the days when you were a quean unthinking, so close to the earth and its smell and its feel that nearly he came from the earth itself!
> From that we all came, you had heard Robert say, but wilder and stranger you knew it by far, from the earth's beginning *you yourself* had been here, a blowing of motes in the world's prime, earth, roots and the wings of an insect long syne in the days when the dragons still ranged the world – every atom here in your body now, that was here, that was you, that beat in your heart, that shaped your body to whiteness and strength,

> the speed of your legs and the love of your breasts when you turned to the
> kiss of your Robert at night – these had been there, there was nothing but
> a change, in a form, the stroke and the beat of a song. (*CH*, 52)

While, however, Chris seems to be involved in a dynamic or tension with
linear time, this too is contrasted with the position of the men in the *Quair*
who repeatedly and whole-heartedly embrace it and its forces; Ewan
Tavendale and the other crofters in Kinraddie, for example, as they march
off to war heralding '*the sunset of an age and an epoch*' (*SS*, 255); Robert with
his belief in social progress and the dawning of a new heaven on earth; and
above all, young Ewan who believes that he has become 'Living History'
(*GG*, 148) and that the bus on which he travels with Ellen is 'the chariot
of Time let loose on the world roaring down long fir-darkened haughs of
history into the shining ways of tomorrow.' (*GG*, 153) As the trilogy
progresses, consequently, the masculine becomes associated with linear
time and what it represents, while Chris, with age, becomes increasingly
at odds with it.

Read in terms of a dynamic between Kristeva's monumental, eternal
time and linear time, then, the *Quair* may, in the characters of Chris and,
among others, her son, be seen as enacting a tension between essentially
masculine and feminine value systems, exploring alternative responses to
time and experience. Within these terms, consequently, the conclusion of
the novel cannot simply be dismissed as 'a bleak truth' that 'there is no final
fulfilment for the woman'[17] but emerges as a rather more complex enactment of a masculine and feminine dichotomy. Ewan may, literally, march
into linear time and history, but these forces have already been aligned with
change and death. Chris, on the other hand, through her decision to step
'out of the world' and return to the enduring land and the 'eternal spring',
may embody a subversively feminine impulse which acts to break through
the 'hirpling clock' of linear time, and reassert the monumental and cyclical
time of eternity. Read thus, her death, if we consider it as such – and the
end of the novel is of course notoriously ambiguous – may not *simply* be a
defeat, but is rather only a change 'in a form' to use her own expression, and
an attempt to reassert the feminine. As Burton puts it, her withdrawal may
then be seen as contributing to 'an understanding of history beyond the
limitations of patriarchy',[18] offering an alternative reading of history which
offers a particularly feminine concept of the dynamics of power within
human experience.

Gibbon's exploration of the tension between linear time and cyclical
'spiral' time is, of course, also reflected in the narrative strategies of the

Quair with its opening 'mythological' sections which elide the great time spans of history, and with its repeated textual practice of non-linear narration whereby the events of the narrative are conveyed retrospectively and out of sequence. Carla Sassi argues that these aspects of the novel, along with its tendencies towards an orality which questions the authority of the written word, and its narrative voice which modulates between character and author, reflect a lack of a fixed centre in Gibbon's trilogy.[19] Sassi suggests that this arises from Gibbon's Scottishness, arguing that national marginalisation leads him to provide a text which subverts centralised authority. For feminist critics, however, these features may all equally be recognised as aspects of *écriture féminine*.

For Kristeva, linear time is also the time of totalising discourse: 'It might also be added that this linear time is that of language considered as the enunciation of sentences (noun + verb; topic-comment; beginning-ending), and that this time rests on its own stumbling block, which is also the stumbling block of that enunciation – death'.[20] Radical writing, or what she elsewhere calls 'poetic language' may, however, be employed as a gesture towards giving voice to that which has been 'made mute' by such discourse. As she puts it in 'Women's Time', it frequently employs strategies to 'break the code, to shatter language, to find a specific discourse closer to the body and emotions, to the unnameable repressed by the social contract'.[21] Such radical writing, in short, gives voice to that which is encapsulated within 'women's time', or what we might describe as the 'semiotic', a 'pre-linguistic' mode often aligned with the feminine.

There is no space here in which to detail all the ways in which the narrative strategies of the *Quair* may be recognised as contributing to such radicalism, although the tendency towards orality and the modulation in the authorial voice outlined by Sassi, among others, are surely relevant. One feature which is perhaps worth commenting upon briefly, is, however, the linguistic strategies of the trilogy. In spite of the novel's acclaimed tendency towards orality it can be surprisingly difficult to read aloud from the *Quair*. This is, perhaps, due to the fact that, as he points out in his note to the trilogy, Gibbon relies not only on 'some score or so untranslatable words and idioms' to render Scots but on 'the rhythms and cadence of the kindred speech that his peasants speak'; rhythms and cadences which operate to disrupt the conventional linearity of language; the enunciation of sentences as 'noun + verb; topic-comment' simultaneously disrupting our readerly expectations and our ability to read aloud fluently.

To use Scots in such a disruptive way was, of course, part of the wider Scottish Renaissance project. By adopting the language of a marginal culture alongside that of its dominant neighbour, Gibbon and others gave voice, in the most simple of ways, to that which had been repressed and silenced. However, the Scots in the *Quair* is employed far more frequently by the narratorial voice than by the voices of the characters, implying that its function is not merely realistic or straightforwardly political but may embody something more subtly radical.

In his essay 'Literary Lights', Gibbon suggests that the work of Scottish writers is frequently 'haunted' by the ghost of the Scots language:

> The English reader is haunted by a sense of something foreign stumbling and hesitating behind this smooth façade of adequate technique: it is as though the writer did not *write* himself, but *translated* himself.
>
> Often the Scots writer is quite unaware of this essential foreignness in his work; more often, seeking an adequate word or phrase he hears an echo in an alien tongue that would adorn his meaning with a richness, a clarity and a conciseness impossible in orthodox English. That echo is from Braid Scots, from that variation of the Anglo-Saxon speech which was the tongue of the great Scots civilisation, the tongue adopted by the basic Pictish strain in Scotland as its chief literary tool. (*Sm*, 125-26)

As a writer, then, Lewis Grassic Gibbon was very well aware of the 'essential foreignness' which he had chosen to put into his work via language, and it would seem that the inclusion of Scots in the *Quair* functions not only at a surface level, but also as a strategy to 'haunt' the 'smooth technique' of Gibbon's narrative; to 'shatter language' and 'give voice to the unnameable' to borrow Kristeva's terms. Notably, for Ewan, Scots is 'that blunted and foolish and out-dated tool' (*GG*, 155), and he ignores his own occasional need for it just as he ignores his alternative selves and those other versions of time which walk along side his own History. For the people of Kinraddie, Scots is a medium through which things inexpressible in orthodox English may be expressed. For Chris it is, like so many other things, an expression of a problematic: both a function and an embodiment of her divided subjectivity, a force which bursts through to unsettle any version of a unified self, just as, arguably, it erupts into the textual world of the *Quair* to disrupt the totalising impulses of discourse.

For Kristeva, language 'is at the service of the death drive' but art, and particularly writing which 'shatters language', exports 'semiotic motility across the border on which the symbolic is established' and allows the artist to '[sketch] out a kind of second birth'.[22] In other words, the disrupting strategies of poetic language – for example, the kind of disruptive linguistic strategies employed by Gibbon in the *Quair* – function to defeat the death-wish of language. By subverting the imperatives of linear time and linear enunciation they give voice to those suppressed others: that is, the semiotic, the eternal, and the monumental; the markers of women's writing which may, for many European feminists, be called particularly 'feminine'. In its strategies of linguistic and narrative disruption, in its insistence on a particularly feminine multiplistic subjectivity, and in its positing of an enactment of 'women's time' in juxtaposition to the linear time of history and politics the *Quair* may, perhaps, be read in terms of such feminist radicalism. Read within the paradigm of 'images of women' criticism, Chris's apparent 'death' at the end of *Grey Granite* must remain problematic. However, European feminism may provide a model whereby her withdrawal can be read more positively; as the embodiment of a feminine rejection of linear time in favour of the 'suppressed alternatives' of women's experience, contributing, as Burton puts it, to a 'shift in conceptualization that will require a different kind of political understanding and activity.'[23] Indeed, read within 'women's time' Chris's decision to retreat at the end of the trilogy, along with many other radical strategies in the *Quair*, may offer a particularly feminine and radically subversive possibility of textual 'second birth'.

Notes

Quotations will be referenced from *A Scots Quair: Sunset Song, Cloud Howe, Grey Granite* (Edinburgh: Canongate Publishing, 1995), ed. with an introd. by Tom Crawford. Quotations from 'The Land' and 'Literary Lights' are referenced from *Smeddum: A Grassic Gibbon Anthology*, ed. by Valentina Bold (Edinburgh: Canongate, 2000), with page numbers given in the text, preceded by *Sm*.

1. Keith Dixon, 'Rough Edges: The Feminist Representation of Women in the Writing of Lewis Grassic Gibbon' in *Studies in Scottish Fiction: Twentieth Century*, ed. by Joachim Schwend and Horst W. Drescher (Frankfurt am Main: Peter Lang, 1990), pp. 289-301 (p. 289). Since this paper was given, a feminist reading of Lewis Grassic Gibbon / James Leslie Mitchell's work has been offered by Christine Kerr in *Lewis Grassic Gibbon: Gender, Sex and Sexualities* (unpub. Ph.D thesis, University of Sussex, 2002).
2. See Isobel Murray's essay in this collection, 'Gibbon's Chris: a celebration with some reservations'.
3. Dixon, p. 298.
4. Sandra F. M. Hunter, *The Role and Status of Women in the Fiction of James Leslie Mitchell/ Lewis Grassic Gibbon* (unpub. MA Thesis, McMaster University, Hamilton, Ontario, 1995), p. 2.

5. Carol E. Anderson, *The Representation of Women in Scottish Fiction: Character and Symbol* (unpub. Ph.D Thesis, University of Edinburgh, 1985), pp. 290 and 295.

6. Anderson, pp. 380-81.

7. Anderson, pp. 329 and 295.

8. Julia Kristeva, who was born in Bulgaria in 1941, is a psychoanalyst and professor of linguistics at the University of Paris. Her work focuses on linguistics, semiotics, psychoanalysis and questions of femininity. Hélène Cixous was born in Algeria in 1938. She also taught at the University of Paris and founded the first research group on the theory of femininity. While these writers have many differences, some fundamental, the concepts of *écriture féminine* and 'radical writing' both place an emphasis on a particularly disruptive style as a key element in 'feminine' discourse and the concepts may be recognised as closely related for the purposes of this essay. For a good introduction to European feminist thought see *French Feminist Thought: A Reader* ed. by Toril Moi (Oxford: Basil Blackwell, 1987) and *New French Feminisms* ed. by Elaine Marks and Isabelle de Courtivron (Brighton: Harvester, 1981) which includes Cixous's essays 'Sorties' and 'The Laugh of the Medusa'.

9. Deirdre Burton, 'A Feminist Reading of Lewis Grassic Gibbon's *A Scots Quair*' in *The British Working-Class Novel in the Twentieth Century,* ed. by Jeremy Hawthorn (London: Edward Arnold, 1984), pp. 34-46 (p. 35).

10. Burton, pp. 38-39.

11. 'Women's Time' was first published as 'Le temps des femmes' in 33/44: *Cahiers de recherche de sciences des textes et documents,* 5 (1979), pp. 5-19 and was translated in *Signs,* 7, (1981), pp. 13-35.

12. Julia Kristeva, 'Women's Time', in *The Kristeva Reader*, ed. by Toril Moi (New York: Columbia University Press, 1986), pp. 187-213 (p. 192).

13. 'Women's Time', p. 191.

14. 'Women's Time', pp. 194 and 196. Kristeva describes two generations of feminists. She identifies the first as concentrating on issues like equal pay and equal footing with men in the workplace, and with the rejection of those attributes traditionally thought feminine or maternal as incompatible with 'insertion' into linear time and history. Second phase feminists, she suggests, reject linear temporality and distrust politics and are interested in 'the specificity of female psychology'. In other words, while first phase feminists sought equality with men, younger, second stage feminists are more concerned with the differences between the masculine and the feminine.

15. 'Women's Time', p. 205.

16. Anderson, p. 330.

17. Anderson, p. 319.

18. Burton, p. 46.

19. Carla Sassi, 'Scottishness and the Nomadic Myth in Lewis Grassic Gibbon's Fiction' in *Appropriations and Inspirations: National, Regional and Sexual Identity in Literature,* ed. by Igor Navrátil and Robert B. Pynsent (Bratislava: Národné literárne centrum, 1997), pp. 94-100 (pp. 97-99).

20. 'Women's Time', p. 192.
21. 'Women's Time', p. 200.
22. Julia Kristeva, 'Revolution in Poetic Language' in *The Kristeva Reader*, pp. 89-136 (pp. 119 and 120).
23. Burton, p. 43.

Gibbon's Chris:
A Celebration With Some Reservations

Isobel Murray

I am a great admirer of *A Scots Quair,* and have been for many years.[1] It is a wonderful trilogy. But I have also frequently stubbed my toe on its imperfections, wishing I could call its author back from the shades for half an hour, to score out lines or phrases that gar me grue. These include the awkward imposition of over-blatant symbolism, which grates as inappropriate. When Chris is pregnant in *Cloud Howe*, Robert famously says: '*Oh Chris Caledonia, I've married a nation!*' Toward the end of *Grey Granite*, Ewan speaks to his mother: 'He said suddenly and queerly, *The Last Supper, Chris*'.[2] And the ponderous unintelligibility of the last sentence of *Grey Granite* makes a disappointing ending. I think the *Quair* is perhaps the most imperfect great work of literature I know. I think it is open in parts to suggestions of over-heightened action, perhaps amounting to melodrama, or inadequate grasp of female psychology and social mores. Maybe this is not surprising, given the pressured haste with which Gibbon composed it. And here I even find myself criticising the feature most generally agreed to be a triumphant success, the presentation of Chris Guthrie. I want to say her characterisation is very imperfect too. But before I start, let me insist that I think the trilogy can survive anything I might throw at it: its language and unique vision and passion ensure that, and cast a spell. I take nothing back that I have ever said in its praise.

I start with a remark from Tom Crawford's Introduction to *Sunset Song* in his fine edition of *A Scots Quair:*

> In this novel Gibbon has created the most convincing female character in Scottish fiction, and so sympathetically, so inwardly, that many of the original readers wondered whether 'Lewis Grassic Gibbon' might be the nom-de-plume of a woman author. (*SS*, viii)

The reviewers were all men. It's true that some early readers, including poet Helen Cruickshank, at first thought it might have been written by a woman, but I don't think it's possible for anyone to think that now, now that the dust has had time to settle. At best, I would argue, Chris might be the most convincing female character in Scottish fiction created by a male author. To outline my case, I place the trilogy – or, in relation to this paper, *Sunset Song* (1932) – beside two other novels of the time, Nan Shepherd's *The Quarry Wood* (1928) and Willa Muir's *Imagined Corners* (1931).

Gibbon is unparalleled in creating the passionate lyricism of Chris's Song. And he is not above learning from his contemporaries, which is praiseworthy. I have pointed out elsewhere how many suggestions he took from Willa Muir, including the portrayal of Chris as composed at different times of warring selves.[3] It was Muir who pioneered this technique in *Imagined Corners*, with both Elizabeth Shand and Elise Mütze. Elizabeth Shand, trying to be a perfect wife, has a waking nightmare experience, 'feeling that she was lost and no longer knew who she was'.[4] When she remembers the name 'Elizabeth Ramsay', her maiden name, the nightmare vanishes. She faces the diminution of her personal identity, but rallies: 'Elizabeth Ramsay she was, but also Elizabeth Shand, and she herself, that essential self which awoke from sleep, had felt lost because she had forgotten that fact' (*IC*, 65).

Elise Mütze also recognises co-existing selves, as she tries to find a 'central self', looking back in some self-mockery at 'Elizabeth the first' and 'Elizabeth the second': 'When she was a little girl Elizabeth the second had been, if anything, a few moments the quicker of the two, and Elizabeth the first was restricted to making sarcastic comments' (*IC*, 147). In the cases of both characters, Muir takes care to analyse carefully the implication of some kind of divided or multiple selves. This means that they are very important in context, pointing up crucial questions about female identity, and they are consistent with other parts of the book. Elizabeth Ramsay has two selves, the original and the married one, and Elise Mütze achieves not only Elizabeth the first and Elizabeth the second, but also what she hopes is a resolution: 'Well! Now I've run away from a tea-party, and most extraordinarily have cornered myself.' (*IC*, 234) This, she thought, was her 'central, dispassionate, impregnable self' (*IC*, 280), but she deserts it and resorts in the end to caprice, taking Elizabeth away with her. But the analysis Muir makes, while progressing, is consistent.

As all his readers know, Gibbon memorably adapted the technique of referring to divided selves in *Sunset Song*, first with the English Chris and the Scottish Chris:

> [T]wo Chrisses there were that fought for her heart and tormented her.
> You hated the land and the coarse speak of the folk and learning was brave
> and fine one day; and the next you'd waken with the peewits crying across
> the hills, deep and deep, crying in the heart of you and the smell of the
> earth in your face, almost you'd cry for that, the beauty of it and the
> sweetness of the Scottish land and skies. (*SS*, 32).

This is a brilliant utterance of the 'self-reflexive you', but we might argue
that Gibbon uses the technique of divided selves too often, and fragments
his heroine too many times in different ways. We remember Chris's
emotional response to her realisation of her pregnancy: 'And Chris Guthrie
crept out from the place below the beech trees where Chris Tavendale lay and
went wandering off into the waiting quiet of the afternoon, Chris Tavendale
heard her go, and she came back to Blawearie never again' (*SS*, 176). Each
usage is effective, but they do not have continuity or consistency, either in
Sunset Song or in the *Quair* in general. It is not necessarily simply a failing of
literal-minded undergraduates that they become puzzled by the Epilude
when Chris says to Robert, '*Oh, my dear, maybe the second Chris, maybe the third,
but Ewan has the first forever!*' (*SS*, 253). And it is perhaps a self too far when
she dreams in *Cloud Howe* of going her own way, 'Chris-alone, Chris-herself,
with Chris Guthrie, Chris Tavendale, Chris Colquohoun dead!' (*CH*, 166).
Gibbon's uses of the technique work locally on each occasion, but do not
build, like Muir's, into an intelligible whole.

I want to suggest also that the intimacy and conviction of Chris's
thought-and-feeling, combined with the marvellously contrived structure
of *Sunset Song*, blinds us to the drama – or even indeed the unlikely
melodrama – to which Gibbon subjects the readers of *Sunset Song*. These
qualities obscure the speed and drama with which events pile up for Chris.

Nan Shepherd's *The Quarry Wood* is much less eventful. In his
Introduction to the Canongate reprint, Rory Watson says that it shows
'what might have happened to Chris Guthrie, had she decided to go to
university after all', and comments that Martha 'makes the same difficult
journey towards intellectual and emotional maturity at a time when such
space was seldom freely given to women'.[5] The action here is much more
mundane. Martha's mother Emmeline has a lot in common with Jean
Guthrie on the face of it. We are told in a dry, dispassionate way of her
circumstances on page 2:

> With base effrontery she married the man she loved, and after twelve
> pinched and muddled years, with her trim beauty slack, two dead bairns
> and a living one mostly nerves and temper, she stood in her disordered

kitchen and fretted that she could not offer her aunt a decent cup of tea. (*QW*, 2)

But Emmeline does not commit suicide, or murder: she hashes her way along, picking up extra bairns to nurture at every turn. Martha goes to university, nurses mother and aunt repeatedly, becomes a teacher, falls hopelessly in love with her best friend's husband, and in a moment of un-Shepherdlike passion exchanges one kiss with him. It's a fine novel, with a minimum of dramatic action, and its only melodrama is in Martha's youthful emotions and imagination.

It is possible to make the action of *Imagined Corners* sound sensational, if you say it starts with a newly married couple arriving in Calderwick, and ends with the bride running off with another woman. But it also is not sensational. The most that happens is that people rebel against the repressive society of Calderwick, and leave, and the main action is internal, a matter of self-discovery for the two main female characters.

Contrast *Sunset Song*. The following actually occurs. Chris is fifteen during the horror of the difficult birth of the twins. There follow in quick succession the move to the Mearns; the 'daftie' going on a sexual rampage which involves Chris and several others; the communal harvest madness; Mother killing herself when she discovers she is pregnant yet again; Mother killing the year-old twins as well; the loss of brothers Dod and Alec, the departure of Will after great strife with his father, leaving Chris alone with her father; Father's strokes, his attempted incest; his death; Chris's decision to stay on the land; her marriage to Ewan, pregnancy and childbirth, the onset of the Great War and the persecution of Long Rob; Ewan's degradation, then his desertion and execution; and after all that she is still a teenager! If not melodramatic, we might at least call this 'heightened realism', perhaps?

The same kind of 'heightened realism' can be seen in the presentation of characters in the three novels. *The Quarry Wood* has a wide range of both sexes, and Martha as main female character is surrounded by strong portraits of women of different ages: the ever-memorable Great Aunt Josephine, Martha's feckless mother Emmeline, her friend Dussie, the intimidating intellectual Lucy Warrender and more. Similarly, in *Imagined Corners* we meet a wide range of characters of both sexes, the women most notable, including, as well as the two Elizabeths, Sarah Murray, Mabel Shand, Aunt Janet and the Watson sisters. But in *Sunset Song* female characters other than Chris are swiftly stripped away or kept in very minor positions. In the whole trilogy, Chris only ever has one equal female friend,

Marget Strachan. We recall that vivid short scene when Marget shows the
adolescent Chris how her future lad will kiss her – 'quick and shameful,
fine for all that, tingling and strange and shameful by turns' (*SS*, 46). But
she is almost immediately removed from the scene, never to return, not
even as a guest at Chris's wedding, let alone a bridesmaid. This function
is performed, for the usually unconventional Chris, by two girls, of no
great significance to the novel or to Chris, one whose first name she doesn't
seem to know. Marget fades from the reader's memory.

    Jean Guthrie, of course, is taken away from Chris as well, by her own
act. And I've always found her suicide affecting and horribly understandable: the birth of the twins was described so graphically that her fear at
another prospective delivery makes sense. (But I've never understood her
killing of the twins – only one even named in the novel, and given a
gender, though they have been part of the family for a whole year. Jean has
apparently no compunction about killing them, although she has fed and
cared for them for a year; and Chris makes little of their deaths: both she
and her father wonder later why Jean left them, but seem to have forgotten
the babies, surely distinct personalities to the whole family by this time.)
The rest of the family is stripped away, leaving Chris and her father alone.
Now Chris is the only sexual focal point on the landscape, in an otherwise
all-male environment, with sexual tensions in all directions, from Chae,
Long Rob, Ewan, and of course Father.

    The local people who were affronted on the publication of *Sunset Song*
perhaps had a point: it *is* drenched in sex, to a unique degree. I am
unfashionable here: it is not my favourite volume of the trilogy, because the
emphasis on sex generally tends to overwhelm other aspects of Gibbon's
vision, and the blissful marriage of young Chris and Ewan is seen as one
where physical happiness is temporarily obscuring deeper differences
between the two, which Gibbon never has an opportunity to develop. In
the end, I find that the treatment of the troubled love between Chris and
Robert Colquohoun, as we see it in *Cloud Howe,* and in retrospect in *Grey
Granite,* has greater depth than the treatment of sexuality in *Sunset Song.*
The subject is so pervasive. We remember the day when Andy the daftie
goes on the sexual spree, and variously follows Mistress Ellison, Maggie
Jean and Chris herself, who is able to take refuge in Pooty's. But we are
struck by John Guthrie's reaction: 'Father raged when he heard the story
from Chris, queer raging it was, he took her out to the barn and heard the
story and his eyes slipped up and down her dress as she spoke, she felt
sickened and queer. *He shamed you then?* he whispered.' (*SS*, 52-3) This
resembles his fury when he finds Chris treading the blankets bare-legged,

when it was 'as though she saw a caged beast peep from her father's eyes' (*SS*, 60). And there is the fearful night during the harvest madness when she hears him lurking outside her bedroom door. We are well prepared for his attempted incest when it comes. Then there is the rest of the harvest madness sequence, which attacks Father first: 'every harvest there came something queer and terrible on father' (*SS*, 67). Then the casual working tink offers to relieve Chris of her virginity, and she does consider it, however briefly. Ewan Tavendale is seen with Sarah Sinclair; Cuddiestoun surprises the manse maid and the minister; people talk about Will and his Molly, and the minister reveals the depth of his hypocrisy in this regard.

I will introduce my final criticism of Gibbon's presentation of Chris with a story that dates back to the first year that I offered a Scottish special subject to Honours students, and I encountered the 'Donald Paterson Syndrome.' Donald was a bright and lively student: I learned later that he and his mate Callum used to rehearse some of their best lines together before the seminar, to get maximum impact – and it worked! But it was unrehearsed, and in a spirit of pure pity that he said to me at a *Sunset Song* seminar – 'Isobel, you're never going to understand the Gibbon thing until you realise that every male reader is in love with Chris.' I saw what he meant, and was grateful for the tip. But since then I have seen it ever more clearly, and with some suspicion. I now see that for all her unique intimacy with the reader, and 'the self-reflexive you', the sexual desirability of the female Chris is regularly seized on by her (male) creator and displayed to the male gaze.

I've often asked female students since Donald Paterson's year whether they have a recurrent need to retreat upstairs to a cold, wintry bedroom, there to undress and inspect themselves slowly in front of the mirror. I've never yet met one who owns up to this tendency, although women's bedrooms are surely warmer now than in Chris's young day. But Chris does this, or something like it, five times in *Sunset Song*, six times in *Cloud Howe* and eight times in *Grey Granite*. Maybe using a word such as voyeurism is unkind and unnecessary, but maybe not. There is an element of titillation here that seems deliberate.

In *The Quarry Wood*, Martha Ironside is not a mirror sort of girl, and I think she is only recorded as looking in a glass twice. This extract shows us a great deal about her with Shepherd's customary economy:

> But what did they all see in her eyes, she queried, staring in the dull and spotty mirror. She could not even tell their colour exactly: they had something in them of Nature's greens that have gone brown, of grass-fields

before the freshening of spring. What did they all see in them? She looked
in the mirror longer than she had ever looked before, searching for her own
beauty. It was not to be found there. (*QW*, 79)

The mirror *is* dull and spotty – and the colour of her eyes is suggested very
specifically; and what other people see in her eyes is nothing she will ever
find by looking in a mirror. Soon after this she looks again, transformed by
wearing the very special frock handed down through the family. This time
she does almost glimpse an elusive, real Martha:

> Wearing it, Martha had an uncanny sense of being someone other than
> herself; as though she had stepped carelessly to a mirror to dress her hair
> and had seen features not her own looking out from the glass. The mere
> wearing of the frock could not have changed her: but like the mirror it
> served to make her aware of alteration; and she seemed to herself farther
> from her folk and her home. Wearing the lustre frock, she had no Ironside
> instincts. She did not belong to the Leggatts. Across the mirror of lustre
> there flitted an unfamiliar Martha with alien desires. (*QW*, 93)

Similarly, Elizabeth Shand in *Imagined Corners* is not a mirror person. She is
gawky and awkward, a girl with a passionate soul and no interest in make-
up, but here she is resolving to be a good wife to the appalling Hector, and
to take care of him as he requires; and sustained by the belief that 'she now
presented the comforting appearance that Hector expected of her':

> She must have known this instinctively, for she first bathed and powdered
> her face, and then put on her prettiest frock. In Calderwick at that time
> it was considered slightly improper to powder one's face by day, but
> Elizabeth excused her daring by reflecting that darkness had already set
> in, although it was not yet five o'clock. She inspected herself in the glass
> and added a string of coloured beads, signs of dawning femininity which
> might have pleased her sister-in-law. (*IC*, 126)

Like Shepherd's narrator, but even more so, Muir's preserves a dry
detachment and amusement toward her characters, who are more complex,
and more insecure than Gibbon's Chris. Elise Mütze, the continental
sophisticate who used to be Lizzie Shand, is no doubt much more used to
utilising the mirror than Elizabeth Shand is. But her author does not take
us there routinely. On this occasion a Calderwick tea-party has irritated
Elise beyond bearing, and she has escaped, only to glimpse something very
interesting in her bedroom mirror:

In that moment of consciousness she caught sight of herself in the long mirror. One cannot look at oneself and remain angry; contrariwise, if one insists on remaining angry one cannot go on looking at oneself. Elise stared; the mirror was like a fog enclosing a ghostly image; gradually the image grew clearer, took shape, and Elise, breaking into a smile, said: 'Hello, Lizzie Shand! Where have *you* been all these years?'
The impetuous, resentful small girl who had hovered in the church and stepped with Elise over the paving stones of Calderwick had come back. (*IC*, 233)

In all these examples the authors are using the simple act of looking in the mirror to convey complex nuances of character and theme. Gibbon's male perspective is a stark contrast.

Gibbon's reflections of Chris, or a small selection of them, seem so blatant when one isolates them. The first is a moving picture of a beautiful, sensual woman looking fully and frankly at her reflection, and incidentally presenting herself to the reader, who is encouraged to dwell on her attractions, and follow the path, even the touch, of the moonlight.

[She] closed the window, shutting out the smells of the night, and slowly took off her clothes, looking at herself in the long glass. [...] She was growing up limber and sweet, not bonny, perhaps, her cheek-bones were over high and her nose over short for that, but her eyes clear and deep and brown, brown deep and clear as the Denburn flow, and her hair was red and was brown by turns, spun fine as a spider's web, wild, wonderful hair. [...] And below face and neck now her clothes were off was the glimmer of shoulders and breast and there her skin was like satin, it tickled her touching herself. Below the tilt of her left breast was a dimple, she saw it and bent to look at it and the moonlight ran down her back, so queer the moonlight she felt the running of that beam along her back. And she straightened as the moonlight grew and looked at the rest of herself, and thought herself sweet and cool and fit for that lover who would some day come and kiss her and hold her, so. (*SS*, 70-71)

The same kind of description is found in the following passage, where the emphasis is less on wonderful hair and more on satin skin and long lines, with a touch of pity for those less well equipped:

And she saw the light white on the satin of her smooth skin then, and the long, smooth lines that lay from waist to thigh, thigh to knee, and was glad her legs were long from the knee to the ankle, that made legs seem stumbling and stumpy, shortness there. And [...] she bent to see if that

dimple still hid there under her left breast, it did, it was deep as ever.
Then she straightened and took down her hair and brushed it, standing
so, silly to stand without her night-gown, but that was the mood she was
in. (*SS*, 147)

Next is a snatch of the pregnant Chris, again admiring her reflection, and
again pitying by contrast other women, here those whom pregnancy does
not become:

[S]he was glad, peeking at herself in the long mirror when she was alone,
seeing gradually that smooth rounding of belly and hips below her frock
– lucky, she had never that ugliness that some poor folk have to bear,
awful for them. (*SS*, 183)

I think I have to call this writing a kind of voyeurism.

There may even be in *Sunset Song* a deliberate, self-conscious acknowledgement of Gibbon's subtle encouragement of voyeurism. We can look
back to the time when the writer's repulsive namesake, the hypocritical and
oversexed Rev Gibbon, came to try for the pulpit at Kinraddie. He preached
a very 'rare' sermon on the Song of Solomon:

It was Christ's description of the beauty and comeliness of the Auld Kirk
of Scotland, and [...] a picture of womanly beauty that moulded itself in
the lithe and grace of the Kirk [...] And in a minute or so all Kinraddie
kirk was listening to him as though he were promising to pay their taxes
at the end of Martinmas.
For it was fair tickling to hear about things like that read out from a
pulpit, a woman's breasts and thighs and all the rest of the things, in that
voice like the mooing of a holy bull; and to know it was decent Scripture
with a higher meaning as well. (*SS*, 55)

Chris may not be, as Tom Crawford claimed, the most convincing female
character in Scottish fiction, but Gibbon seems aware that he has taken
pains to make her physically and in detail the most attractive!

I think I have said enough to illustrate aspects of the novel which are
less than totally satisfactory, if one can resist the spell. But as I said at the
start, the trilogy effortlessly survives my carping. To remind us how completely Gibbon triumphed at the end of the day, let me quote what Jessie
Kesson wrote to Douglas Young some years ago. *Sunset Song* was published
just before she turned sixteen, and it was very definitely forbidden reading
in the orphanage at Kirkton of Skene:

To read it, I 'snecked' myself inside our dry lavatory next to the pig's sty. And although I had 'written' bits and pieces ever since I could *spell!!!* – it was then I had my first conviction that I'd be a writer, in my reaction to *Sunset Song* – in the dry lavatory. 'That's MY book', I protested to myself. 'He's written MY book!' I so identified with Chris Guthrie.[6]

Notes

1. See, for example, 'Lewis Grassic Gibbon: *A Scots Quair*' in Isobel Murray and Bob Tait, *Ten Modern Scottish Novels* (Aberdeen: Aberdeen University Press, 1984), pp. 10-31; 'Action and Narrative Stance in *A Scots Quair*' in *Literature of the North* ed. by David Hewitt and Michael Spiller (Aberdeen: Aberdeen University Press, 1983), pp. 109-20.
2. Lewis Grassic Gibbon, *Cloud Howe* (1933), reprint ed. and introd. by Tom Crawford (Edinburgh: Canongate, 1988), p. 139; *Grey Granite* (1934), reprint. ed. and introd. by Tom Crawford (Edinburgh: Canongate, 1990), p. 201. Further quotations from *A Scots Quair* will be referenced in the text from the Canongate Classics edition (1995), which includes Crawford's editions of all three books (1988, 1989 and 1990).
3. Isobel Murray, 'Selves, Names and Roles: Willa Muir's *Imagined Corners* offers some inspiration for *A Scots Quair*', *Scottish Literary Journal* 21:1 (1994), pp. 56-64.
4. Willa Muir, *Imagined Corners* (1931) in *Imagined Selves*, introd. by Kirsty Allen (Edinburgh: Canongate, 1996), p. 64. Page numbers for subsequent references will be given in the text from this edition, preceded by *IC*.
5. Nan Shepherd, *The Quarry Wood* (1928) in *The Grampian Quartet*, introd. by Roderick Watson (Edinburgh: Canongate, 1996), p. viii. Page numbers for subsequent references will be given in the text preceded by *QW*.
6. Jessie Kesson, quoted in Isobel Murray, *Jessie Kesson: Writing Her Life* (Edinburgh: Canongate, 2000), p. 81.

From *Grey Granite* to Urban Grit: A Revolution in Perspectives

David Borthwick

Grassic Gibbon's *Grey Granite,*[1] despite dating from 1934, provides a narrative model for describing urban life, and working class life, that is constantly borrowed from in contemporary Scottish fiction. Most recently, Gibbon's example can be seen in the juxtaposed voices and narratives utilised by Irvine Welsh. It strikes me that both Gibbon and Welsh have portrayed an urban sphere which is in a state of cultural and economic crisis. The working classes of both Gibbon's Duncairn and Welsh's Edinburgh share a level of change and uncertainty characterised by the machinations of corporate economics. In *Grey Granite* and, indeed, within Welsh's vision of Edinburgh, dependence on low-paid labour and handouts from the state are central to the survival of many protagonists. Gibbon's 'broo men' and Welsh's 'dole-moles' and addicts are characterised by their economic unproductiveness. They are unable to contribute fully to society and, furthermore, to a society in which material wealth and economic success determines rank.[2] The examples of both Gibbon and Welsh illustrate what Jürgen Neubauer has called 'problem populations' which are 'redundant, stranded and bored'.[3]

Ian S. Munro, referring to an article by William Montgomerie, makes the point that Gibbon's Duncairn is 'a city without a history, without development, without depth, without background'.[4] To a non-Scottish reader, Welsh's Edinburgh is equally unknowable. Of course, Gibbon's city is entirely fictional while Welsh's Edinburgh is a fictionalised representation of a real location.[5] However, without a Scot's background knowledge, Welsh's Edinburgh, too, is without history or depth. Welsh's references to Montgomery Street or the Meadows occupy the same status as the Windmill Steps or Craigneuks to the uninformed reader. The fictional Duncairn, like the fictionalised Edinburgh, is 'anonymous and voiceless despite the tumult of traffic and noise of its inhabitants'.[6] The communal 'you' voice, expressing 'generally acknowledged truths'[7] that summed up community opinion in Kinraddie and Segget has been lost in the city of Duncairn. The city's voices are stratified and fragmented according to geography and class. Duncairn's working-class 'keelies' have no voice that can sound out across the city: their voice is confined to the slums of Paldy Parish and the Cowgate. In Welsh's fictionalised Muirhouse and Wester Hailes, there is no communal voice whatsoever which can express working-class experience in a holistic way. Nonetheless, these two fictional cities are only knowable by the multiple voices of their inhabitants, and it is these voices, and working-class voices in particular, that I will explore.

Gibbon's Duncairn is socially, geographically and ideologically stratified. The multiple voices of the city make Duncairn a city of ideas; they cut across the boundaries of class, and represent in themselves commitments, ideologies and obsessions. These commitments range from Neil Quaritch's view that the Douglas Scheme[8] is 'the Only Plan to Save Civilisation' (*GG*, 51), to John Cushnie's desperate attempts to retain his 'improved' status. We have Miss Murgatroyd's ultra-conservative Unionist Ladies. So too, there is the Reverend MacShilluck's congregation, hermetically sealed in Craigneuks, with only the *Daily Runner* to rely on for happenings outside their own district of the town. The *Daily Runner* provides ready-made modern parables for MacShilluck that affirm the dignified status of his parishioners in opposition to what he perceives as 'the atheist, loose-living times' (*GG*, 58) encouraged by the political activists in Footforthie. The class-based ideologies of geographically situated groups in the middle and upper-classes perpetuate their own social identities, using a communal voice that is constantly in agreement with itself. However, it is not a communal voice recognisable to the inhabitants of Kinraddie or Segget. Gibbon lets us know that the gossiping 'you' voice of these communities, expressing 'generally acknowledged truths' and largely using a Scots vocabulary, is not suitable as a communal voice for the inhabitants of Craigneuks. Gibbon employs an external narrator to report events and to sum up a communal sentiment. The narrator does so as Craigneuks reads the newspaper over breakfast on the morning following the riot at Gowans and Gloag's. We are told: 'all Craigneuks read the news with horror, every word of it' (*GG*, 122). While Gibbon's narrator is mocking and satiric as he describes the rich breakfasts enjoyed in Craigneuks, he *does* succeed in conveying a communal sentiment that is fitting. He ends this narrative with Craigneuks' resolution on the strikers: '[s]omething would have to be done about them' (*GG*, 122).

The class-system in Duncairn is held firm by agreement regarding issues that consolidate 'gentry' identities in opposition to those sections of the population which are geographically removed in peripheral areas of the town and, furthermore, traditionally employed in manual, low-paid forms of work. The alarm in Craigneuks at news of 'Red' tendencies among the 'keelies' arises because such agitation threatens to upset the status-quo of the class system in the town. News of Communist agitation also unnerves the residents of wealthy areas of the town, because *their idea* of the working classes is disrupted by it. Among Duncairn's gentrified inhabitants, the working-class in themselves exist as an idea rather than as a reality. This is seen when news of 'Red' agitators among the Footforthie 'keelies' filters up to Craigneuks courtesy of the *Daily Runner*. The town fathers immediately view 'Reds' and working-class 'keelies' as being distinct. Lord Provost Speight puts the incident down to 'Communist agents, paid agitators who were trained in Moscow' (*GG*, 58). For Speight, the problem does not originate among the working-class in Duncairn. He uses a general comment, regarding the consequences of Communism in Russia, in order to offset the riot's relevance to any unrest in Duncairn. In this way, he affirms his *own ideas* of the identity of the Duncairn workers. He is reported as saying that 'the working-class was sound as a bell' (*GG*, 58). During the strike, when workers who 'scabbed' are attacked, the *Daily Runner* also differentiates between 'Red' strikers and Duncairn's idealised vision of the working-class. The strikers are accused of doing 'awful things' to 'working folk that were coming decent-like from their jobs' (*GG*, 122). To the higher orders of Duncairn – the gentry – the 'keelies' of Footforthie do not exist as a social reality. At the end of the novel, as the hunger march is organised, the *Daily Runner* sub-editor takes the following line: 'Hunger – there was none anywhere in Duncairn' (*GG*, 196). In Gibbon's fictional city, the working-classes are a homogeneous and indistinct entity, existing for the bourgeois only as an idea. John Cushnie's 'feeungsay' speaks of 'the Communists, coarse beasts' who are 'aye stirring up the working-class' (*GG*, 173). Her opinions can be seen to be representative of the views of the Duncairn 'gentry', and her speech regarding the town's working classes is given as follows: 'they could be led astray by agitators, they'd no sense and needed to be strongly ruled' (*GG*, 173).

An exploration of contemporary class politics can be found in Irvine Welsh's 1995 novel *Marabou Stork Nightmares*.[9] In the novel, Roy Strang and his family return from a disastrous attempt at emigration to South Africa. The family has left a South Africa still deep within the apartheid regime. As a white family in South Africa, the Strangs have enjoyed special privileges. Before they leave, Roy contemplates his re-instalment into a Scottish working-class housing scheme. He finds that, as a result of the apartheid regime, he has gained new insights into the family's forthcoming living conditions. He explains:

> Edinburgh to me represented serfdom. I realised that it was exactly the same situation as Johannesburg; the only difference was that the Kaffirs were white and called schemies or draftpaks. Back in Edinburgh, we would be Kaffirs; condemned to live out our lives in townships like Muirhouse or So-Wester-Hailes-To (*MSN*, 80).

While in South Africa, Roy's Uncle Gordon, with whom the family lodge, expresses various opinions regarding his servants. Roy recounts one such sentiment: '[e]ven the good ones needed white people to look after them, to provide them with jobs and homes' (*MSN*, 65). Gordon's sentiments echo those of John Cushnie's 'feeungsay' in *Grey Granite* in their insistence on provision and rule for those seen as weak and inferior. Ironically enough, throughout the Strangs' stay in South Africa, Roy's Uncle Gordon provides the family with a home, and initially finds Roy's father a job. Welsh is not saying, of course, that Roy and his family are somehow Scottish 'Kaffirs'. What he *is* saying, however, is that, in the context of Scotland, they are analogous to the oppressed population of Johannesburg. While in South Africa, Roy notes that Johannesburg looks to him like 'a large Muirhouse-in-the-sun' (*MSN*, 61). On his return to Scotland, he says: 'Edinburgh had the same politics as Johannesburg: it had the same politics as *any city*' (*MSN*, 80, my italics). He describes his scheme as 'a concentration camp for the poor' (*MSN*, 22). Similarities between Roy's Edinburgh schemes and Duncairn's districts of Paldy Parish and the Cowgate are fairly apparent. Roy is trapped in a world of 'self-contained camps with fuck all in them, miles fae the toon' (*MSN*, 80). In Welsh's present-day depiction of Edinburgh, the 'problem populations' mentioned earlier – those who are economically unproductive, who cannot contribute fully to society – are situated geographically on the peripheries of a city dominated by capitalist economics. In this way, they exist outside the mercantile city in the same way that Duncairn's working-classes live in decentralised areas where they exist, not as social reality, but as an idea: in terms of social homogenisation, there is not much that separates a 'keelie' from a 'schemie'.

Gibbon's Duncairn exists as a city of ideas. It is a city that Gibbon represents as being composed of numerous voices, each one with its own concerns, ideals and obsessions. It is not only social class that divides and stratifies various areas of Duncairn, but commitments to varied ideologies. In the case of Duncairn's working classes it is ideas, particularly political ideas, that help them to achieve solidarity. When the workers are talking of, or participating in, political action, a communal 'you' voice operates, expressing the 'general truths' of working-class experience at that particular time. Even before Ewan's political agitation gets underway, it is clear that empathy with the Labour movement gives cohesion to individual workers' experiences. We are told: 'somehow when a chap knew another had a father who'd been Labour you could speak to him plainer, like, say what you thought' (*GG*, 48). When Jim Trease is recruiting for the hunger march, it is the sight of the names of friends and acquaintances that motivates men to sign up: 'you saw Will's there and Geordie's and Ian's and even old Malcolm's – Christ, you could go if they were going' (*GG*, 198). The communal 'you' voice also appears during the initial march to the Provost's house. The singing of the broo men 'gave a swing to your feet and you felt all kittled up and high' (*GG*, 54). The men are convinced that '[t]hey couldn't deny you, you and the rest of the Broo folk here, the right to lay bare your grievances' (*GG*, 54). Of course, the broo men cannot become a tangible social reality to the more economically successful inhabitants of Duncairn, and the marchers *are* denied this right. However, there is a sense in which the working class inhabitants of Duncairn remain a cohesive community even in failure. They, too, assert their own identity within their own parishes of the town, and define themselves in opposition to those who oppress them. When pepper is thrown in the face of policemen at the gates of Gowans and Gloag's, the arrival of the *Daily Runner* in working class areas produces 'a growl of laughing and cursing' (*GG*, 124), rather than the social outrage felt in Craigneuks. Even the broo men, who could potentially poach jobs at Gowans and Gloag's during the strike, resolve not to do so and to remain in solidarity with those of their own class. The narrator tells us that these men 'gave a bit rub at their hunger-swollen bellies – ah well, they must try the PAC again' (*GG*, 124). Within the working-class parishes of Duncairn, political agitation provides a communal voice as well as a carnival atmosphere generating a feeling of both escapism and hope. The inaction of the unemployed men is converted into action. As the workers' communal voice states at one stage: 'Communionists like Big Jim might blether damned stite but they tried to win you your rights for you' (*GG*, 55). Communist politics might be viewed as 'damned stite' but they are nonetheless symbolically unifying. Politics lends a voice to the workers that *can* be heard across Duncairn, asserting its own existence.

In Irvine Welsh's working-class vision, no such political motivations exist. Furthermore, no unifying ideas or ideologies are exercised. In Welsh's fictionalised Edinburgh, the only 'generally acknowledged truth' is that violence holds currency in the social sphere. Early in his life, Roy Strang works out a simple formula: 'if you hurt them, they don't laugh' (*MSN*, 35). Within Strang's housing scheme, power and violence are synonyms. Following an attack on a female classmate, Roy realises '[t]hat was it wi the power [...] you just had to take it. When you took it, you had to hold onto it. That was all there was to it' (*MSN*, 106). Social status in Welsh's vision of working-class Edinburgh runs along very simple lines: the more physically violent you are, the more respect is accorded you. In Welsh's infamous 1993 novel *Trainspotting*,[10] Renton sums up this equation as he accompanies the sociopathic Begbie to the house of an acquaintance. He says: '[s]trutting doon the Walk wi Begbie makes us feel like a predator, rather than a victim, and ah start looking fir cunts tae gie the eye tae' (*T*, 308). In the company of Begbie, Renton gains status by association. Renton's social sphere is divided up simply into those classified as 'predators' and 'victims'. No class solidarity exists: every individual must affirm his own status as 'predator' at all costs, lest his public image be reduced to that of 'victim', with obvious consequences. The only form of politics that *does* exist in Welsh's urban vision is that of the soundbite. Roy joins a group of football casuals and, as his group violently assaults visiting Glaswegian supporters, he recalls Winston Churchill's statement that 'the Germans were either at your feet or at your throat'. This quote is ridiculously reinterpreted to apply to those whom he opposes. Regarding his opponents, he says: '[*b*]*ack doon tae they cunts and they're fuckin swarming all over ye*' (*MSN*, 172). Churchill's sentiment is applied to an inappropriate context, yet acts as a form of self-justification for Strang. It amounts to a temporary ideological position regarding those whom he opposes. His own violent reputation is affirmed, and his actions are justified in his own mind.

Ironically, however, Roy does realise at one stage that he is contributing to the fragmentation of his own community through violence and other illegal activities. He realises that he should be in solidarity with his own class, and in opposition to the contemporary equivalent of Duncairn's moneyed classes. Regarding the managers in his workplace, he says: 'these are the cunts we should be hurtin, no the boys wi knock fuck oot ay at the fitba, no the birds wi fuck aboot, no oor ain Ma n Da, oor ain brothers n sisters, oor ain neighbours, oor ain mates' (*MSN*, 200-1). Strang briefly recognises that all his aggression is exercised upon his own class. Welsh's commitment to the depiction of the working-classes in Edinburgh ensures that he largely excludes voices from outside that sphere. Just as the working-

classes remain largely out of sight, out of mind, to the inhabitants of
Gibbon's Craigneuks, it is the *middle-classes* that remain invisible to Welsh's
working-class protagonists. Speaking again of his employers, Strang states:
'it's like ah'm jist invisible tae thaim n they are tae me'. He continues:
'these cunts wi dinnae even fuckin see. Even when they're aw aroond us'
(*MSN*, 200-1). Welsh effectively maroons his characters in their own urban
sphere: their own invisibility on the economic margins of the city is counter-
defined by their blindness to those who are economically prosperous and
geographically removed. Arguably, this blindness contributes to the
atomisation and lack of solidarity within their urban space. If a more
prosperous life cannot be seen, it is hard to aspire to that life or, alternatively,
to mobilise oneself against those who live it at your expense. Rather than
solidarity and political campaigning to attain a better life, Welsh's
protagonists seek to escape from their lives altogether. The euphoric
experiences obtained through the use of drugs appear again and again in
Welsh's depiction of working-class Edinburgh. Even Roy's violence at
football matches is defined in terms of a 'swedge buzz': the euphoric
experience that he gains owing to an adrenaline high during the act of
violence. In *Trainspotting*, Swanney's cocktail of drugs is described as 'his
ticket to better times' and 'that wee *private heaven* the uninitiated pour scorn
on' (*T*, 321, my italics). This commitment to a private heaven shows no
desire for solidarity. Nowhere in Welsh's fiction is there a 'you' voice, the
voice of a community or a parish. Indeed, the number of first-person
narratives contained within *Trainspotting* alone bespeaks a location in which
the self is preserved and valued above all else. In Welsh's novella 'A Smart
Cunt',[11] Brian ponders what he can do to aid 'the emancipation of working
people in this country'. He says: 'the answer is a resounding fuck all'. In
preference to political thinking, he decides: 'I think I'll stick to drugs to get
me though the long, dark night of late capitalism' (*AH*, 240).

It must be noted here, however, that the political ideas which aid
solidarity and cohesion within the working-class parishes of Gibbon's
Duncairn are *not* unproblematic. In *Grey Granite*, Gibbon largely portrays
the political life of the working-classes in terms of the progression of
Ewan's ideals; that is, the political machinations that the reader is privy to
are largely those which either affect Ewan's vision or which are the product
of Ewan's organisation. As Ewan's political aims become more extreme, a
dichotomy emerges between his initial commitment to the welfare of the
working-classes of Duncairn and his commitment to revolution on an
international scale. During Ewan's Socialist phase, his Young League has
the aim of persuading the workers '*of whatever party to join together and stop*

the old squabbles and grab life's share with their thousand hands' (*GG*, 106). In his speech following the tanner hop, Ewan describes the rights that he feels the workers are denied. He says: *'every one should have a decent life and time for dancing and enjoying oneself, and a decent house to go to at night, decent food, decent beds'* (*GG*, 106). The support of the workers is gained, not only through rhetoric, but through entirely practical issues that affect every member of Duncairn's working-class. However, as Ewan's Communist philosophies develop, the political action he encourages has less to do with Duncairn's oppressed than it has to do with his own personal philosophies and commitments. The workers at Gowans and Gloag's engineer a strike, not for decent housing and decent food, but to be in solidarity with Chinese workers who are assumed to be the potential victims of the shell cases and gas canisters that Gowans has put into production. When the strike is over, however, the Gowans and Gloag's communal 'you' voice expresses the following opinion: 'if the Chinks and the Japs wanted to poison one the other, why shouldn't they? – they were coarse little brutes, anyhow, like that Dr Fu Manchu on the films' (*GG*, 177). For the workers of Duncairn, the strike may have heightened class solidarity within their own communities, but it has done them little good personally. They have picketed Gloag's pointlessly for an ideology that is quickly disregarded. Soon enough, too, they are working with poisonous gas themselves, and there is *no word* of any agitation from Ewan on this subject until the plant explodes with loss of life. At this point, Ewan effectively betrays his fellow workers by using the incident as propaganda to further his own Communist beliefs. He suggests that 'it had all been deliberately planned to see the effect of poison gas on a crowd' (*GG*, 187). In a counter-attack, the gentry-friendly *Daily Runner* subtly suggests that Communist terrorism may have been to blame for the explosion: 'hadn't there been similar occurrences abroad inspired by the Asiatic party of terrorism?' (*GG*, 195). In this war of propaganda, the only losers appear to be the workers of Duncairn. Ewan's initial commitment to Duncairn's workers is subsumed beneath his commitment to international Communism. Ewan betrays the local to support a much wider cause. He is now far more concerned with the coming of revolution: it is 'a great black wave' that will succeed by 'swamping the high places with mud and blood' (*GG*, 181). Both Ewan and Trease seem resigned to the fact that an element of corruption and betrayal at the personal and local level is required to further the international cause of Communism. However, the character of Ewan seems susceptible to a much more serious failing in the context of his political activism. Ewan's ambition to 'be History', 'LIVING HISTORY

ONE-SELF' (*GG*, 148) is surely an idealistic and *personal* ambition rather than a specific commitment to the workers of Footforthie and beyond. Ewan and Trease may be committed to Communism, but they are also fundamentally corrupt. Indeed, Ewan and Trease are so engrossed in their own idea of what it is to be a worker that they are convinced that 'THEY THEMSELVES WERE THE WORKERS' (*GG*, 181); yet they share no common problems with those whom they purport to identify. Their *idea* of the identity of the workers is filtered through Communism. Just as the inhabitants of Craigneuks share a communal idea of the workers, so too do Ewan and Trease share a different idea of the same class. As Jim Trease says: *'it's me and you are the working-class, not the poor Bulgars gone back to Gowans'* (*GG*, 147). This statement is obviously ridiculous. Just as the gentry feel that the working class need to be guided and ruled on *their* terms, so too do Ewan and Trease have ideas of the workers and the *way* they must be led to emancipation. Neither the idea of the workers held by those in Craigneuks, nor the idea of the workers held by the idealistic Ewan, does anything but damage and betray the class that they purport to represent. Although the workers of Duncairn are given a chance to sound a public voice across Duncairn, to assert their existence in the face of bourgeois ignorance, they are not in control of the voice that is sounded. They remain an oppressed 'problem population' both in the eyes of the economically-successful Craigneuks gentry, and in the eyes of political idealists who would harness the workers for their own ends.

If, as I have argued, Duncairn exists as a city of ideas, however flawed they may be, then Irvine Welsh's fictionalised Edinburgh is a city that is completely devoid of ideas but for those which encourage personal gain. In *Trainspotting*, Renton criticises capitalism's 'materialism and commodity fetishism' (*T,* 343). He rejects what capitalism has to offer in his, now infamous, 'choose life' speech: '[c]hoose life. Choose mortgage payments; choose washing machines; choose cars; choose sitting oan a couch watching mind-numbing and spirit-crushing game shows, stuffing fuckin junk food intae yir mooth' (*T*, 187). Welsh's protagonists are *entirely aware* of the capitalist system that oppresses them. During one of his coma-dreams, Roy Strang holds a conversation with Dawson, in which he argues about the effects of capitalism upon the working classes. Dawson points out that, in previous eras, there existed within communities, 'a shared understanding of the world' (*MSN*, 45). This has been replaced, he argues, with 'empathy with the profit system', in which advertising and commodities motivate the individual to gain wealth and possessions at the expense of the greater good of the community. Ironically, though, Welsh's protagonists have such 'empathy with the profit system' that they directly mimic the system that they purport to reject. They buy and sell drugs – commodities – that are no different from any other commodity but for their illegality. They are entirely guilty of the 'commodity fetishism' that Renton so vehemently rejects. Even Pete Gilbert, the big-time drug dealer whom the Trainspotters meet in London, has his activities described as follows: '[h]e'd buy and sell anything. For him, it was strictly business, and he refused to differentiate it from any other entrepreneurial activity' (*T*, 339). The system that oppresses Welsh's protagonists, characterising them by their economic unproductivity, confining them to their housing schemes on the periphery of a mercantile city, is the very system that Welsh's protagonists mimic for want of a better ideology. Welsh's protagonists essentially accept that no better equivalent to rampant capitalism exists. The profit system dictates that a 'private heaven', such as the one Swanney achieves with his cocktail of drugs, can be purchased if one has enough money to do so. A 'private heaven' is preferable to communal oppression. Life can be escaped from via the back door, and the future – the very thing that Ewan Tavendale must rely on – can be denied until the next fix is required.

Thomas Crawford is exactly right in his description of the *Quair* as a whole, and *Grey Granite* within it, as 'a method of *thinking* about contemporary morals and politics in aesthetic terms' (*GG*, xv). Each stratified viewpoint and voice in *Grey Granite* represents a part of the social equation that made up Gibbon's view of a Scottish city. If this is the case, Welsh's protagonists are a means of asserting that communal ideas and morals are dead; that rampant individualism, expressed through the purchase of commodities, is the only communal ethic left in play; and, furthermore, that this communal ethic must be expressed in isolation: a 'private heaven' that cannot be shared. A private heaven requires a private voice, and Welsh's fictionalised Muirhouse and Wester Hailes sound no communal voice to prove their own existence. Furthermore, Welsh's disparate voices suggest no hope, and no desire, for class emancipation. It must be noted that, while Duncairn's 'keelies' are misrepresented by the politics of their time, their social cohesion – their 'you' voice – at least remains true to their communal experience while they actively search for a representative voice. However, the corrupt and ultimately unrepresentative voices offered to the workers of Gibbon's Duncairn by Ewan Tavendale and Jim Trease demonstrate that, largely, the 'you-voice' of Duncairn's workers is doomed to fail, and to be failed, by the ideals that attempt to harness it. Given this fact, it can be posited that Welsh's vision, such as it is, represents the contemporary result of the successive failure of the working-classes to find a representative voice; the subsequent lack of hope, and a final descent into a solipsistic commodity-obsessed culture. Gibbon's investigation into the class-politics of a Scottish city, then, retains a lasting legacy in contemporary Scottish writing. His achievement in *Grey Granite* is not only to define a Scottish city at a certain time in history but, as my comparison with Welsh's work shows, to define aspects of class division and social injustice that are relevant irrespective of the age from which his work is viewed.

Notes

1. Lewis Grassic Gibbon, *Grey Granite,* in *A Scots Quair* ed. and intro. by Thomas Crawford (Edinburgh: Canongate, 1995). All future references to this text will be indicated by the abbreviation *GG.*
2. In my opening statements, I am indebted to Ian Haywood's book *Working Class Fiction from Chartism to Trainspotting* (Plymouth: Northcote House, 1997), in which he argues that 'significant fractions' of the contemporary working class have been submerged 'into a heterogeneous, proletarianised underclass of alienated social groups, defined by their economic unproductiveness and an inability to participate fully in society' (p. 141).
3. Jürgen Neubauer, *Literature as Intervention: Struggles over Cultural Identity in Contemporary Scottish Fiction* (Marburg: Tectum Verlag, 1999), p. 97.
4. Ian S. Munro, *Leslie Mitchell: Lewis Grassic Gibbon* (Edinburgh: Oliver and Boyd Ltd., 1966), p. 176.
5. See Ian Campbell, 'Lewis Grassic Gibbon and the Mearns', in *A Sense of Place: Studies in Scottish Local History,* ed. by Graeme Cruickshank (Edinburgh: Scotland's Cultural Heritage, 1988), pp. 15-27. Ian Campbell has argued that Gibbon's Duncairn is, in fact, a fictionalised version of Aberdeen. He states that the identification of Duncairn with Aberdeen is 'a private one to those who are reasonably familiar with the district' (p. 18).
6. Munro, p. 177.
7. A paraphrase from the article by Graham Trengrove in *Scottish Literary Journal,* 2, (1975), pp. 47-62. Trengrove points to the use of a stylistic community 'you' voice in *Sunset Song* as a device for 'powerfully suggesting a homogenous body of opinion in Kinraddie' (p. 49).
8. Thomas Crawford explains, in his notes to the Canongate Classics edition of *Grey Granite,* that the Douglas Scheme was a theory of social credit, proposing that 'the government should distribute national dividends in order to spread purchasing power and thus increase consumption' (p. 211). The leading proponent of this idea was Major Clifford Hugh Douglas (1879-1952), hence the naming of the scheme.

9. Irvine Welsh, *Marabou Stork Nightmares* (London: Jonathan Cape, 1995). All future references to this text will be indicated by the abbreviation *MSN*.

10. Irvine Welsh, *Trainspotting* (London: Minerva, 1994 [1993]). All future references to this text will be indicated by the abbreviation *T*.

11. From the collection *The Acid House* (London: Vintage, 1995 [1994]), pp. 177-289. All future references to this text will be indicated by the abbreviation *AH*.

Shouting Too Loudly: Leslie Mitchell, Humanism and the Art of Excess

William K. Malcolm

One of the keenest passages of self-analysis by James Leslie Mitchell/Lewis Grassic Gibbon (for simplicity's sake, I'll employ his own name throughout this essay) occurs in the course of a letter to his friend Helen Cruickshank, dated 18 November 1933 and written at the very peak of his popular success. This famous letter begins with him thanking her for accepting the dedication of *Scottish Scene* and providing an update on his latest publishing plans. Having dispensed with the formalities – charmingly modulated, as ever – Mitchell then proceeds to more intimate literary matters, in a paragraph whose very sensitivity he acknowledges immediately afterwards when he describes it as witnessing him 'pouring forth my soul abroad'. In this seminal passage Mitchell writes:

> Sorry you didn't find Spartacus up to Naomi's [Naomi Mitchison's] standard. (But rather like comparing the Bible to the Rig-veda, they're so unalike!) It's going very well, in spite of the pathological horrors. Or probably because of them [...] Yes, horrors do haunt me. That's because I'm in love with humanity. Ancient Greece is never the Parthenon to me: it's a slave being tortured in a dungeon of the Athenian law-courts; Ancient Egypt is never the Pyramids: it's the blood and tears of Goshen; Ancient Scotland is never Mary Queen: it's those serfs they kept chained in the Fifeshire mines a hundred years ago. And so on. And so with the moderns: I am so horrified by all our dirty little cruelties and bestialities that I would feel the lowest type of skunk if I didn't shout the horror of them from the house-tops. Of course I shout too loudly. But the filthy conspiracy of silence there was in the past! – and is coming again in Scotland, in a new guise, called Renaissance, and Objectivity, and National Art and what not. Blithering about Henryson and the Makars (whoever these cretins were) and forgetting the Glasgow slums.[1]

I believe that detailed deconstruction of this passage yields vital keys to an understanding of Leslie Mitchell's creative approach and, more pointedly, to his achievement as a supreme humanist writer, whose work was directly inspired by human life in all its myriad forms – and indeed as a humanitarian writer, whose writings were at their most pungent when confronting pressing moral and social concerns.

At the beginning of the quoted paragraph, Mitchell can be seen responding with quite uncharacteristic equanimity to Helen Cruickshank's negative comparison of his recently published historical novel *Spartacus* with the work of Naomi Mitchison. He deflects the criticism by pointing to the invidious nature of all literary comparisons, using a suitably grand analogy ('rather like comparing the Bible to the Rig-veda, they're so unalike!'). His following defence, outlining his motivation as an artist (and as a man), develops a compelling momentum which has a psychological immediacy that gradually reveals Mitchell's mature literary mindset.

Having picked up initially on Helen Cruickshank's misgivings regarding the violent tenor of *Spartacus*, Mitchell then comments blandly about his general progress ('It's going very well') before adding the apparently simple rider, 'in spite of the pathological horrors'. The conventional view that he subscribes to here is that his success has been achieved despite his mental preoccupation, taken to an unhealthy pathological extreme, with unspecified 'horrors'. However, he immediately turns this qualification on its head, musing: 'Or probably because of them.' This shift from 'despite' to 'because' is fundamental to an understanding of Mitchell's motivation as a writer: the 'pathological horrors', the demons that he cannot escape in his mind are, by extension, a strength in his art, rather than the supposed weakness.

From here, Mitchell moves on to generalise about his personal obsession with acts of cruelty, confessing, 'Yes, horrors do haunt me', before directly attributing this condition to his humanism, reasoning: 'That's because I'm in love with humanity.' Now fully warmed to the topic, he embarks upon a sweeping trawl of historical atrocities which he personally feels blot out corresponding wonders, itemising his *bêtes noires* from Ancient Greece, from Ancient Egypt and from Ancient Scotland with captivating parallelism. The next logical development is to update the picture, but with the striking addition of an awareness of the communal responsibility for this perceived malaise:

> And so with the moderns: I am so horrified by all our dirty little cruelties and bestialities that I would feel the lowest type of skunk if I didn't shout the horror of them from the house-tops.

Then comes the most revealing sentence in this whole moral tirade: 'Of course I shout too loudly.' That presumptive 'of course' is crucial to Mitchell's declaration, elevating it to a kind of strategic mission statement demarcating deliberate intent on his part. Overstatement is not just a temperamental habit; he is not just confiding an unchecked propensity to rant and rave; overstatement is an essential part of his considered literary response. Subsequently, circumstantial justification for this disposition is laid at the door of his contemporaries who evidently have become distracted from the pressing social issues of the day and who have turned towards consideration of specious aesthetics, bound up in nationalist politics. The broken syntax degenerating towards the end of the paragraph to an untypically vague catch-all ('and what not') reflects the writer's animation. Finally, Mitchell loses his poise when in passing he directs unwarranted invective at the medieval Makars, condemning his peers for: 'Blithering about Henryson and the Makars (whoever these cretins were) and forgetting the Glasgow slums'.

Mitchell regains self-control for the remainder of the letter, but his splenetic outburst in this paragraph highlights an inescapable truth about his art as a whole: it is predicated on the belief that the artist has a moral obligation for the realistic positing of human suffering – in past, present or future – at the very core of his aesthetic. This grim perspective, ineluctably homing in on the egregious flaws in human behaviour, is very much a tragic vision, where human nobility is all but undermined by life's darker forces. Leslie Mitchell was much more deeply absorbed by the social, moral and spiritual darkness of the twentieth century than by the apprehension of the wan light beyond. And his neo-tragic predilection to 'shout too loudly', Lear-like, as a voice from the darkness, lies right at the heart of his achievement as an imaginative writer.

Mitchell's emotional humanism, his passionate interest in all peoples, frequently manifested as a humanitarian concern for the poor and the downtrodden, is all-pervasive in his writing. In his essay 'The Land', he even strikes his personal mantra, proclaiming, 'Humanity right or wrong!'[2] His natural engagement with the welfare of ordinary folk can be traced from his school essay books, penned at thirteen years of age, brimming with wry and touching cameos of local and historical characters. And of course this simple preoccupation is most vividly captured thereafter in the characterisation in his mature writings, most prominently in his affectionate relish of human foibles and quirks and eccentricities throughout the Scottish novels and stories.

The peculiarities of Mitchell's background conditioned his move towards an outspoken forthrightness. In addition to his natural sensitivity, he was very much isolated within his family, with parents and half-brothers standing firmly at an intellectual and emotional remove; at school, by virtue of his academic ability and disposition; and even within the community, where the smothering northeast farming conservatism traditionally undermined basic human rights at home, in the workplace, in society at large (for example with regard to the female role); and where the prevailing political fatalism painted a bleak picture for the crofters' welfare. Protest against such a stifling background had of necessity to be trenchant.

Intensified by environmental circumstances, Mitchell's innate humanism naturally led to his consistent and dogged pursuit of left-wing causes throughout his life, from his schoolboy rebelliousness through his early adult radicalism, galvanised by the outbreak of the Russian Revolution and, closer to home, the first hand – and hands-on – experience of Red Clydeside. From this, the noble 'history of a revoluter' (as he concisely described his socialism to Naomi Mitchison),[3] moved through a douce anarchist phase, encompassing an interest in pacifism and diffusionism, to, finally, a thrawn acceptance of the necessity of Marxist militancy and Communist Party activism.

Mitchell's left-wing political ideology was underpinned by a series of formative shocks in his personal life. His own family experience of the grind of crofting life confirmed that the city certainly did not have a monopoly on poverty. However, the six months he spent living in post First World War Glasgow exposed him to a social tableau of unparalleled squalor and ugliness. This was compounded by his later army experience which developed further images of human degradation and brutalisation, prefiguring the fictional representation of Ewan Tavendale's corruption later in *Sunset Song*, as well as occasionally throwing up dramatic scenes of death and physical mutilation. And tragedy even erupted in his personal life, in the form of the near fatal miscarriage suffered by his wife Ray in 1925, an event which scarred him so deeply that scenes depicting the pains of childbirth recur insistently in his writing, extending from private poetry striving after personal catharsis to his first novel *Stained Radiance*, and running right through to *A Scots Quair* itself.

Subsequently, Leslie Mitchell can be seen forging his own individual brand of *littérature engagée* which is in keeping with the later definition coined by the French Marxist Louis Aragon, involving clear social commitment dependent upon the personal 'inner necessity' of the artist. Max Adereth's essay, 'What is *"Littérature Engagée"*?' throws valuable light upon the symbiotic relationship between a radical writer's personal principles and his artistic credo:

> '*Littérature engagée*' is the application of commitment to the special field
> of literature. Its one and only requirement is that the writer should take
> part in the struggles of the age, and it urges him to do so, not because
> it is presumptuous enough to decree where his artistic duty lies, but,
> more modestly, because it knows the value of such a source of
> inspiration. Committed literature has no special themes, styles or
> methods – it is distinguished only by greater realism and by the
> author's attitude to life. These do not, by themselves, create a work of
> art, but they do enhance its quality. They help literature to make us
> aware of our true condition and to increase our sense of responsibility.
> In addition to providing aesthetic enjoyment, *littérature engagée* fulfils a
> 'social function'.[4]

This conception preserves the dual ideal of the author's living social commitment and of the realistic character of his artistic response to the *zeitgeist*
while offering a more flexible framework than the severe dogma of socialist
realism which Leslie Mitchell was strongly influenced by – though never
absolutely thirled to – in the 1930s.

In Leslie Mitchell's own *littérature engagée*, it is his searing protest at
social and moral injustice that is most true to his 'inner necessity', and
which time and again dominates his writing. In his most mature essay on
the role of the revolutionary writer, published in *Left Review* at the end of
his life, Mitchell took this theory a step further, when he spelled out the
revolutionary writers' collective function as being to constitute 'a shock
brigade of writers'.[5] His own strategic tendency to 'shout too loudly' thus
repeatedly bursts to the fore with fierce directness elsewhere in his nonfiction, achieving an all-embracing conviction, as in his famous indictment
of the squalor of Glasgow: 'There is nothing in culture or art that is worth
the life and elementary happiness of one of those thousands who rot in the
Glasgow slums.' (*Sm*, 102) The author's moral imperative thus culminates
in an ideological trade-off between social and aesthetic concerns – a set of
priorities characteristically reversed by Hugh MacDiarmid, who declared
defiantly in his 1946 essay on Mitchell that he himself 'would sacrifice a
million people any day for one immortal lyric'.[6]

The darker manifestation of Mitchell's humanism – the concentration
upon acts of violence and suffering – even obtrudes in his historical
writings. The painstakingly researched academic works on the ancient
American Maya revolve around imaginative empathy with the ordinary
Indians in the ancient Mayan theocracies, who fall victim to physical
torture and blood sacrifice. Again, this makes for harrowing reading; yet
while Mitchell's historical erudition *per se* counts for little nowadays in the

light of modern research, his imaginative humanism genuinely illuminates his recreation of the ancient world.

However, it is in his fiction that Mitchell's predisposition to 'shout too loudly' is most marked, and indeed most convincing. His early fiction typically highlights contemporary social problems at home and abroad within a range of forms and to varying degrees of success. But it is in *Image and Superscription* and *Spartacus*, two of Mitchell's mid-period novels, that he expressly yokes his humanism to a representational style that I would term 'the art of excess'. These novels thus provide an enlightening comparison as experiments in *littérature engagée* – the first taking the form of the quest, the second that of the historical novel.

Finally published in March 1933 following a protracted period of gestation, *Image and Superscription* stands at the very core of Mitchell's *oeuvre* between *Sunset Song* and *Cloud Howe*.[7] It demands further exploration as an unjustly neglected novel which directly and indirectly indicates the wellspring of his artistry. *Image and Superscription* witnesses Mitchell working towards the 'art of excess' by assembling shocking images culled from the distant and recent past, images which evoke a truly convincing sense of horror. Despite structural flaws, as *littérature engagée* the novel is raw and strident and ultimately a qualified success, its narrative following a familiar pattern in Mitchell's fiction as a symbolic pilgrimage representing the quest for light in the darkness of modern life. In its picaresque sweep, jumping episodically from place to place, Gershom Jezreel's tale discloses a litany of human atrocities from the past and, most distressingly, from the early twentieth century. The early portion of Jezreel's narrative constructs a biography shaped by darkly ambivalent forces, with a tyrannical and brutalised father – John Guthrie taken to extreme – tormenting a warmly sympathetic mother who inevitably abandons her family. Subsequently exposed to 'all the wild, dreadful things of human life' (*IS*, 29), Gershom logically develops a philosophy which wavers between the pagan and the absurdist, in which consciousness of human suffering blocks the cultivation of any positive form of personal belief whatsoever.

In a narrative which moves swiftly between settings as disparate as Chatham, Palenque, the Gulf of Mexico, Kentucky, and various European locations from Paris to Mitchell's home area of Welwyn, scenes of human cruelty from diverse eras and places cry out in agony – in the exotic form of a sacrificial statue in a Mayan temple or in the domestically humdrum, yet even more shocking, physical persecutions of an abusive father. Two viscerally realistic scenes stand out in this torrent of brutality. Firstly, the report of Ester's traumatic witnessing of a particularly savage Ku Klux

Klan killing, involving the sadistic murder of a victim's widow and her unborn foetus, gains additional shock-effect from Mitchell's authorial gloss affirming its factual basis. The second peculiarly potent example of Mitchell's 'art of excess' focuses on Gershom's suffering at the Front in the First World War. The specific experience of the trenches is tackled much more directly here than in *Sunset Song*, with the protagonist's own physical and mental torture being accompanied by graphically observed battlefield scenes, centring upon the excoriating sight of a dead Saxon soldier suspended on the barbed wire, 'like Saint Peter of legend, crucified upside down and with head to earth'. (*IS*, 202) The moral charge developed in these scenes fully sustains a vision of the grotesque character of life as a whole, a vision possessing a bracing integrity that has a strong affinity with Chris Guthrie's 'philosophy of change'. Human life is thus perceived as a trivial part of the organically evolving life force:

> Life was no flower, it was mindless, the crawling of a mindless fecundity, changing and passing, changing and passing. Man was a beast who walked the earth, snarling his needs and lowing his fears, and with other beasts he would perish and pass, a ripple on the cosmic mind that itself was mindless. (*IS*, 193)

The book's idealistic resolution, with Gershom finding personal romance and 'salvation' in the sanguine affirmation that 'man's a hero, not a beast by nature 'n' intention' (*IS*, 226) is correspondingly slight and ineffectual. Thanks to the author's heart-rending cries of protest, the earlier image of human barbarity remains largely undiminished at the end of this sprawling, yet undeniably arresting work of fiction.

The outstanding success among Mitchell's English novels is *Spartacus*,[8] published only five months after *Image and Superscription*. So what is the secret of its success? I would argue that this historical novel succeeds, as the author tacitly suggests in his letter to Helen Cruickshank, precisely because, more fully than all the others, it fulfils his literary objective to 'shout too loudly'. Dorothy Tweed, the book's dedicatee and the staunchest supporter of her writer friend, told me in 1989 that she herself could not bear to pick the book up after her initial encounter with her presentation copy. Mitchell's historical novel is indeed nothing like Mitchison's authentic sagas, but is an unavoidable expression of pain and of rage which represents his most articulate channelling of his moral indignation and humanism. It is also, in my view, his single most balanced and perfectly integrated work of *littérature engagée*.

Mitchell complimented Mitchison in his 1934 essay 'Literary Lights' as 'the one writer of the "historical" novel in modern English who commands respect and enthusiasm', observing how *The Conquered* and *Black Sparta* 'light up the human spirit very vividly and truly' (*Sm*, 129). In a short but memorable correspondence with Mitchison, Mitchell went further in his praise, hailing in the very highest terms the central characterisation of her classic study of ancient Marob, *The Corn King and the Spring Queen*, and actually confiding his fears prior to the publication of *Spartacus* that she would beat him to the subject of the gladiators' revolt, as 'it was so essentially hers'.[9] The admiration, at least so far as historical fiction was concerned, was not reciprocated, however. Mitchison disliked *Spartacus*, complaining in 1983 that the novel lacked true historical veracity:

> It didn't seem to me that he had thought enough about the nature of the Roman Empire and that things don't just repeat themselves. He had put it into modern terms without understanding what the ancient terms were.[10]

Yet this is to misunderstand Mitchell's actual intentions in the novel. Over sixty years after its first appearance, the author's focus now appears satisfyingly modern, in a work that is less historical reconstruction than political abstract. Spartacus's dramatic life story has regularly been endowed with overt political significance in modern times, famously being cited in the revolutionary writings of Voltaire and in the subversion leading to the French Revolution; and influencing the radical stance adopted by Karl Liebknecht and Rosa Luxemburg and their fellow Spartacists in Germany just over a decade before Mitchell's book.

At its most fundamental, then, Mitchell's *Spartacus* dramatises a successful class insurrection orchestrated by a primitive neo-Leninist form of dictatorship of the proletariat against the forces of social repression; and despite the failure of the rebellion, a glimpse is afforded finally of the ideal of a fair and just society established within a popular body that is in essence an international brotherhood. The concentrated narrative promotes the slaves' viewpoint, unflinchingly probing incidences of individual and mass cruelty perpetrated by men upon fellow men. Casual or organised acts of the utmost savagery are commonplace, from the original rebellion at Capua through the epic encounters in what the slave-girl Elpinice accurately classes as 'WAR' (*Sp*, 32): the bloody defeats of the armies of Clodius and Furius in Campania, of Cossinus in Salenae, of Varinus in Lucania, of Manius outside Mutina; the retreat south from the cusp of conquering Rome itself. The brutality continues unabated in the saga of the unsuccessful exodus to

Sicily and the final heroic defeat by Crassus at Calabria, culminating in the reprisals of the Romans with mass crucifixions along the Appian Way.

Timeless left-wing political responses are adumbrated paradigmatically in the course of the slaves' battle for freedom: the universal condemnation of slavery, the denunciation of social injustice, the promotion of basic egalitarian values and of the moral rights of the individual, the delineation of the ultimate goal of the ordinary people to win – by force if necessary – political self-determination. Yet ultimately the novel's power rests upon the balanced way in which the moral indictment standing at its heart is sustained. The use of Kleon's consciousness as the emasculated victim of the Roman empire allows for objective rendering of acts of the extremist violence. As 'there were no tears in the body that had lost its manhood' (*Sp*, 14), the institutionalised cruelty of Roman society subsequently is relayed graphically, with little emotion.

This counterpoints with the depiction of Spartacus himself. Introduced initially as a 'bandit' who kills a retiarius in gladiatorial training in sheer mindless rage (*Sp*, 19), he does learn to shed tears, in increasing abundance. His sensibility, like Ewan Tavendale's in his early idealistic phase in *Grey Granite*, is the one that 'shouts' with uninhibited moral and emotional fervour. Spartacus, indeed, assumes the role of symbolic avenger, as a political icon heroically pitted against the forces of oppression. Yet he is also 'the Voice of the voiceless' (*Sp*, 194) – the custodian of the conscience of the oppressed slaves throughout their 'orgy of hate' (*Sp*, 39). His own aggression, significantly, is tempered by a generous humanism which embraces the mixed races among the slave army and even extends to conquered foes. Accordingly, while the brutality in *Spartacus* is realised with shocking intensity, it is not gratuitous but is firmly harnessed to Mitchell's moral and political objective to dramatise the full horror of the human capacity for cruelty – and subsequently to affirm the full extent of the redemptive Christ-like force required to counter it, and to conquer it. Critically, Spartacus's inspirational anger at injustice is tempered latterly by his mature compassion for all peoples – crystalised in his proclamation before he marches on Rome in the ultimate vision of a post-revolutionary society in which 'even the Masters will not be enslaved' (*Sp*, 136).

The magnificent climax of the novel – a close-up of Kleon's individual death agony – is clinically conceived to wring maximum pathos from the tragedy of the slaves' defeat. Mitchell systematically traces Kleon's physical deterioration in the pain of his individual wounds, his dehydration and self-defecation, through to his increasing vulnerability to scavenging beasts. His disjointed and slowly diminishing stream of consciousness is in turn disturbing and exhilarating, with flashback charting dramatic escapades which graduate into a closing apotheosis which fuses Spartacus's martyrdom with Christ's suffering. This climactic vision denotes a dynamic authorial engagement with the 'pathological horrors' of human history. For here, in contrast to *Image and Superscription*, Mitchell also moves towards achieving a genuine imaginative exorcism of the horrors. In *Spartacus*, in fact, Mitchell's humanism coalesces with his absurdism: within the spiritual barrenness of life, Spartacus's nobility is radiant, as Kleon finally 'went into unending night and left them [Spartacus and Christ] that shining earth' (*Sp*, 210). The final legacy of Spartacus's revolt, then, is that it paved the way for the even more enduring radicalism of Christ and of Christian doctrine. The apparently innocuous comment opening the book: 'It was Springtime in Italy, a hundred years before the crucifixion of Christ' (*Sp*, 3) is thus charged with meaning by its repetition at the novel's close. The very final (or, more accurately, non-final) dash in the last line of the text subtly reduces the sense of tragedy created by Spartacus's demise and hints at vaguely defined hopes concerning the future of humanity.

The same phenomenon of the author's demonstrable capacity to 'shout too loudly' is also in evidence in the most famous Grassic Gibbon fiction – although it is generally more understated and subtly synthesised. *Sunset Song*, *Cloud Howe* and *Grey Granite* all draw their inner strength from the author's moral protest at harsh social conditions prevailing in the Scottish countryside, in the town and in the city. *Sunset Song* perhaps convinces most in the intimately crafted individual tragedies of the crofters – ordinary people caught up in malevolent forces of which they have no understanding. The lasting power of *Sunset Song* lies in the crowning of the rumbustious humour of the earlier sections and of the lyrical nature-loving rhapsodies of Chris Guthrie with the pathos of Ewan Tavendale's fate. And in terms of 'shouting loudly', Robert Colquohoun's closing threnody for Long Rob, Chae Strachan, John Guthrie and Ewan Tavendale may be eloquently wrought in its disciplined construction as a sermon, yet it has a profound emotional impact. But even this is not enough for the author, who embellishes the whole effect with the lyrically achieved rural setting and the poignancy of the accompanying bagpipe lament, fastidiously set out in musical notation. This crafted synthesis arguably shows Mitchell fulfilling his artistic aim to 'shout too loudly' most convincingly, with the overwhelming sense of human waste and loss finally pointing purposefully towards the future.

The specific techniques employed in the second and third volumes of the trilogy emulate the success of the first, with a strong predilection for literary overkill again being very much in evidence. The social commentary upon deteriorating conditions throughout the 1920s is sharply presented in *Cloud Howe* through individual melodramatic anecdotes largely attesting to the spinners' continuing misfortunes, but also including emotive agitprop-style episodes such as the quasi-biblical parable of the Kindness family's symbolic rejection by society at large, designed to generate orthodox left-wing indignation at social injustice. And of course the personal trauma of Chris's miscarriage reflects metaphorically the still birth of the General Strike, with Robert's own individual demise – dramatically obliterating the pages of the pulpit Bible in a gush of crimson blood – capturing with near hyperbole the full import of his personal political failure. Mitchell thus again deploys Robert's ministerial function through his dying sermon to give a rhetorical flourish to the set piece placed at the novel's finale.

Grey Granite again witnesses the author aiming to 'shout too loudly', this time in a voice and a literary style specifically fashioned to deal with the austere social and political circumstances being addressed archetypally in the urban novel. Young Ewan Tavendale obviously emerges as the author's main political vehicle; it is through his moral empathy and his accelerated political apprenticeship that the novel's key political themes are elucidated. The parallel with *Spartacus* is instructive, with Ewan's increasing militancy also being shaped by his sensitivity to signs of squalor and deprivation amongst the proletariat at large. His heightened social conscience, expressed in a series of powerful interior monologues, is clearly the author's main means of enunciating his austere political theme – that hard-line communist activism represents the sole hope for the ordinary people to gain improved social conditions. In 'shouting too loudly', Ewan's moral homilies and political apologias develop a growing fervour and provide convincing counterbalance to Chris's peasant fatalism.

Mitchell borrowed techniques from the European novel and particularly from Soviet socialist realists such as Gorki and Gladkov in order to develop the art of his urban novel. He is still sadly underestimated for his use of Eisenstein-like political montage to highlight the stock nature of the kneejerk opposition of reactionary elements of society (the press, the police, local councillors); for the translation of his rural folk narrator into an anonymous communal urban voice (with multiple names – John, Peter, Thomas, Neil, Jim, Sam, Rob); and for the introduction of the highly imaginative Marxist symbolism employed judiciously throughout the book to capture the desirability of the Marxist ideal.[11] Yet it is Ewan's plaintive – and desperate – humanitarianism that pulls the whole novel together. While Chris struggles to find meaning beyond 'the fleshless grin of the skull and the eyeless sockets at the back of life' in the regenerative powers of the natural world,[12] Ewan seeks his destiny in more pragmatic political activities. Ironically his mute disappearance on the road to political oblivion – or martyrdom – constitutes the single most telling authorial statement in the whole trilogy. Ewan's sacrifice to the cause is absolute.

As a humanist, Leslie Mitchell directed his work towards clear moral, social and political ends – most forcefully in the works where he shows a propensity to 'shout too loudly'. An ironic side-effect of his intense humanitarianism was the implosion of his belief in the whole force of art itself, including his own. He poured scorn on Henryson and the Makars as 'cretins', purely because he felt they were being revived at the wrong time, a time when more pressing social and political issues were begging to be addressed. In his polemic on Glasgow, he even goes so far as to proclaim a willingness to sacrifice all art for just the remotest possibility of some kind of social relief. Yet, paradoxically, it was precisely in this absolute dedication to the overriding aim to 'shout too loudly', to sublimate his art to the articulation of the austere vision of the revolutionary writer, that Leslie Mitchell found his true literary voice. Louis Aragon has observed that the truly committed writer should aim to leave of himself 'une image vraie', a true image.[13] In this sense, *Spartacus* and *A Scots Quair* embody Leslie Mitchell's true humanist profile.

Leslie Mitchell's death at thirty-four years of age means that his writings are wholly, by definition, those of a young man. His search for solutions to moral problems, to social problems, to political problems, to philosophical problems, had the urgency of a young man. In the final analysis, Mitchell's *littérature engagée* is more compelling in its dramatisation of the image of the 'horrors' of life themselves than in its almost desperate efforts to superscribe them. 'Of course' he shouted too loudly. And of course we appreciate why he did so. We still heed, and need, his voice today.

Notes

1. Leslie Mitchell, letter to Helen B. Cruickshank, 18 November 1933, National Library of Scotland MS 26109.
2. Lewis Grassic Gibbon and Hugh MacDiarmid, *Scottish Scene or The Intelligent Man's Guide to Albyn* (1934), reprinted in *Smeddum: A Lewis Grassic Gibbon Anthology* ed. by Valentina Bold (Edinburgh: Canongate, 2001), p. 95. Further quotations from *Scottish Scene* will be referenced in the text, preceded by *Sm*.
3. Leslie Mitchell, letter to Naomi Mitchison 10 August 1933, National Library of Scotland Acc. 5885.

4. Max Adereth, 'What is *"Littérature Engagée?"?'* in *Commitment in Modern French Literature* (1967), reprinted in *Marxists on Literature*, ed. by David Craig (Harmondsworth: Penguin Books, 1975), pp. 445-85.

5. Lewis Grassic Gibbon, 'Controversy: Writers' International (British Section)', *Left Review* 1 (1935), pp. 179-80.

6. Hugh MacDiarmid, 'Lewis Grassic Gibbon – James Leslie Mitchell' in *The Uncanny Scot*, ed. by Kenneth Buthlay (London: MacGibbon & Kee, 1968), p. 161.

7. J. Leslie Mitchell, *Image and Superscription* (London: Jarrolds, 1933). For full details of the background to *Image and Superscription*, see William K. Malcolm, *A Blasphemer and Reformer* (Aberdeen: Aberdeen University Press, 1984), p. 96. Quotations will be referenced in the text preceded by *IS*.

8. J. Leslie Mitchell, *Spartacus* (London: Jarrolds, 1933). Quotations will be referenced in the text from the Polygon reprint of 2001, prefaced by *Sp*.

9. Leslie Mitchell, letters to Naomi Mitchison 10 August 1933 and 'Tuesday' undated [1933], National Library of Scotland Acc. 5885.

10. Naomi Mitchison, letter to the present writer 21 September 1983.

11. A full analysis of the formative literary influences in *Grey Granite* is given in *A Blasphemer and Reformer*, pp. 150-57.

12. Lewis Grassic Gibbon, *Cloud Howe* (1933) in *A Scots Quair*, ed. by Tom Crawford Edinburgh: Canongate, 1995), p. 20.

13. Quoted in Adereth, 'What is *"Littérature Engagée"?'*, p. 461.

Ecstasy Controlled:
The Prose Styles of James Leslie Mitchell and Lewis Grassic Gibbon

John Corbett

> It is strange how Scotland has no Gilbert White or H.J. Massingham to
> sing its fields, its birds, such night as this, to chronicle the comings and
> goings of the swallows in simple, careful prose, ecstasy controlled.
>
> Lewis Grassic Gibbon, 'The Land' (Sm, 94)[1]

Lewis Grassic Gibbon's prose style is without doubt one of the most
powerful contributions to the success of *A Scots Quair*. Different aspects of
it have prompted critical comment, and its experimental nature is the
subject of several brief but telling comments by Gibbon himself,
particularly in his introduction to *Sunset Song*, and in 'Literary Lights':

> [T]here is no novelist (or, indeed prose writer), worthy of the name who
> is writing in Braid Scots. The technique of Lewis Grassic Gibbon in his
> trilogy *A Scots Quair* [...] is to mould the English language into the
> rhythms and cadences of Scots spoken speech, and to inject into the
> English vocabulary such minimum number of words from Braid Scots as
> that remodelling requires. (*Sm*, 135)

Gibbon's preface to *Sunset Song* closely echoes this passage, and both stand
as a corrective to those commentators who would argue that Gibbon's
literary prose is a naturalistic, or even a literary form of broad, north-east
Scots.[2] Gibbon was clearly at pains to distinguish his prose style from both
the 'authentic' transcribed speech of the Mearns, and from such a literary
'Braid Scots' as was then being practised in poetry by Hugh MacDiarmid.
In 'Literary Lights', Mitchell describes 'Gibbon' as a writer of *English*,
whose literary prose in *A Scots Quair* and the Scottish short stories conveys

an *impression* of Scots speech. When he was not anxious that the style would become 'intolerably mannered' (*Sm*, 135), his attitude to his prose might well have been akin to James Barke's summation of Fionn MacColla, which he quotes approvingly in 'Literary Lights':

> 'Fionn MacColla, in English, it may be noted, is far away the finest example of the Gaelic influence. In a very profound sense, his English is the finest Gaelic we have.' (*Sm*, 137)

Mitchell perceived problems for Scottish prose writers adopting English both as a literary and a non-fictional medium. Ironically, given his own linguistic experimentation in *Spartacus*, he criticises A.J. Cronin's novels for their 'Latinized barbarization of the English language' (*Sm*, 131-32), and he begins his withering assault on Ramsay MacDonald by attacking his use of language: 'English remains for him a foreign language: its terms and expressions, its unique twists of technique, he has followed and charted laboriously, competently, and unintelligently' (*Sm*, 140). The invention of 'Lewis Grassic Gibbon' allowed Mitchell the freedom to experiment with an English prose style that would include some elements of Scots, and effectively to make a virtue out of the necessity for a Scottish writer of 'foreignising' the English tongue. But how does Gibbon's style compare to that of 'James Leslie Mitchell', for whom, no less than Cronin and Ramsay MacDonald, literary English was, in some respects, a foreign language?

In 'Literary Lights', Gibbon criticises John Buchan's narrative style:

> He writes it all in a competent, skilful and depressing English: when his characters talk Scots they do it in suitable inverted commas: and such characters as do talk Scots are always the simple, the proletarian, the slightly ludicrous characters. (*Sm*, 131)

This is the Scottish narrative tradition that *Sunset Song* reacts against. Gibbon articulates his Scots terms (which amount to many more than 'some score or so') through an unconventional English narrative voice, which blends seamlessly with the voices and thoughts of the characters. The Scots terms include nouns (e.g. *daftie, futret, creature*), verbs (e.g. *swithering, louping, sleeking*), quantifying adjectives (as in *a bit walk*) and intensifying adverbs (as in *fell early*).[3] The Scots vocabulary tends towards the colloquial, and especially the evaluative – the nouns are descriptive of people (often negatively; for example *futret* describes Mistress Munro), and the adjectives and adverbs belittle or intensify.

It is perhaps important to note the opportunities spurned by Gibbon to make his narrative more densely Scots. For example, he writes *out* (not 'oot' – though orthographic traditionalists might balk at the <oo> spelling), *just* (not 'juist'), *holding* (not 'haudin'), *all* (not 'aa' or 'aw'), *eyes* (not 'een'), *thought* (not 'thocht'), *creature* (not 'cratur'), and so on. If Gibbon had wanted to write prose in dense 'Braid Scots', the opportunities were available. This evidently was not his intention. The vocabulary in *Sunset Song* is idiosyncratically eclectic: like *creature,* such words as *brave* ('braw'; 'handsome'), and *childe* ('chiel'; 'young man') are given the spelling of the cognate English term, even when these spellings evoke a different sense or a poetic archaism. Also archaic are the spellings of *meikle* ('muckle'; 'great') and *quean* ('quine'; 'young girl'). *Queans* appears in this spelling in Burns's 'Tam o' Shanter' (l.151), where it rhymes with 'teens' rather than with, say, 'lines', as in the north-east. In short, Gibbon's use of vocabulary adapts for English prose the synthetic approach to Scots poetry favoured by his friend, MacDiarmid: some archaic Scots and English items are mingled with general Scots terms, as well as a few regionalisms from different localities, though mainly north-eastern. The result is a literary construction of Scottish speech, rather than an 'authentic' recreation of the spoken Scots of Angus. As we shall shortly see, Gibbon's use of imported, 'un-English' terms in his prose extends to *Spartacus.*

However, perhaps even more telling than the use of 'foreign' terms in the English of *Sunset Song* and *Spartacus* is their distinctive 'rhythm and cadence'. Prose rhythm in general is difficult to analyse, involving as it does the ordering of words syntactically to produce an 'aural' effect, if only in the silent reader's mind. As D.W. Harding puts it: 'In all prose, utilitarian included, the words are being grouped into patterns according to two systems, simultaneously operative: patterns of sense and syntax, and patterns of sound and movement.'[4] The syntax and the sound of *Sunset Song* both work towards the same end: the fostering of a sense of conversational intimacy.

Conversational intimacy is possibly the most telling consequence of one of the most discussed syntactic features of *Sunset Song,* namely the idiosyncratic use of 'self-referring you' (that is, the use of 'you' in the narrative when Chris seems to be 'talking to herself' and thus allowing the reader to eavesdrop on her thoughts).[5] *Sunset Song* shares some of the conventions of 'real' conversational narratives as recorded by sociolinguists interested in the structures of oral storytelling, namely the focus on key protagonists; the use of simple phrases and clauses, loosely linked (if at all) by coordinating conjunctions; the shading of narrative into direct speech to dramatise key events; and the expression of the narrator's own attitude by exclamations and evaluative asides.[6] These 'oral' features are evident in passages such as the following:

> Chris watched him go, sitting in the front of the box-cart, Clyde in the shafts, the cart loaded down with corn for the Mill, and Ewan turning to wave to her from the foot of Blawearie brae. And all that afternoon he was away she fretted from room to room, oh! she was a fool, there was nothing could happen to him! And when at last he came back she ran out to him, fair scared he was at the way she looked, and thought her ill, and when she cried she had missed him so he went white and then blushed, just a boy still, and forgot to unyoke Clyde left in the cold, he was kissing Chris instead. And faith! for the bairns of farmers both they might well have had more sense. (*SS*, 169)

Here Gibbon's crafted literary prose reproduces some of the features associated with a well-told spoken anecdote: the loosely-coordinated sentence structure (e.g. each sentence begins with 'And'), the narrator's exclamation ('faith!') and the final evaluative coda ('for the bairns of farmers both they might well have had more sense'). It is such characteristics that partly convey the impression of speech.

In addition, the syntax of *Sunset Song* has rhythmic implications, often commented on, not least by Gibbon himself.[7] For many critics, the rhythm is highly evocative: 'Recurring alliteration and rhythmic anapaestic prose show the traces of a past that still survives, and reproduce the pulse of living and working.'[8] However, the function and nature of prose rhythm are difficult to determine. Aristotle's *Rhetoric* states the issue succinctly by noting that 'the primary function of prose rhythm is to be neither wholly unrhythmical nor full poetical metre.'[9] Derek Attridge further notes that 'poetic rhythm is a heightening and an exploitation of the rhythm of a particular language'.[10] The question to ask, then, is what the 'natural' rhythm of Scots and English might be, and how prose exploits that rhythm in such a way as it begins to be perceived as 'poetically' significant.

The 'natural' rhythms of English and Scots have changed over the centuries. Both have their origins in Anglo-Saxon verse, which is believed to have been trochaic in nature: its words were made up of stressed stems followed by unstressed grammatical endings. However, as Anglo-Saxon dialects evolved into English and Scots, these endings withered away, and their grammatical functions were taken over by unstressed words such as articles and prepositions, both of which *precede* the stressed lexical item. Rising rhythms, that is, iambs and anapaests that move from unstressed to stressed syllables, therefore became the 'norm' in English and Scots.[11]

Linguistically, present-day English and Scots both make use of the same basic resources for rhythm and metre. Any differences in the distribution of rhythmic and more general poetic features that may be discerned can be considered a matter of taste and tradition rather than an inherent quality of the languages.

Gibbon's task in *Sunset Song,* then, was to draw on the linguistic resources English shares with Scots, and fashion a rhythmic quality that could be identified as Scottish, whilst losing neither the 'dignity' of literary prose nor the 'spontaneity' of everyday speech. As in Aristotle's time, of all the poetic rhythms, the iambic is most closely identified with everyday speech: iambic pentameter, after all, is the basis of most English dramatic verse. Anapaestic rhythm, as the alternative 'rising rhythm' would seem to be the likeliest candidate for a novelist wishing to mark out his prose as 'other', and, as we shall shortly see, this is what Gibbon employs to mark *Sunset Song* as rhythmically 'un-English' – which the reader interprets in this case as 'Scots'.

In a discussion of the rhythm of a celebrated passage in the novel, Macafee contrasts the iambic patterns used when Chris talks of learning and her 'English' self, with the anapaestic patterns used when she speaks of the land and her 'Scots' self. In the excerpt below, I have italicised the stressed syllables to show one possible (rather exaggerated) reading that demonstrates the switch from 'English' iambs ('so *sharp* and *clean* and *true*') to 'Scots' anapaests ('for a *while,* for a *while*'):

> *Scots* words to *tell* to your *heart* how they *wrung* it and *held* it, the *toil* of their *days* and un*end*ingly their *fight*. And the *next* *min*ute that *passed* from you, you were *Eng*lish, *back* to the *Eng*lish *words* so *sharp* and *clean* and *true* – for a *while*, for a *while*, till they *slid* so *smooth* from your *throat* you *knew* they could *nev*er say *any*thing that was *worth* the *say*ing at *all*. (*SS*, 32)

For prose, this passage is surprisingly regular in its rhythms, with anapaests largely dominating except where the 'English words' are mentioned. This is not to say that in everyday speech, Scottish speakers use more anapaests than English speakers. Commenting on this passage, Macafee observes, 'Gibbon has made an anapaestic rhythm stand for a Scots voice and an iambic one for an English voice. He has done this by associating the two rhythms with the two dialects (or languages) *within the text*. This stylistic effect has no basis in external reality.'[12]

This claim demands a certain degree of qualification. Gibbon makes an iambic rhythm 'stand for an English voice' within *this part* of the text.

Gibbon frequently uses iambic 'bursts' for descriptive passages where no 'English voice' is implied, as in the following excerpt from another part of the novel. Here, I have shown the stressed (—) and unstressed (U) syllables, and again italicised the syllables I have chosen to stress.

U   U   U — | U— | U — | U U — U
So they were *douce* and *safe* and *blithe* in Bla*wea*rie
U   U —| U   U — |U U   — | — U | —(U)
though Kin*rad*die was *un*co with *Chae Strach*an gone.

(SS, 194)

Here we find the same switch between iambs (*'douce* and *safe* and *blithe'*) and anapaests ('though Kin*rad*die was *un*co with *Chae'*) without the suggestion that one stands for an English voice while the other stands for a Scots voice. The rhythmic variation simply prevents the dominant anaepaestic pattern from becoming too monotonous. In short, Gibbon's employment of rhythm is not over-schematic: particular rhythms cannot always be associated with one specific meaning (such as Chris's Scottishness or Englishness). However, allied to the content of particular passages of the text, pronounced contrasts in rhythm can take on contingent meanings. And, certainly, the preponderance of marked anapaestic rhythms in the novel as a whole does suggest a non-English 'other', and therefore in this instance 'Scottish', cadence.

In *Spartacus,* too, Mitchell experiments with prose style to construct a sense of an 'other', in this case the multicultural members of the Free Legion and their Roman adversaries. As Ian Campbell has observed, Mitchell imports Latin and Greek terminology into *Spartacus* in a manner similar to the way he imports Scots terms into *Sunset Song*;[13] for example (Latinisms italicised):

> The Gauls had been shepherds and labourers, but the others *vulgares* of the household, *ostiarii, pistores, coqui*, bed-chamber slaves and slaves of the bath. [...] Their backs were scored with *cicatrices*, for their mistress had been Petronia, wife of C. Gaius Petronius, strong in belief that a well-flogged slave was a willing slave. (*Sp*, 10)

Graham Tulloch has noted that the language of *Sunset Song* is difficult to classify, being a mixture of elements, and the same is true of *Spartacus.*[14] In the latter novel, the obvious Latinisms tend to be technical terms (and therefore 'untranslatable') but occasionally a 'gratuitous' Latinism appears, as in *cicatrices,* which could equally well be 'scars'. The effect is to give the prose style of *Spartacus* the appearance of what Lawrence Venuti would call a 'foreignising translation', that is, a translation from another language that calls attention to its translated quality. Foreignising strategies include the use of borrowed terms, dialect vocabulary and sudden shifts of register from formal to informal.[15] Mitchell's use of Latinate terms in *Spartacus* can be read as a foreignising strategy; but so too can his use of Scots terms in *Sunset Song*. Both point to a half-elided 'other' behind the English prose – one Scottish, one the multicultural underclass of the Roman Empire.

If the use of 'foreignising' vocabulary in *Sunset Song* and *Spartacus* is surprisingly similar, nevertheless the narrative voice, grammatical characteristics, rhythms and cadences of the novels are generally different, with a few significant exceptions. *Spartacus* has a conventional omniscient narrator, the typical voice of a dispassionate historian, and there is no trace of the experimental 'self-referring you' we find in *Sunset Song*. The reader is placed in the position of an observer of historical events, not the intimate acquaintance of a preternaturally knowledgeable member of a community, and of its central character. The central character of *Spartacus* is at best an enigma, at worst a cipher:[16] his history is early shrouded in amnesia, and his status shifts from rebel, to proto-communist, to monarch, to token of the 'innumerable Christ', all according to the demands of the narrative. Spartacus is enigmatic because we are never given his view of the events of the novel in the way we see the events of *Sunset Song* partly through Chris Guthrie's eyes: the narrator keeps Spartacus ever aloof, distant and cold.

The most marked feature of the syntax of *Spartacus* is a tendency towards descriptive participial constructions, complex sentences, and marked clause structures (i.e. clauses that depart from the conventional English sequence Subject + Verb + Complement). English participial structures are often used when translating 'ablative absolute' constructions in Latin. The 'ablative absolute', as every classically-trained schoolchild once knew, was a Latin noun phrase whose inflected grammatical structure has no modern English equivalent, e.g. *Caesare duce* (literally 'Caesar leader') or *Numā rēge* ('Numa king'). The schoolchild wishing to translate the full grammatical force of these phrases would have either to insert a participle ('Caesar *being* leader', 'Numa *being* king') or find a way of paraphrasing the expression more 'fluently', for example, 'under Caesar's leadership', or 'in Numa's reign'.[17] Mitchell's use of participial phrases is particularly redolent of schoolboy Latin and deliberately 'unfluent':

When Kleon heard the news from Capua he rose early one morning, and
being a literatus and unchained, crept into the room of his Master. ... (*Sp,* 3)
He paused ceremonially, *being mad,* and chanting an oft-told tale. (*Sp,* 8)
Kleon, *being Greek,* looked contemptuously on Thracians. (*Sp,* 28)

Grammatical inversions also indicate the 'otherness' or 'un-Englishness' of
the narrative, for instance:

Above the ridged Italian hills uprose the sun... (*Sp,* 18)
One man who was quarrelsome he slew with his own hands. (*Sp,* 20)
These the Jew had no desire to engage. (*Sp,* 101)

The un-Englishness of these constructions lies in the marked sequence of
clause elements: the Subject + Verb + Complement sequence is disrupted
in each case, and a more flexible 'Latinate' word order is substituted.

Ian Campbell remarks positively on the Latinate style of *Spartacus,*
arguing that 'carefully used' it 'functions powerfully to give the reader a
sense of involvement'.[18] The pleasures afforded by Latin allusion are complex, however, and different in origin from those afforded by the 'Scots' prose
of *Sunset Song.* Hugh Osborne, in a discussion of the function of embedded
Latin tags in the novels of nineteenth-century writers such as Trollope,
argues that the apparently gratuitous use of 'disguised' Latin translations
into English functioned to reinforce the sense of a common public-school
background amongst their readers, an elite-pleasing device that went out of
fashion with mass literacy later in the century.[19] It might seem perverse to
accuse Mitchell of conscious elitism in such a revolutionary tract as *Spartacus,*
but part of its pleasure for a dwindling number of readers trained classically,
whether by the master in the public school or the local *dominie,* must surely
be located in the recognition of Mitchell's skill in constructing something
that gives the flavour of a Latin translation. By comparison, the appeal of
Sunset Song is altogether less dry and more resonant: it gives the flavour of
intimate conversations with a living community.

The cold aloofness of the character of Spartacus is partly the result of
denying the reader access to his perspective, and in general the emotions
of the characters in the novel are frequently distanced by impersonal
grammatical realisations that construct them simply as 'media' through
which passions work. Impersonal constructions using *there + verb,* or the
choice of an emotion rather than a person in Subject position, reduce the
responsibility of the characters for the emotions they feel. For example,
consider the episode in which Crixus is waiting in vain for Spartacus to
reinforce his troops at Garganus:

> And *for some reason* he thought of the woman Elpinice [...] And so strong
> upon him *did this imagining grow* [...] Then on Crixus *there came a fine
> gaiety* [...] And in that early-morning light there clung to his eyelids a
> fine web from the night-time mist; and *the wonder of that on his eyelids was
> strange on his spirit* for a moment. (*Sp*, 120; italics added)

There is no reason why this passage could not have been written with Crixus
as the grammatical Subject, e.g. 'Then *Crixus* imagined Elpinice for some
reason... *He* suddenly felt gay... *He* wondered at the strangeness of the
night-time mist on his eyelids'. The effect of Mitchell's grammatical choices
is to present the characters as vessels through whom externalised emotions
– imaginings, gaiety, wonder – pass 'for some reason'. The characters
become, effectively, subject to rather than responsible for their passions in
this historical drama. As the reader's sense of the characters' control over
their destiny is diminished, they become the 'shadowy cup bearers' of the
author's intentions, as Kleon prophesies, somewhat ironically (*Sp*, 218).

The deliberately 'stilted', 'un-English' grammar of *Spartacus* therefore
results in a prose style that is distinct from that of *Sunset Song*. The reader
is set at much more of a distance from the actors in the drama, who play
out their roles often at the mercy of externalised, brutalising emotions. The
reader is never allowed to look at the drama with the intimacy of Chris
Guthrie's perspective, via self-referencing 'you', for example, and, as Ian
Campbell also notes, the cardboard quality of the characters in *Spartacus* is
reinforced by the monotonously-repeated character traits with which each
is saddled. In comparison, our access to the complex motivations of at least
the main characters in *Sunset Song* raises them above such two-dimensional
stereotypes.

Yet in some superficial respects certain passages in *Spartacus* do
resemble *Sunset Song*, particularly when Mitchell wishes to heighten the
emotional impact of a passage, such as Spartacus' death or the crucifixion of
Kleon. In the former episode (*Sp*, 232), the loose linking of clauses with
coordinate conjunctions might seem to resemble the free-wheeling, spoken
mode of the Scottish novel. This passage also has the episodic style of a
spoken narrative, but other aspects work against a colloquial impression:
the capitalisation shouts out that this is a SIGNIFICANT MOMENT, and the
mock-Latin participial constructions ('and inflicting many wounds', 'and,
being surrounded by a great number') again remind us that this is
reconstructed *written* Roman history. The episodic nature of the narrative
here serves mainly to quicken the pace and thereby heighten the drama.

There are certain passages in *Spartacus* that, like *Sunset Song,* have a

marked anapaestic rhythm; however, these tend to be passages of heightened
action, the more lyrical descriptive passages of countryside description, or,
at the end, the death agony of Kleon (*Sp*, 235):

```
U   —  | U     —  |  U  U —|U U —
he fought and marched and debated again,                          1
U    —  |U U   — |U  — |U U— | — U
heard cry in his ears the myriad slave voices,                    2
—   U | —   U |U    —  |U  —  | U  —  |U —
heard the ghost of that Hope and Promise wail away                3
U U  —  | U    —  |U — |U — |U U —
as the morning came upon the Appian Way.                          4
```

Although not quite as marked, perhaps, as in *Sunset Song,* there is a
discernible alternation of iambic and anapaestic rhythms here, certainly in
'lines' 1, 2 and 4. The marked switch from trochees to iambs in 'line' 3
arguably has the mimetic effect of imitating the repetitive 'wailing away'
of the 'Hope' and 'Promise'. The relatively high distribution of anapaests
overall, obviously, cannot be attributed to some notional 'Scots speaking
voice' as in *Sunset Song* – rather it is designed, as is the quick succession of
narrative phrases at the death of Spartacus, to heighten the emotional
impact of a passage whose significance is already, arguably, over-wrought.
Edwin Morgan suggests that 'Mitchell's final image is one of the book's
many dramatic reverberations, with which the reader must come to terms
in his or her own way. Its boldness is its defence.'[20] The overtly rhythmical
nature of the prose here does underline the boldness of the vision, but in
the context of a comparison between Spartacus and Christ – even Christ as
the kind of revolutionary who leads his comrades in Aleksander Blok's
poem, *The Twelve* – the passage seems to strain for effect.

The move from linguistic description to literary interpretation and
evaluation is always problematic. As Stanley Fish observed, the problem
with stylistics is not that it fails, but that it always succeeds.[21] Thus the
linguist can point to anapaestic rhythms in passages of *Sunset Song,* and
speak at one moment of the typical cadences of the Scottish community,
and point to anapaestic rhythms in (albeit fewer) passages in *Spartacus* and
arrive at a different interpretation. Harding warns, 'There is always the risk
of attributing to rhythm an expressive significance that stems in reality
from other features of language.'[22] In prose, rhythm can do only a few
general, although important, things,[23] for example:

(a) a marked rhythm (e.g. a preponderance of anapaestic 'feet') can 'heighten' the language of *a particular passage*, that is, our attention is particularly drawn to the content, whose – for instance – lyrical, dramatic or reflective nature will therefore be more pronounced. The use of anapaestic paragraphs in *Spartacus* can be related to this function.

(b) the use of a given marked rhythm relatively consistently *throughout a novel*, as in *Sunset Song*, gives it a coherent unity. As we have seen, the significance of the rhythm is not intrinsic, however, except insofar as it is 'unnatural' in English prose, and therefore useful in expressing 'otherness'.

(c) once a pattern has been set up, there is the possibility of deviating from it and creating *patterns of contrast*, as in the iambic and anapaestic patterns we see in both *Spartacus* and *Sunset Song*. In particular passages, the rhythms may attract 'local' interpretations, as in the contrast between English ('iambic') and Scots ('anapaestic') Chris in one passage in *Sunset Song*. However, these local interpretations are not necessarily sustained across the entire novel.

(d) the use of anapaestic rhythms in both *Spartacus* and *Sunset Song* are *emotionally suggestive*. Attridge comments: 'Though the association of rhythmic qualities and emotional states is no doubt in part a matter of cultural conditioning, it seems likely that there's a physiological connection as well, since emotions manifest themselves directly in the way we expend muscular energy.'[24]

Despite the fact that this last quality of rhythmic prose – 'emotional suggestiveness' – is the most elusive to the analytical linguist, it may well be that this is the quality that Mitchell or Gibbon valued most. In 'The Land' Gibbon speaks with admiration for the 'controlled ecstasy' of the 'careful prose' of two English writers on natural history, Gilbert White (1720-1793) and H.J. Massingham (1888-1952). A glance at some of their writings indeed shows a mastery of the use of prose rhythms in the service of natural description. Perhaps influenced by these favoured writers, Gibbon structures his prose with the desire both to evoke and control intense emotion. The novelist, however, is not content to offer the reader detailed and uplifting glimpses of natural beauty. The allusion in 'The Land' to the 'controlled ecstasy' of White and Massingham is followed immediately by Gibbon's meditation on the cruelty of his fellow human beings:

> When I hear or read of a dog tortured to death, very vilely and foully, of some old horse driven to a broken back down a hill with an overloaded cart of corn, of rats captured and tormented with red-hot pokers in bothies, I have a shudder of disgust. But these things do not move me too deeply, not as the fate of the old-time Cameronian prisoners over there, three miles away in Dunottar; not as the face of that ragged tramp who went by this afternoon; not as the crucifixion of the Spartacist slaves along the Appian Way. (*Sm*, 95)

The 'controlled ecstasy' of the Scottish prose writer, by implication, should arouse a 'shudder of disgust' for the horrors that people inflict upon each other. For this reader, *Spartacus* certainly evokes revulsion at the many cruelties powerfully described. However, there is an uneasy feeling that the 'ecstatic' nature of the description, heightened by the careful prose, amounts to a near pornographic rendering of physical and sexual abuse, as in the following description of Gaius Cassius:

> In his years of debauchery he had also become infected with leprosy, and, inflamed in the colds of the northern province, this disease had vexed him to the edge of insanity again and again, finding its only relief in heated baths and the ministrations, night upon night, of great numbers of girls from the stud-farm. A patrician, Gaius Cassius was a man of culture, and knew that without the strong hand of the Law men would live in misery and fear. And, groaning in pleasure, he would fondle the horrified children. (*Sp*, 143)

The heightened language and the detailed description of abuses from an external viewpoint might suggest that the suffering in *Spartacus* is 'on display', in part at least for our vicarious gratification. The reader closes the covers of the book feeling uneasily complicit with Kleon's short-lived Master, amongst whose favourite books is 'the *Nine Rapings* of the Greek Ataretos' (*Sp*, 4). Part of the problem is, as Edwin Morgan points out, the sexual violence so graphically described is made to represent the problems of civilisation for which there is ultimately no solution. For Morgan, the virtue of the novel is in the 'shaking experience' it uniquely offers[25], but since no prophetic vision is achieved other than the infinite recycling of torture and martyrdom, the uncomfortable charge of voyeurism is hardly dispelled. Endless variations on the *motif* of the crucifixion of a warrior-slave do not function as a political call to arms, no matter how impassioned they might be.

In contrast, *Sunset Song* complicates the narrative perspective by constructing a narrative voice that takes us inside the community and inside the female protagonist's head. This perspective complicates our understanding of violence and gender politics, as when Chris narrowly avoids being the victim of sexual assault, possibly even rape, at the hands of two ploughmen:

> But it hadn't seemed fun to her, dead earnest rather; and lying that night in her bed between the cold sheets, curled up so that she might rub her white toes to some warmth and ease, it was in her memory like being chased and bitten by a beast, but worse and with something else in it, as though half she'd liked the beast and the biting and the smell of that sleeve around her neck, and that soft, unshaven face against her own. Sweet breath he had had anyway, she thought, and laughed to herself, that was some consolation, the tink. (*SS*, 91)

Here, rather than postitioning the reader as a reluctant voyeur of Chris's experience from an external perspective, Gibbon collapses the distance between reader and character. We see the attack through the eyes of the frightened victim as well as (in a heightened, 'ecstatic' language) her growing recognition of her own sexuality, aroused by the attack. And we empathise with her attempt to regain control of her body physically by warming it, and symbolically by appraising her attacker's attractiveness before contemptuously dismissing him as 'the tink'. Nothing of this complexity is found in the parade of atrocities that make up *Spartacus,* although there is no doubting the serious intent of the exhibition. In *Sunset Song,* the fluid narrative perspectives situate the reader in a privileged position: we have unparalleled and sympathetic access to the intimate perceptions of the community and the main character of the novel. In contrast, the narrative voice in *Spartacus* is that of an ancient historian, the characters are more caricatured and less rounded, and the reader is positioned rather like William Howard Russell, the Times correspondent who watched the Charge of the Light Brigade from a nearby hill amongst other 'war tourists' – distant spectators to tragedy on an epic scale.

Gibbon's overall concern with prose style was the structured evocation of the 'controlled ecstasy' he found, for example, in the writing of favoured natural historians. He too fashioned skills necessary to convey both emotional immediacy and descriptive accuracy; however, his goal was to turn this power towards the evocation of compassionate rage against human

injustice. While *Spartacus* attempts this in an unremitting catalogue of
horrors, whose ecstatic description uneasily compromises the reader in the
act of reading them, *Sunset Song* offers a more rounded narrative of both joy
and everyday cruelty, no less horrifying in places for its greater artistry and
moral complexity.

Notes

1. Lewis Grassic Gibbon and Hugh MacDiarmid, *Scottish Scene or the Intelligent
   Man's Guide to* Albyn (London: Jarrolds, 1934), p. 304. Quotations from
   Scottish Scene will be referenced in the text from its reprint in *Smeddum: A Lewis
   Grassic Gibbon Anthology* ed. by Valentina Bold (Edinburgh: Canongate, 2001).
   Quotations from *Spartacus* (London: Jarrolds, 1933) are from the edition
   introduced by Edwin Morgan (Edinburgh: B&W Publishing, 1996),
   indicated by *Sp*; those from *Sunset Song* (London: Jarrolds, 1932) are taken from
   the edition ed. and introd. by Tom Crawford (Edinburgh: Canongate, 1988),
   indicated by *SS*.
2. See, for example, Ramon Lopez Ortega, 'Language and Point of View in Lewis
   Grassic Gibbon's *A Scots Quair*' in *Studies in Scottish Literature* 16 (1981), p. 150:
   'The language of *A Scots Quair* successfully renders the country speech of the
   North Eastern Lowlands, usually known as Lallans, Synthetic or Braid Scots, a
   direct descendent from the Old English dialect Northumbrian.' This claim is
   at best misleading, confusing as it does spoken and literary forms of Scots.
3. See also Graham Tulloch, 'The search for a Scots narrative voice' in *Focus on:
   Scotland*, ed. by Manfred Görlach (Amsterdam: John Benjamins, 1985), p. 173.
4. D.W. Harding, *Words into Rhythm: English Speech Rhythm in Verse and Prose*
   (Cambridge: Cambridge University Press, 1976), p. 133.
5. See Graham Trengrove, 'Who is you? Grammar and Grassic Gibbon' in *Scottish
   Literary Journal* 2:2, 1975, pp. 47-62.
6. See, for example, Ronald MacAulay, 'Remarkably Common Eloquence: The
   Aesthetics of Urban Dialect' in *Scottish Language*, No. 14-5, 1995/6, pp. 66-80.
7. For example, Ivor Brown in the foreword to the Pan edition of *Sunset Song*
   (1973), p. xii; Ortega, p. 152; see also Caroline Macafee's more extended
   analysis in her unpublished workbook written for a distance-learning M.Phil
   in Scottish Literature: 'Unit 3A: Modern Scots' (Department of Scottish
   Literature, University of Glasgow: no date), pp. 102-11.
8. Ortega, p. 152.
9. Aristotle, *The Art of Rhetoric*, Book III, Chapter 8. This translation is H.C.
   Lawson-Tancred, *Aristotle: The Art of Rhetoric* (Harmondsworth: Penguin:
   1991), p. 230.

10. Derek Attridge, *Poetic Rhythm: An Introduction* (Cambridge: Cambridge University Press, 1995), p.4. Although this introductory textbook explicitly deals with poetry rather than prose, its discussion of free verse and phrasing is particularly useful for an analysis of *Sunset Song*.

11. For further detail see C.M. Millward, *A Biography of the English Language* (Fort Worth: Holt, Rinehart and Winston, 1989), esp. p.134; and for a case study of prose rhythm in a period of change, see J. Smith 'Language and Style in Malory' in Elizabeth Archibald and A.S.G. Edwards, eds. *A Companion to Malory*, (Cambridge: D.S. Brewer, 1996), pp.97-113.

12. Macafee, p.111; original emphasis.

13. See the Introduction to James Leslie Mitchell's *Spartacus* edited by Ian Campbell (Edinburgh: Scottish Academic Press & ASLS, 1990), pp.xxiv-xxv.

14. Tulloch, p.173.

15. See Lawrence Venuti, *The Translator's Invisibility: A History of Translation* (London: Routledge, 1995).

16. Edwin Morgan in his introduction to the 1996 edition suggests this is a virtue: 'Spartacus is a true hero in that he retains something enigmatic, alien, unexplained', p.x.

17. The schoolbook that jogged my memory is Peter Milne, *Latin Sentences* (London: Longman, 1963); see the section on ablative absolutes on pp.47-8.

18. Campbell, p.xxv.

19. Hugh Osborne, 'Hooked on Classics: Discourses of allusion in the mid-Victorian novel' in *Translation and Nation: Towards a Cultural Politics of Englishness* ed. by Roger Ellis and Liz Oakely-Brown (Clevedon: Multilingual Matters, 2001), pp.120-66.

20. Morgan, Introduction, p.x. Morgan also notes the comparison between Spartacus and Blok's Christ in *The Twelve*.

21. Stanley Fish's assault on stylistics and some counter-attacks are reprinted in Jean Jacques Weber, ed. *The Stylistics Reader: From Roman Jakobson to the Present* (London: Arnold, 1996). See particularly pp.94-137.

22. Harding, p.153.

23. cf. Attridge, pp.12-20, on the functions of rhythm in poetry.

24. Attridge, p.14.

25. Morgan, Introduction, p.xiii.

The Rendering of Community Voices in Lewis Grassic Gibbon's Short Stories

Catriona M. Low

Lewis Grassic Gibbon's short stories share a similar narrative technique with *A Scots Quair*. Of the five stories published in *Scottish Scene*, the book co-written with Hugh MacDiarmid in 1934, four are set in the farming countryside of the Mearns, and these – 'Smeddum', 'Greenden', 'Clay' and 'Sim' – will be the focus of this discussion.

The short stories are narrated by an anonymous community voice, gossipy and critical, like the Kinraddie voice of *Sunset Song*, and the Segget voice of *Cloud Howe*. In the trilogy, the narrative alternates between the community voice and the points of view of central characters – often Chris's, but also, for example, Else Queen's, and Ewan's. The technique of switching points of view can also be seen from time to time in the short stories, but the occasional shifts tend to be between different representatives of the community, only very seldom involving the consciousness of one of the central characters. The impact of the short stories, to a great extent, is achieved by the gap the reader perceives between the community's interpretation of events, and reality. To move into the consciousness of a central character in these stories would lessen their effectiveness. In 'Clay', however, the use of Rachel Galt as a focaliser for short sections of the narrative, significantly alters the tone and mood of the story, as will be discussed later.

The style of the community narrator in these stories is conversational and heavily descriptive, with imagery taken from the farming environment. Characters are often identified with beasts and the similes associated with the characters are frequently repeated throughout the story; in 'Greenden', for example, George Simpson has a 'sappy red face like an ill-used nout's' and in 'Smeddum' Meg Menzies is likened throughout to a 'meikle roan'.[1] Some critics have felt this habit of repetition is overdone,[2] but I would suggest that the repetitions further reinforce the sense of these stories being 'heard' rather than 'read', functioning like the repeated epithets in orally-delivered traditional tales. The metaphors used are also completely in keeping with the character or personality of the narrator, whose selection of imagery is dependent on and informed by the daily life around him/her. Not only do the descriptions add authenticity to the narrative voice, they are also vivid and robust and, more often than not, contribute to the humour in the tales. In 'the speak', Gibbon captures the essence of the community character: the eagerness to find fault with one's neighbours, to mock people's failings and bluntly observe their physical oddities, and to judge and moralise about the rest of the village. As in *A Scots Quair*, the folk-narrator is at times malicious, relishing the misfortunes of others; generally, however, the tone tends to be matter-of-fact, unsympathetic and insensitive to the emotions, motivations and problems of the central characters. Nevertheless, the crony narrator has some redeeming features: humour, particularly, but also the ability to paint a vivid picture of the people, their daily lives and the land itself.

In 'Smeddum', I would argue, the voice of the community is at its most likeable and entertaining. There is no real malice and cruelty in the depiction of Meg Menzies and her family: the unfairness found in the 'Greenden' voice, or in the coarse Segget voice of *Cloud Howe*, is absent here. Indeed, the narrator from time to time introduces the phrases 'folk said' or 'some said' to the more insulting remarks, thus attributing the nastier comments to un-named others. Meg's tendencies to roughness and vulgarity are gleefully pointed out, however, and the community reveals itself eager to see her come-uppance: 'And folk laughed right hearty, fegs! that was a clour for meikle Meg Menzies, her daughter a thief!'(*Sm*, 40). However, the narrator cannot hide an enjoyment of Meg's exploits, and has a respect and admiration (albeit grudging) for her attitude:

> There was a fair speak about that at the time, Meg Menzies and the vulgar words she had used, folk told that she'd even said what was the place where she'd skelp the bit doctor's wife. And faith! that fair must have been a sore shock to the doctor's wife that was that genteel she'd never believed she'd a place like that. (*Sm*, 37)

Meg Menzies provides opportunities for entertaining gossip and this, in the eyes of the community, makes her likeable.

Unusually in Gibbon's short stories, the community voice in 'Smeddum' also demonstrates sympathy for an individual. In Meg's case this is because Will Menzies is 'as coarse a little brute as you'd meet, bone-lazy forbye, and as sly as sin' (*Sm*, 36). The narrator mentions Meg's 'soft side' and comments: 'Rampageous and ill with her tongue though she was, you couldn't but pity a woman like Meg tied up for life to a thing like *that*' (*Sm*, 36). Nevertheless, it emerges that the community is mistaken: unlike some women who feature in the short stories,[3] and despite her own reservations revealed at the end, Meg clearly has deep feelings for her man. Will Menzies' death provokes a characteristically blunt remark by the community voice: 'he drank himself to his grave at last, less smell on the earth if maybe more in it'; however, immediately a note of genuine concern for Meg is introduced: 'But she broke down and wept, it was awful to see, Meg Menzies weeping like a stricken horse' (*Sm*, 37). Typically in the short stories, the community voice finds situations like this amusing; there is usually a certain relish at the misfortunes of others. This is even more prevalent when the unfortunate individual is perceived as non-conformist, and Meg Menzies' 'smeddum' certainly marks her as different from the rest of the community. In one very significant way, on the other hand, Meg is shown to conform very strongly to community values: she is a hard worker. In the opening description the narrator notes: 'if ever a soul had seen her at rest when the dark was done and the day was come he'd died of the shock and never let on' (*Sm*, 35), and throughout the story the narrator continues to refer to Meg's industriousness. Not only does she work 'about the house', she takes on her man's work in the parks too: 'she'd yoke up the horse and the sholtie together, and kilt up her skirts till you'd see her great legs, and cry *Wissh!* like a man and turn a fair drill' (*Sm*, 36). Meg, by virtue of her hard work, deserves the community's respect and admiration. In this way, Gibbon shows the criteria by which the community judges an individual, and where its values lie.

'Smeddum' shows the Mearns' community's attitude to one of its own; in contrast, 'Greenden' deals with the experiences of 'incomers' to the area: a couple from the city, strangers to the farming life. With no background in farming, and little real conception of what is involved, physically or emotionally, the Simpsons are, according to the crony narrator, 'ill-suited' for farm-work: 'Ay, they'd find it a change from their Glasgow streets; they didn't know what it was to work, the dirt that came from the towns' (*Sm*, 24). This comment is revealing. Firstly, it articulates the prejudice felt by the rural community to anyone from outside. There is a tendency for the community to feel that it is looked down on by town-dwellers for being less sophisticated, and it uses attack as the best form of defence. In his essay 'The Land', Gibbon writes of the country people's suspicion and wariness, as they are 'an order sneered upon by the little folk of the towns, their gait is a mockery in city streets, you see little waitresses stare haughtily at their

great red, sun-creased hands' (*Sm*, 87). The narrator of 'Greenden' delivers
a judgement on the Simpsons because they are representatives of a separate
and potentially hostile community. Secondly, as we saw in 'Smeddum', the
comment illustrates the value the rural community places on the work
ethic through claiming moral superiority over its urban counterpart by
virtue of 'hard work'.

The narrator feels that the Simpsons are doomed to fail, and mocks their
ignorance of the rigours of farm life. It is difficult enough for those who have
a lifetime's experience of farming to scrape a living, so what chance have
these outsiders? There is no serious malice in the community's attitude; nor
is there much sympathy: the folk-voice, as representative of the majority, is
initially fairly indifferent to the couple and events at Greenden. It is
interesting that in 'Greenden' the narrative voice is careful to attribute the
most malicious remarks to the Murdochs. It is Murdoch of Mains who
makes the disparaging comment about old Grant at the beginning of the
story, 'fair strong in the hands if weak in the head'; and he provides the first
description of the Simpsons' ignorance of farming practice, in his tale of
Pittendreich's roller. Only once is Murdoch questioned or censured in any
way: 'everybody knew that the Murdoch brute could lie like a tink when the
mood was on him.' (*Sm*, 23, 24) Later, the narrative shifts briefly to the voice
of Mistress Murdoch, who supplies the community with the unflattering
portrait of Ellen Simpson: 'the creature fair got on to her nerves with her
flitting here and her tripping there, and her laugh, and the meikle eyes of
her in the small doll face that she had' (*Sm*, 26). The community bases its
opinions of the Simpsons on the 'evidence' presented by the Murdochs. As
the story progresses, and George Simpson becomes a frequent visitor and
friend to the Murdoch family, the community voice becomes more
sympathetic in tone towards him, while becoming more antagonistic to
Ellen. Any doubts about the propriety of Simpson's flirting with Jeannie
Murdoch are quickly dismissed by the narrator: 'no harm in their fun, folk
'greed about that: the poor stock was no doubt in need of a laugh, him and
that wife with her flutterings that fair set your hackles on edge' (*Sm*, 29).
George Simpson is now a 'pretty, upstanding childe' – a marked contrast to
the earlier description of his 'sappy big face, and a look on that face as
though some childe had ta'en him a hard kick in the dowp' (*Sm*, 30, 25).
The community voice has assimilated the Murdochs' view. Significantly, it
is the Murdochs' new barn which proves the final straw for Ellen Simpson
and prompts her suicide. The barn blocks out her only source of comfort –
the view of the sun on the hill – just as the Murdochs' negative opinion has
influenced the rest of the community and left her isolated.

Webster, the grocer, is the only one of the community to care about Ellen Simpson, noticing (or sensing) her loneliness and her husband's selfishness, though even he is not sensitive enough to the seriousness of her mental state to intervene until it is too late. Initially the grocer is described as 'a kindly stock' (*Sm*, 25), but the community changes its mind, as it did in its view of Simpson, and Webster later is distanced from the community by the narrator:

> He never told the story in a neighbour-like way, he never did that, and he wasn't much liked, for he'd never much news to give a body when you spoke to him at the tail of his van and would drop a bit hint that you'd like to know why the Gordon quean was getting gey stout, and if Wallace was as coarse as they said to his wife, and such newsy-like bits of an interest to folk. He'd just grunt when you spoke and start counting the eggs, and say he was damned if he knew or cared. (*Sm*, 31)

The grocer's antipathy to gossip is found suspect by the 'folk', who relish juicy stories about their neighbours and find his stance somewhat threatening, as it uncomfortably reminds them of their own 'coarseness'.

The farm of Greenden is an 'ill place', according to the narrator, simply because the land is poor; the Simpsons can be mocked because they were ignorant enough of the country to make a bad bargain. Yet the narrator does not refute the fleeting connection Webster makes when confronted by Ellen Simpson's mental instability, that the previous tenant of Greenden, old Grant, 'also had whispered and whispered like that' (*Sm*, 32). The narrator recognises the loneliness of the place, and seems partly to sense its oppressive, claustrophobic atmosphere in the description of the farm in the opening paragraph: the biggings are 'old and right dark', and the view from the door is a 'jungle, near, lost from the world' (*Sm*, 23). Later in the story, the folk-voice describes the unsettling feeling experienced at Greenden, but attributes blame for this to Ellen rather than the environment:

> [S]he'd set you at unease till you'd sit and wonder what ailed yourself – till going up home through the dark you'd be filled with fancies daft as a carrying woman, as though the trees moved and the broom was whispering, and some beast with quiet breath came padding in your tracks; and you'd look, and 'twas only a whin that you'd passed. (*Sm*, 30)

Webster, although unable to fully comprehend Ellen's fear of the place, nevertheless has more sensitivity than the rest and, when he finally confronts Simpson, calls the farm '*that hell of a Den*' (*Sm*, 33). The difference between Ellen Simpson, Webster and perhaps also old Grant, on the one hand, and the rest of the community on the other, is the factor of imagination. Like the positive characters in *Sunset Song* – Chris, Long Rob and Chae Strachan, among others – these people are marked as outsiders by being more imaginative and sensitive than the remainder of the community, which sees these traits as weakness. Gibbon's implication in the characterisation in 'Greenden' is that George Simpson is accepted by the community because they recognise him as one of their own: by the end of the story, he has emerged clearly to be an unimaginative, insensitive, selfish man, with no conception of (let alone interest in) his wife's feelings.

In 'Clay', the central character, Rob Galt, having spent too many years working as foreman on his father's farm, decides to leave and take on his own croft. The family move to Pittaulds, and Rob changes from a loving husband and father, who 'spoiled them both, the wife and the quean, you'd have thought them sugar he was feared would melt' (*Sm*, 71), to a man so obsessed by the land and the work, he neglects his family in the process. Any profits he makes are put straight back into the farm, and the family live in the most meagre conditions:

> He worked from dawn until dark, and still later, he hove great harvests out of the land, he was mean as dirt with the silver he made; but in five years' time of his farming there he'd but hardly a penny he could call his own. Every meck that he got from the crops of one year seemed to cry to go back to the crops of the next. (*Sm*, 76)

This is a fair, if blunt, description of the crofter's lot. The crofting system relied on family labour, which inevitably meant unlimited working hours, and the crofter was always financially vulnerable; one imprudent decision, or one bad harvest, and he would bear the full brunt of his loss. In the eyes of the community, Rob Galt is not wrong to place the needs of his croft over the needs of his family, and therefore escapes the caustic criticism we might expect from one of Gibbon's crony narrators.

Indeed, it is interesting to note that the tone of the narrator in 'Clay' is markedly different when dealing with Rob Galt from what it is in the opening of the story. In the first three paragraphs the narrator introduces the Galt 'brood' in most uncomplimentary terms, and catalogues a list of their failings. Initially likened to vermin, the Galts are then described as cheats and thieves, and criticised as vulgar gossips. There are two more serious allegations, however. The narrator accuses the Galts of bad farming practice: 'So soon's they moved into some fresh bit farm they'd rive up the earth, manure it with fish, work the land to death in the space of their lease, syne flit to the other side of the Howe with the land left dry as a rat-sucked swede.' (*Sm*, 70) Furthermore, according to the narrator, the Galts will also stoop as low as to defraud their neighbours:

> And often enough as he neared his lease-end a Galt would break and be
> rouped from his place [...] And if you didn't know much of the Galts you
> would be right sorry and would bid fell high. Syne you'd hear in less than
> a six months' time that the childe that went broke had bought a new farm
> and had stocked it up to the hilt with the silver he'd laid cannily by before
> he went broke. (*Sm*, 70)

Rob Galt, however, is introduced as 'the best of the bunch [...] lightsome and hearty, not mean like the rest' (*Sm*, 70); and throughout the story, the narrator resists making harsh judgements of his behaviour. Rob's obsession with the land is merely 'daft'. The narrator refrains from commenting on Rob's behaviour towards his wife and child, and although the community voice never goes as far as empathising with Rob, the absence of the vicious-ness of the opening paragraphs suggests he is accorded a certain amount of respect.

In 'Clay' Gibbon uses a more complex narrative technique than in the other stories, and this also contributes to the difference in tone. It is worth pointing out that this is the only story in which the gender of the commu-nity voice is explicitly revealed as female: 'he fair was a deave as he sat by your fire, he and your man would start in on the crops' (*Sm*, 74). This female voice continues for almost two paragraphs, and after illustrating Rob's obsession with his work on the land, she comments on Rachel who 'fair was a scholar'. The compliment to Rachel is immediately followed by an aside that reveals the woman's pride in her own child (however misplaced it may be): 'no better than your own bit Johnnie, you knew, the teachers were coarse to your Johnnie, the tinks' (*Sm*, 74, 74-75). The passage has the effect of making the narrator less 'faceless', as we glimpse a little of her own family life. She is no longer just an anonymous representative of the community; she has a clearer 'individual' identity. At times, the narrative moves from the community voice to the point of view of one of the central characters; for example, the change in Rob since taking on the croft is highlighted in a short passage narrated from Mrs Galt's point of view: 'you could hardly believe it still was the Rob that once wouldn't blush to call you his jewel, that had many a time said all he wanted on earth was a wife like he had and land of his own. But that was afore he had gotten the land.' (*Sm*, 76) More commonly, however, the focaliser is Rachel:

And he bent down and picked up a handful of earth and trickled the stuff through his fingers, slow, then dusted it back on the park, not the path, careful, as though it were gold-dust not dirt. So they came at last to the moor he had broken, he smoked his pipe and he stood and looked at it, *Ay, quean, I've got you in fettle at last.* He was speaking to the park, not his daughter but Rachel hated Pittaulds from that moment, she thought, quiet, watching her father and thinking how much he'd changed since he first set foot on its clay. (*Sm*, 76)

As 'Clay' progresses, Rachel's point of view takes over from the community voice more frequently, and the story ends with Rachel's thoughts. The story is therefore told not simply from an observer's detached point of view; it is also narrated by those most deeply affected by events at Pittaulds, and this heightens the emotional impact of the Galts' tragedy, and affords the reader a deeper understanding of Rob and his family.

William Malcolm considers 'Sim' to be the 'most readily expendable' of the Scots stories and sees it as taking the 'simple form of a character study' and being a 'simple moral homily against the vice of avarice'.[4] I would argue, however, that 'Sim' is less straightforward than Malcolm claims. Given the unreliability of the community voice in its opinions in the other short stories, it would be foolish to trust its judgement of Sim. The story delivered by the narrator is an indictment of Sim Wilson's less admirable qualities and his final come-uppance, but the moral homily (if such it is) is not simple. Avarice is not the only vice of which Sim is guilty:[5] indeed, the early part of the story concentrates on his sloth, and informs us that he is 'the only sweir soul in the hash of the Howe' (*Sm*, 58). In fact, the narrator takes pains to show that most of the 'seven deadly sins' are present in Sim, or his family: his mother – from whom no man is safe – is guilty of lust; and his auntie, being a 'meikle big creash of a woman' (*Sm*, 58), represents gluttony. As a young man, Sim is prone to pick fights when he is drunk, thus being guilty of wrath, and it is his pride in his younger daughter which brings about his inevitable downfall.

Nevertheless, Gibbon's portrait of Sim is ambivalent. The reader finds Sim, in some respects, a fairly likeable character, in that he questions the values of those around him, instead of meekly accepting that the community's way is the only way. In contrast to his peers, Sim has aspirations: '*Show me a thing that is worth my trauchle, and I'll work you all off the face of the earth!*' (*Sm*, 59); he sees no value in toiling for the benefit of other people, preferring to work for himself. Sim can be criticised for callous selfishness in his treatment of his wife and elder daughter, but he is a man who 'gangs his ain gait', to use a favourite Scots expression: a trait which is usually admired in the North East psyche. His independent nature is emphasised throughout the story by the descriptions likening him to a cat, with 'glinting green eyes' (*Sm*, 58). The narrator, however, despises Sim for his ambition and independence.

At the beginning of the story, Sim is described as coming from 'fell queer stock, his mother a spinner at the Segget Mills, his father a soldier killed by the Boers' (*Sm*, 57). He is, therefore, an outsider in the eyes of the farming community, and this is the foundation of the narrator's prejudice. Sim's own attitude, of course, does not help: as a boy, he sees farm-workers as *'fools'* for their *'sossing and chaving'* (58), and by showing no respect for the work ethic, he antagonises the community. When Sim takes his first fee, he is 'as sweir as ever' (*Sm*, 59) and sneers at the others in the bothy. However, a reader with knowledge of the feeing system recognises that Sim's laziness is exaggerated by the narrator: Sim 'stayed on for a four-five years' (*Sm*, 59), and no ploughman would be kept at term-time if his work was less than satisfactory.

Sim wants more from life than the dull routine of farm labour, and shocks the bothy by articulating this: *'And we'll get up the morn and slave and chave for that red-headed rat — and go to our beds and get up again. Whatever for, can you tell me that?'* (*Sm*, 59). This sentiment is not too far removed from Gibbon's own comment in 'The Land': 'Yet it was waste effort, it was as foolish as the plod of an ass in a treadmill, innumerable generations of asses.' (*Sm*, 93) I am not implying that Gibbon intends us wholly to accept Sim's point of view. Sim's methods in attempting to escape the treadmill are undoubtedly flawed: he sets himself a goal, but in attaining it, discovers no lasting satisfaction. However, he has imagination which the majority of his peers lack, and this, at least, is to his credit.

The role of the foreman in 'Sim' is a significant one. A 'canny-like childe', he has a fatalistic philosophy in life: 'there were some that had aye to be looking ahead, and others looked back, and it made little odds, looked you east, looked you west, you'd to work or to die'. He is the only one with any time for Sim, and occasionally in the story, we see events from his point of view: 'Well, he'd gotten the thing, good luck go with him, the foreman thought as he tramped away home up through the grey of the morning mists with the bothy lightless and grey in the dawn, leaving Sim with his hard-eyed quean; you hoped he'd not eat her, that's what he'd looked like.' (*Sm*, 59, 64, 63)

The foreman sees the folly of Sim's approach to life but, unlike the rest of the community, does not mock him. They fall out eventually, when Sim laughs at the foreman's attitude to education, but a few years later when

he has married and has a family of his own, he remembers Sim: 'And
sometimes he'd mind of that sweir brute Sim and the speaks of his in the
bothy long syne: *Well, what's it all for, all your chaving and care?* And when
he'd mind that the foreman would laugh and know that most likely his
stomach was wrong'. (*Sm*, 65) The foreman now, it is implied, recognises
an element of truth in Sim's attitude, by noticing a similar impulse in
himself. However, he dismisses the feeling by putting it down to an unset-
tled stomach. Nevertheless his 'difference' from the rest of the community
is tacitly acknowledged.

The folk-voice which relishes Sim's eventual downfall is clearly shown
to be narrow-minded, petty and hypocritical, preaching on Sim's vices,
while being oblivious to its own. 'Sim' is indeed a 'moral homily', but is
just as much a censure of a community as it is of an individual.

A Scots Quair is not just Chris's story, it is the story of a society. Similarly,
these four short stories are not simply the stories of Meg Menzies, Ellen
Simpson, Rob Galt and Sim Wilson: the community is as vital a character
as the main protagonists. The community may reveal its unpleasant side –
this is Segget after all, not Thrums – but Gibbon's narrators are always
entertaining, and this is their saving grace. Despite all the evidence
mustered against them, it is difficult to be totally hostile to a narrator who
likens a new born baby to 'an ill-boiled swede' (*Sm*, 65). In the novel, *The
Thirteenth Disciple*, an explanation of the community need for gossip is
given through a description of Aunt Ellen: 'The little woman was a
romantic – a romantic starved of legitimate romance. Books were beyond
her, art was not even a name, music was mouth-organs and melodeons.
Only the ethically unsavoury was left to provide her with colour and excite-
ment and the light that never was.'[6] Gibbon's short stories may point out
the deficiencies of the community, but they also remind us to celebrate the
art of the tellers of good tales.

Notes

1. Valentina Bold (ed), *Smeddum:A Lewis Grassic Gibbon Anthology* (Edinburgh:
   Canongate, 2001) pp. 28, 36. Further references to this volume will be given in
   parenthesis after quotations preceded by *Sm*.
2. For example, Graham Trengrove criticises *Sunset Song* for 'the insistence on
   perceiving Ewan as a cat (eleven references)'. See Graham Trengrove, 'Who is
   You? Grammar and Grassic Gibbon', *Scottish Literary Journal* 2.2 (1975), p. 58.
3. Mistress Grant in 'Greenden' 'near dropped the teapot' at the prospect of
   meeting her man in heaven (*Sm*, 23), and Sim Wilson's mother laughs at the
   news of her soldier husband's death (*Sm*, 57).

4. William K. Malcolm, *A Blasphemer and Reformer* (Aberdeen: Aberdeen University Press, 1984), p. 75.
5. Sim's wife Kate is actually more avaricious than her husband. She only agrees to marry Sim when she discovers he has a farm of his own.
6. James Leslie Mitchell, *The Thirteenth Disciple* (1931), reprinted (Edinburgh: B & W Publishing, 1995) p. 35.

From Exile:
The Poetry of Lewis Grassic Gibbon

Valentina Bold

> O happy are we who find not what we seek
> Who follow dreams across the fringe of day.[1]

Lewis Grassic Gibbon's poetry has, up till now, been neglected. Hidden
away in the manuscript room of the National Library of Scotland and the
Department of Special Collections in the University of Aberdeen, only a
few items had previously been published until my anthology of Gibbon's
work, *Smeddum*, came out in 2001. Some of the poetry was evidently
written for publication – in the manuscripts held by the National Library
of Scotland, there is a table of contents, as well as draft versions of the
finished poems – other pieces seem to have been written largely as therapy
poetry, in response to personal and intellectual crises.

The poetry primarily expresses the viewpoint of an exile. Exact dates,
except in a few cases, are difficult to ascertain, and much of it seems to have
been written outside Scotland, either in the Middle East or from Welwyn
Garden City. Looking back to real and metaphorical lands left behind, the
poet creates an atmosphere which is at once melancholic and hopeful.
Occasional pieces mention fellow-exiles, particularly those who share the
speaker's political and personal agendas, such as 'Rupert Brooke' (*Sm*, 190)
or Keats in 'Rhea, Remembered Suddenly' (*Sm*, 181). More often, however,
Gibbon's poetry explores states of being cast adrift, intellectually and
geographically, from present bearings.

This distanced poetry can be divided into four categories, focussing on
literal, political, spiritual and emotional displacements. The first looks at
exile in its spatial and temporal senses: the subject is either physically far
from home or excluded from a pre-civilisation golden age. In the second,
Gibbon explores the notion of the political exile, separated (sometimes

violently) from those who share his ideas. This is linked to a group of poems exploring states of spiritual separation from the religious establishment. A final set considers emotional varieties of exile, usually self-imposed.

The poems of physical and temporal exile bring together past and present, and deal with (often unearthly) encounters between the two. This group is usually set at night, a setting which enhances their sense of liminality. For instance, 'In Exile' (*Sm*, 173-74), written in Ludd in 1922, invokes the tangible power of the remembered image while 'chill through the dull, white night / The bare trees shiver'. A 'Dream-self' crosses 'sund'ring leagues of sea' to join the narrator before dawn. This female 'Shadow Love' is as sensual as one of Lawrence's women, or as Chris Guthrie can be, as she comes 'out of the darkness, softly shod' and 'like dew to thirsting desert sands'. Stark shades of white and grey combine with images of decay: 'dead, crackling grasses' and 'Dead almond leaves'. These austere images anticipate the bleakness of parting in Eliot's 'Marina' (1930).[2] Gibbon's poetry as a whole is full of poetic resonances. In 'Peace: To the Irene of Kramelis' (*Sm*, 198), 'Death came forth to guide my falt'ring feet, / Unveiled, and lo! 'twas you': a passage reminiscent of Robert Buchanan's 'The Lifting of the Veil' in *The Book of Orm* (1870) in which the 'ineffable Face' is mystically revealed.[3] Gibbon's suggestion of a personal revenant here is, however, closer to the ballad world of 'The Daemon Lover'.

'Song of a Going Forth: Written for the Hegira of the Evelpidae' (*Sm*, 211) is more positive, celebrating the adventure of journeys into self-imposed exile: 'Let us go forth and venture beyond the utmost plain! / Beyond the utmost beetling crag where wilting sunsets wane!' This exile purposefully rejects 'the dead days and the old' and bravely states, even when 'the end draws nigh: who knows? / Let us go forth!' Optimistic in the face of death, the poem brings to mind the fearless imagery of Psalm 23: 'Yea, though I walk through the valley of the shadow of death, I will fear no evil: for thou *art* with me; thy rod and thy staff they comfort me.' Gibbon's poem, however, appears to advocate solidarity between people rather than following a faith.

'Morven' (*Sm*, 212-13) is a more straightforward poem, dealing with the return of an exile to his Scottish home. Atypically of Gibbon's poetry, this is written in Scots. The poem opens in a joyful way, recalling the happy trekking of James Hogg's 'A Boy's Song', and paralleling the resonant Scots of Soutar's 'Bairn Rhymes', with a trace, too, of Stevenson's 'A Mile an' a Bittock' where lads go out by moonlight, 'Abüne the burn, ayont the law'.[4]

> Ayont the brig and up the brae
> The lichts glint ane an' twa
> On the kin'ly hills o' Morven
> An' the shielin' in the snaw.

The Scots is more conventional here than in Gibbon's individualistic language in *A Scots Quair*. This exile, tired of life, approaches home in a couthily Christian way – 'Mony's the weary year sin' laist / We saw the gloamin fa' / On the God-loved hills o' Morven' – finding that the 'canty, couthy fouk' of Morven offer solace from 'the touns an' stour an' a' / O! The miles are lichtsome, lassie', / Tae the shielin' in the snaw!' This is an exile who seeks relief in the land and the folk left behind, as the landscape, in a way which resembles Keats's images in 'Walking in Scotland', is understood as being populated by the past and its people.[5]

'On a Vernacular Society' (*Sm*, 218-19) is less sympathetic to its subjects, exploring the experience of the civilised barbarian, situated 'amidst the hills of Rome, / Sated with almonds and red Tuscan wine' and weeping for the lost, 'redwood stockade and the auroch's lowe'. Having forgotten their language – 'Such rhyme and radiance Latin never knew. / They swore to this in Latin' – their nostalgia is solely sentimental; when one man suggests returning through the Alpine passes to home, they believe 'some evil god disported with his brains' and return to the 'perfumed baths' of Rome. Perhaps there are echoes here of the unreflecting nostalgia Gibbon found among émigré communities in the Middle East, as profiled in his 'Polychromata' series of stories (*Sm*, 223-419).

Contemporary exiles are treated in an even more caustic way in 'Nostalgia. A Parody' (*Sm*, 188-89) with its colonial cry, 'Hot lemonade and sweaty beer! / In Cairo it's damned hot this year'. The 'poor blighter / Who's the present sweating writer' yearns for Camberwell and (in a moment which brings to the reader's mind John Major's future devotion to cricket and warm beer) Gibbon imaginatively enters the English exile's mind:

> Oh, ginger-pop upon the lawn,
> Oh, glistening sandwiches of brawn!
> And empty bottles on the grass,
> And boards that warn all who trespass.

Gibbon understands the loaded meaning of home to the exile, and particularly the power of place-names (as evocative to the Englishman here as those of the Mearns were to Gibbon in his Scottish fiction): Sydenham, Dogkennel Hill, Camberwell Green where 'fish fry', Big Ben, the Thames, Wormwood

Scrubbs and 'Southwark's fair and stately pubs'. People within the landscape are also remembered with (tongue-in-cheek) affection as, with a nod to 'The Love Song of J. Alfred Prufrock', 'purring policemen come and go / (Go and come, for all I know)'.[6] The punchline summarises the present degenerate nature of this place, as a 'great fat motor-bus' passes 'through glade and dene and dell' to (the previously prestigious) 'Ruskin's home – and Camberwell'.

More attractive role-models than the expatriate are treated in the political poetry, often dealing with marginalised and oppressed heroes like the forcibly-exiled 'Spartacus' (*Sm*, 185-86). This celebrates a hero 'who lived for Freedom when the Night / Had hardly yet begun'. Although Spartacus fell, the poet celebrates his memory in a lyrical image:

> Long as on the shore
> The washing tides shall crumble cliff and nore
> Remembered shalt thou be who dauntless gave
> Unto the world the lordship of the slave!

Spartacus' struggle for freedom, then, is as vital for the present as for the past.

In Gibbon's poetry, as in his prose, the near-past and the present (what he saw as the product of a corruptly advanced civilisation) is a political wasteland which demands heroic action. This is no simplistic vision, however; even those considered to be heroic, it is suggested, can be unwittingly involved in a capitalist conspiracy. 'Vimy Ridge: Seven Year's After' (*Sm*, 183), recalls the recapture of this place by the British in April 1917, in preparation for the offensive in Flanders. The futility of victory is implied in the poem's gruesome images:

> Sleep on, poor fools, sleep on:
> Your bones have paved
> Ways unto bloody wealth,
> And left enslaved
> Dreams that ye kissed alone.

At once dismissive of the action, and sympathetic to the sacrifices of 'Christ's comrades', the poem brings to mind the bleakness of Wilfrid Owen's 'The End' where the Earth itself cries for the war dead: 'Mine ancient scars shall not be glorified. / Nor my titanic tears, the seas, be dried'.[7] The theme of the unglorified dead, lost in war, is taken up again in *The Thirteenth Disciple* (1931), and there are echoes too of MacDiarmid's' 'Innumerable Christ' as the 'poor fools' of Gibbon's poems await the resurrection of a better world which will, implicitly, never come.

For the speaker in some of these poems, the hell on earth of the early twentieth century is made bearable only by the existence of political heroes from whom the poet is detached by space and time. 'Lenin: 1919' (*Sm*, 194) recalls the leader with awe and with respect; although '"His shadow lies on Europe"', this is a shadow to be welcomed: 'I see your eyes, / Steadfast and cold, unutterably wise, / Look westward where the ling'ring sunset dies'. His voice brings 'A prayer or a command?' and, as Lenin moves, 'all the nations of the Earth, / Shuddering in pangs of agonising birth' cry out: 'How long, O Lord?' And the hero answers: '*It comes.*' The whole has an atmosphere which brings to mind the evocative snowscapes of Blok's 'The Twelve'.[8]

There is real affection expressed for those who have been martyred in the cause of political freedom: these are the comrades who support Gibbon's self-imposed exile. 'On the Murder of Karl Liebknecht and Rosa Luxembourg' (*Sm*, 200) celebrates the lives of the 'Splendid Two' and is a call to activism for the future. Their 'mighty Task' has a quasi-religious flavour as 'the longed-for Dawn shall glint our Spears, / And the Splendid Two return', in a left-wing version of the Second Coming. So too, in 'The Communards of Paris' (*Sm*, 199), those gone are not to be grieved for; rather, 'Yours is the glory, Pioneers of Dawn!' In this sense, the poet's exile is seen as merely a temporary state. A state of joy will come, as asserted in the short piece 'A Communist's Credo' (*Sm*, 203):

> *Yesterday*, yours; *Today* – it is a sea
>   Where writhe and foam the tides of storm
>   And shine
> Mist-spume o'erhung; but in the still, stark
>   Hours
> Reading the stars, I know *Tomorrow* mine!

Such faith in the future could be described as a politicised spirituality. There is evidence of this, of course, in Gibbon's prose as well as his poems.

Gibbon's poetry often expresses a profound and subtle faith. 'At the Last' (*Sm*, 195-96), comes close to being a hymn, showing the influence of a Christian education and echoing, again, the powerful sentiments of Psalm 23:

> When the last hours shall tread with silent feet,
> When the last dream-sad eventide shall fade,
> When the last night shall veil its starry hosts:
> I shall be unafraid.

This, however, is not a looking forward to an afterlife. Rather, it is a trust that Death will end the hard labour, the lusts and desires of being alive: 'Yea, were the gift of God's own splendour wrought / I should not live again'.

In his poetry, as in prose pieces like 'Forsaken', Gibbon explores the nature of Christianity and of Christ, suggesting a more complex vision than that put forth in his damning essay on 'Religion'.[9] Perhaps recalling his own time in the Middle East, he wryly comments in 'Christ' (*Sm*, 192-93) on the tourist guide's introduction to the holy places: 'They point each resting-place / Whereon he sat and wept and gabbled prayers / Unto his childish God'. In these places, 'dim legends [are] blown down dim and blinded years', and the true story of Christ is lost: He 'Who loved the People, was the harlot's friend, / And blessed a robber with his dying breath'. This compassionate (and forgotten) Christ is the people's hero, like Spartacus, whom the writer valued so highly. Similarly, in the enigmatic 'Lost' (*Sm*, 187-88), God stands in 'aged form' in London, and is bewildered by a preacher's message. God asks, 'Who is Christ?'; 'And blown / About the streets that night the voice of One / Cried terribly, "My Son!... My only Son!".'

In contrast to the despair informing the poem just mentioned, 'The Day God Died' (*Sm*, 201) welcomes God's final exile from the world. Despite the title, there is no pessimism here. The poem opens abruptly, as stark and ostensibly emotionless as any ballad: 'God died one morn / As dawn sprang red'. The rising sun does not notice, Earth does not lose its 'gladness'; men continue to work 'for love and bread' and the lark sings on: 'Being born of song and Eternity, / Fashioned of no sick dreams / Nor sprung of any lie'. Ultimately, Nature is pleased, and the forests whisper: 'The world is better / Since God has died.' This piece expresses a preference for the human and the living over creeds and creed-makers.

Gibbon's poetry, ultimately, is a mixture of despair and hope, faith in humanity, and a quantity of personal *angst*. While there is not in his poetry the interest in psychoanalysis found, for example, in the early work of Edwin Muir, he does in the poetry explore emotional states more overtly than in his fiction. The exile has, at least, experienced love at first-hand. 'Lines written in a "Happy-thoughts" album presented to Ré, August, 1923' (*Sm*,174-76) is in praise of 'she [sic] against whose living sun all praise/Is candle-light' and expresses the joy of one who has 'glimpsed in staggering lines / The Beautiful and True'. In this poem, Gibbon seems to suggest that women are more soulful than men and, in a complimentary sense, more primitive. They are, in short, particularly in touch with the numinous.

'Six Sonnets for Six Months' (*Sm*, 176-180) treat the whole experience of love as a phenomenon which is the opposite of exile, bringing the lovers in contact with fundamental truths. This cycle, despite touching on the dangers of 'love grown stale' as well as the terrible losses love can involve, is infused with the concept of renewal. Seasons pass and spring comes again, in Sonnet 'IV: An Old Theme'. Throughout his poetry (as in his prose), Gibbon uses the cycle of the year to express human hopes of renewal: as in 'Vision' (*Sm*, 182), where 'the Hand of Change' sets 'a sign for eyes of gods and men:/That that which is shall fade and die and fall,/And Springtide comes again'. Like MacDiarmid, Gibbon owed a tonal debt to John Davidson, and the way in which he parallels the year's passing with human losses and renewals is reminiscent of Davidson's 'Spring Song' and 'Sunset'.[10] On the other hand, in Sonnet 'VI: The Lovers', those who 'made to Life the sacrifice of Death' find solace in oblivion. The poem's conclusion is both peaceful and paradoxical: 'for that they gave, and bring in tears again,/The love that makes our hearts remember then'. Women, here, understand love more profoundly than men. They are at one with nature, almost as part of a living landscape, as in the knowing heroine of 'V: To My Lady Rhea': 'And when you bring my message to her, lo!/She'll smile through tears. She heard it long ago.'

The poetry also explores the experiences of those exiled from love. 'The Unbeloved', for instance, (*Sm*, 195) observes that, 'true love is power to long, to yearn, to fail!', and portrays the dangers of reciprocal love becoming stagnant and 'a draggled thing, most wretched, stripped and bared!' Darker still, 'Dead Love' (*Sm*, 203-4) is powerfully sad and understated. Having looked, 'far down through all the rayless way [...]' where your soul lies', the speaker sees, 'as when the atheist prays [...] a stranger-soul'. Burnt by the 'dreaded pyre' of dead love, the lovers stand 'explorers back from out that land' and, with a sudden note of comfort, 'you stretch your hand./Not unto me – but where the dawn/Will tinge the eastern roses'. 'Réponse' (*Sm*, 196) explores a similar theme, pondering, 'Were then the hills stirred, shaken with our love? [...] Not so, for these were strong – O little we'. Similarly, 'Song' (*Sm*, 193) – several pieces have 'song' in their title, perhaps unsurprisingly for a poet familiar with the lyric traditions of the North East – looks back to first love from the position of the exile: 'That you will never find,/Never again'. The speaker has left far behind 'the first sweet kiss of the first sweet maid' and, ultimately, 'the path you will never find/Never again'. The statement invests the whole with a blunt finality characteristic of Gibbon's poetry.

More horrifically, the enigmatic 'The Romanticist' (*Sm*, 199) is a poem of enforced exile and unspecified suffering:

> They took the thing I love
> Horror and shuddering shame:
> Twisted the flesh in rotting agonies,
> Spattered in filth the mouth
>   that called my name.

Perhaps, as the title could suggest, this is meant ironically, but still the ending is despairing: 'I saw her heart stand pure and clean and white: / Yet turned and fled'. Much of Gibbon's poetry has this desperate edge, typical of his period and the post-*Waste Land* environment. Often detached from a sense of security, Gibbon's poems commemorate the exile's state of mind.

Gibbon's poems are, overall, explorations of the experiences of exile, focussing on the experiences of those separated from their physical and spiritual homes and those who may rescue the twentieth century from its political fall from grace. The writer, in investigating various experiences of separation, may not always achieve the lucidity of his finest prose but his imaginative renditions make this poetry both intriguing and revealing. Moreover, reading the poetry offers new insights into the work of a great Scottish writer whose work is now gaining the detailed consideration it deserves.

Notes

1. Lewis Grassic Gibbon, 'The Rainbow Road', in *Smeddum: A Lewis Grassic Gibbon Anthology*, ed. by Valentina Bold (Edinburgh: Canongate, 2001), pp. 176-77. All subsequent references to Gibbon's poems are to this edition, with page numbers given in parentheses after the titles and preceeded by *Sm*.
2. T.S. Eliot, 'Marina' in *Collected Poems 1909-1962* (London: Faber and Faber, 1974), pp. 115-16.
3. Robert Buchanan, 'The Lifting of the Veil', *The Poetical Works of Robert Buchanan* (London: Chatto & Windus, 1884), pp. 280-81.
4. James Hogg, 'A Boy's Song', *Remembrance* (1831), pp. 74-75. Robert Louis Stevenson, 'A Mile an' a Bittock', *Poems* (London: Dent; New York: E.P. Dutton, 1946), pp. 104-05.
5. John Keats, 'Walking in Scotland', *The Poetical Works of John Keats*, ed. by William T. Arnold (London: Macmillan, 1933), pp. 293-94.
6. Eliot, *Collected Poems 1909-1962*, pp. 13-17.
7. Wilfred Owen, 'The End', reprinted in Walter de la Mare, *Come Hither* (Harmondsworth: Puffin, 1973), p. 181.
8. Alexander Blok, 'The Twelve' in *Scanning the Century: The Penguin Book of the Twentieth Century in Poetry* (Harmondsworth: Penguin Books, 2000), pp. 26-27.

9. Lewis Grassic Gibbon, 'Forsaken', 'Religion', reprinted in *Smeddum*, pp.46-57, 152-67.
10. See the non-fiction too: for instance, 'The Land', reprinted in *Smeddum*, pp.81-97. John Davidson, 'Spring Song' and 'Sunset', in *John Davidson: A Selection of his Poems* ed. and introd. by Maurice Lindsay, with preface by T.S. Eliot and essay by Hugh MacDiarmid (London: Hutchinson, 1967), pp.85,96.

Lewis Grassic Gibbon and the Scottish Enlightenment

Gerard Carruthers

Lewis Grassic Gibbon's great project in *Sunset Song* and elsewhere in his fiction and prose was to elucidate the historical and cultural location of the peasantry of the Mearns. For Gibbon, however, a substantial impediment to his acceptance of an imaginative empathy with the 'common folk' lay in the misty romantic myths which he perceived to envelop Scottish history. As he writes in 'The Antique Scene' (1934):

> Few things cry so urgently for rewriting as does Scots history, in few aspects of her bastardized culture has Scotland been so ill-served as by her historians. The chatter and gossip of half the salons and drawing-rooms of European intellectualism hang over the antique Scottish scene like a malarial fog through which peer the fictitious faces of heroic Highlanders, hardy Norsemen, lovely Stewart queens, and dashing Jacobite rebels. Those stage-ghosts shamble amid the dimness, and mope and mow in their ancient parts with an idiotic vacuity but a maddening persistence.

Gibbon continues:

> Yet behind those grimaces of the romanticized or alien imagination a real people once lived and had its being [...] Behind the posturings of those poltergeists are the lives of millions of the lowly who wiped the sweats of toil from browned faces and smelt the pour of waters by the Mull of Kintyre and the winds of autumn in the Grampian haughs [...] who were much as you or I, human animals bedevilled or uplifted by the play of the forces of civilization in that remote corner of the Western world which we call Scotland.[1]

What we find here is the characteristic impulse of the Scottish Renaissance movement of the 1920s and 1930s to dissociate itself from a powerful point of traditional cultural pride of nearly two hundred years standing: the ability of Scotland to do history. Quite explicitly, Gibbon identifies the eighteenth-century period of Enlightenment, with its 'salons' of 'European intellectualism', as that milieu generating the most potent iconic images of Scotland to which he so objects. Gibbon is not wrong in his identification of Scottish Enlightenment icon-minting. It is during this period that two of those figures to which he refers, Mary, Queen of Scots and Charles Edward Stuart, are adopted into the mainstream pantheon of Scottish identity. Previously marginalised in Scottish history and discarded as 'losers' in religion and politics, both figures in a highly retrospective manner become part of the national imagination. Earlier in the eighteenth century Mary Stuart does not enjoy any real cultural coinage; not even within the iconography of Jacobitism, where we might perhaps expect it. By 1790, however, Robert Burns, influenced by the reappraisal of Mary which was promulgated by the Enlightenment historians William Tytler (1711-92) and William Robertson (1721-93), is able to write his delicately emotive 'Lament of Mary, Queen on Scots on the approach of Spring'.[2] Mary appears again as a sly, though not uncharming and pathetic, figure in Walter Scott's *The Abbot* (1820) where, to some extent, she is explained as a product of her generally inconstant historical context; deviousness is not simply the result of personal predilection but of political necessity and mortal survival. In the meantime Mary had already completed her Enlightenment and Romantic disinterment in a spectacular repatriation to Europe with Friedrich Schiller's tragic treatment of her for the German stage in 1800. Charles Edward Stuart features in a raft of sentimental Jacobite songs from at least the 1780s – where again Burns plays an important role in the dissemination – and appears somewhat attractively in Scott's *Waverley* (1814). What was it that inspired such representation and, indeed, rehabilitation of these previously derided and repressed elements of Scottish history from the eighteenth century, a phenomenon at which Lewis Grassic Gibbon bridles?

Broadly speaking, the environmental and psychological school of historiography represented by David Hume, Adam Ferguson, William Robertson and others broke down some of the religious and political sectarianism of earlier eighteenth-century Scottish culture. The first element of environment meant that Scottish historians attempted to read historical peoples and personages, at least to some significant extent, according to the mores of their times and to the state of civilised development inherent in their society. Even more importantly, perhaps, the second element of psychology was at once both objective and imaginative, according to Adam Smith's philosophic concept of sympathy outlined at length in *The Theory of*

Moral Sentiments (1759). Again, we might turn to creative literature of the Scottish Enlightenment period to see this in clear cultural action. This literature is even-handed: it considers with some measure of sympathy Catholic monarchs and would-be monarchs, who were previously judged to be bywords in black despotism, but also brings in from the cold figures at the opposite end of the ideological spectrum. We see the literary fruits of such impulses in 1794 when Burns provides a poetic celebration of the fashioners of the Solemn League and Covenant, seeing them as champions of 'freedom'.[3] He does so as part of an Enlightenment-led project in transformational comparative history; in this case we glimpse the radical potential of Enlightenment as, implicitly, a parallel is drawn between seventeenth-century opponents of tyrannical kingship and the same phenomenon of the revolutionary 1790s. Thus, those previously thought to be anachronistically theocratic are newly seen to be of pertinence to a modern, secular age. To take another example, in James Hogg's *The Brownie of Bodsbeck* (1818), the author shows the persecuted Calvinist hillfolk as heroic, deeply communitarian and battling against royalist forces at least as 'fanatical' in their violence as the Covenanters are in their beliefs. Extremism, then, is universal under certain fraught circumstances and not solely generated by the Scottish dissenters. We might even argue that in the deranged Calvinist protagonist of Robert Wringhim in *Confessions of a Justified Sinner* (1824), we find sympathy (albeit in a neutral sense, such as the thinking of Adam Smith provided for) alongside censure of the warped faith in predestination which the character embodies. Crucially in this regard, sympathetic explication is found as Wringhim's dysfunctional family background colliding with the Calvinist doctrine of the Elect is seen to play a crucial part in the formation of his rebarbative behaviour. Such focalised, environmentally pressured fiction provides a direct antecedent to the practice of Gibbon, for instance, in his depiction of that manifestation of the 'unco' guid', John Guthrie in *Sunset Song*.

So far, then, while agreeing with Gibbon that eighteenth-century Scotland was a period of historical image-making, I have suggested that the Scottish Enlightenment's effect on the national imagination of Scotland might be interpreted rather differently from Gibbon's view of it as merely precipitating a one-dimensional romantic iconography. Gibbon's attitude to the historical generation of the icons of the nation is familiar with the views of Hugh MacDiarmid and Edwin Muir in their diagnosis of Scotland as a false or unreal place; Gibbon identifies, fairly precisely, 'sham historians of a sham nation'. Importantly, however, he also acknowledges his own period as generating a national imagery at least as collectively quixotic and as colourfully eccentric as anything coined by Enlightenment Scotland. In his essay, 'Glasgow' (1934), he writes:

> I like the thought of a Scots Republic with Scots Border Guards in saffron kilts – the thought of those kilts can awake me to joy in the middle of the night. I like the thought of Miss Wendy Wood leading a Scots Expeditionary Force down to Westminster to reclaim the Scone Stone: I would certainly march with that expedition myself in spite of the risk of dying of laughter by the way. I like the thought of a Scots Catholic kingdom with Mr. Compton Mackenzie Prime Minister to some disinterred Jacobite royalty, and all the Scots intellectuals settled out on the land on thirty-acre crofts, or sent to recolonize St Kilda for the good of their souls and the nation (except the hundreds streaming over the Border in panic flight at the sight of this Scotland of their dreams). I like the thought of the ancient Scots aristocracy revived and set in order by Mr. George Blake, that ephor of the people: Mr. Blake vetoing the Duke of Montrose is one of my dearest visions. I like the thought of the Scottish Fascists evicting all those of Irish blood from Scotland, and so leaving Albyn entirely deserted but for some half-dozen pro-Irish Picts like myself. I like the thought of a Scottish Socialist Republic under Mr. Maxton – preferably at war with royalist England, and Mr. Maxton summoning the Russian Red Army to his aid (the Red Army digging a secret tunnel from Archangel to Aberdeen). [...]
>
> But I cannot play with those fantasies when I think of the hundred and fifty thousand in Glasgow. They are a something that stills the parlour chatter. I find I am by way of being an intellectual myself.

And he concludes: 'There is nothing in culture or art that is worth the life and elementary happiness of one of those thousands who rot in the Glasgow slums.'[4] Here, Gibbon talks himself into a position where all mythologising of identity is irrelevant in the face of the most basic economic necessities. He moves from comedy to grim social reality as a kind of shock tactic, and one can understand why in the face of the malnutrition and endemic disease suffered by the working classes during the 1930s. Gibbon even appears somewhat embarrassed that he is an 'intellectual' himself, or one who might play imaginatively with the possibilities of cultural identity. One can reasonably retort in the face of all this reductionism that humanity – even the most impoverished class – does not live on bread alone. And as Enlightenment writers understood, the empathetic imagination must always be on the lookout for new possibilities in describing the universals of the human condition beyond its mere physical wants or class condition, whatever the latter may be. Scottish literature,

influenced by the Enlightenment, ranged widely in its depiction of
historical period, social station and psychology. The icons created in the
process were not only those of romantically doomed would-be rulers (whose
image and ideology, in any case, mattered – often very deeply – to such
substantial groupings as Highlanders, Catholics and Episcopalians among
the Scottish population) but included also, through that characteristic
even-handedness of the Enlightenment, a more ostensibly demotic turn in
the numerous imaginative examples which celebrate the peasantry.

In the passage from 'The Antique Scene' quoted at the outset of this
essay, Gibbon himself speaks with a recognisable post-Enlightenment voice
when he demands attention to 'human animals bedevilled or uplifted by
the play of the forces of civilization.' Gibbon's Enlightenment lineage here
is one of those really rather obvious points of continuity in Scottish culture
seldom grasped due to Scottish criticism's angst-ridden obsession with
narratives of discontinuity. The anthropological emphasis of the Scottish
Enlightenment, in its pronounced interest in the states of primitivism and
civilisation, initiates a strong Scottish intellectual tradition that runs
through the work of Hugh Millar and William Robertson Smith and which
continues to the late nineteenth century in its most spectacular exemplar,
in the studies of mythology by J.G. Frazer.[5] Gibbon's phrase, 'the human
animal' (which he explores in one of his most famous essays, 'The Land'
(1933), an essay true to his personal icon-smashing approach to history) is
very much an Enlightenment perception.[6] Such a perspective is filtered and
imaginatively nuanced in the writing of Gibbon's greatest forerunner in the
essaying of Scottish country life, Robert Burns. We might call to mind here
particularly Burns's 'To A Louse' (1785) where the narrator ironically
berates a loathsome insect for its presumption in clambering over a young
lady in her Sunday-best. The poem, of course, works toward the conclusion
that under our clothes (which metonymically stand also for the cloak of
civilisation), human beings are merely part of the animal kingdom. The
poem's lines in its final stanza, 'O wad some Pow'r the giftie gie us / To see
oursels as others see us!' – one of the most celebrated pieces of couthy
Burnsian wisdom – is extracted quite directly from a writer Burns hugely
admired, Adam Smith in his *Theory of Moral Sentiments*.[7] The phrase, 'To see
oursels as others see us!' is, in Burns's usage, both a recognition of Smith's
agency of sympathy as the necessary cement of society, and, at the same
time, it represents something of a shudder. 'To a Louse' displays a tone of
tender sympathy toward Jenny, the louse-afflicted individual. An implied
narrator is sympathetic to Jenny in classic Smithian fashion as he observes
her fragility. He sees her aimed-for sartorial and toilet effects easily under-

mined by vulgar, disrespecting nature. Besides this sympathy, however, we have the shiver of the poet's recognition of human transience: what is all our dressing up physically or socially (our 'airs in dress an' gait') in the face of the natural process (including death, where our bodies are scoured by the insect world)? Burns's engagement here with Smithian sympathy shows very well the interface between the Enlightenment consideration of 'primitive' nature and the notion of the civilised self. A philosophic vignette arising out of the writings of the Scottish Enlightenment, 'To a Louse' is one of those poems which really ought to put paid to the idea of the eighteenth century as absolutely bifurcated between Enlightenment and vernacular Scottish cultural values, though it is certainly oxymoronic enough in its location of a 'Gibbonesque' 'human animal.'

Gibbon is very much heir to Burns as his fiction frequently features attention to the body and the faulty human, 'civilised' attempt to hide this physical reality.[8] However, Gibbon is also interested, we might say, in disembodiment. We find this when we turn to that well-known passage in *Sunset Song* dealing with the 'two Chrisses', the English and the Scottish. The most traditional literary theory of Scotland would see this 'split personality' as a sign of crisis and dangerous national confusion. What happens, on the other hand, if we apply the concept of sympathy and see Chris in classic Smithian fashion as standing in healthy manner outside of herself? In the novel, naturally enough, her perception of her two selves causes her to be a little perplexed. She thinks that 'two Chrisses there were that fought for her heart and tormented her.'[9] In her resulting character, though, we find no dissociated Robert Wringhim, but rather a stillness, a centre of calm; for the most part, a stoicism in the face of her irreconcilable public or social self, or selves, that are almost equally 'Scots' as well as 'English' cultural constructions. Symbolically, her healthy, outward 'centredness' is signalled by her periodic visiting of the Pictish standing stones which represent a time, a 'golden age' even, prior to that trajectory of civilisation which had created the national, class and gender divisions that ultimately comprise the divided Chris. Gender, of course, enters into this 'split personality' as well. A female Chris exchanges Chris Guthrie for Chris Tavendale and single self for pregnancy and motherhood yet is still herself. For Gibbon, it may be the case that Chris is a somewhat traduced historical character but in her what pertains is an instinct for refusing to be merely a site of contradiction. She has final resort, in characteristic modernist fashion, to a primeval consciousness (or moral sense) that stands ultimately beyond anything that her contemporary cultural context imposes upon her by way of identity.

It should be acknowledged that Lewis Grassic Gibbon indulges in rather bizarre ethnic theorising where the pre-civilised 'golden age' of 'Scotland' is located as prior to the coming of the 'Keltic vandals' and so dissolution begins, long before English 'cultural invasion'.[10] Gibbon's insistence on spelling the word with a 'K' is derived from references by the Greek chroniclers to the 'Keltoi'. In a number of places in both fiction and non-fiction, Gibbon implies that the peasant stock of the Mearns is the remnant of the pre-Celtic, Pictish people. Somewhat ironically, then, both his identification of distinct and separate Pictish and Celtic peoples in Scotland and the idea of a prelapsarian golden age are derived from the Greek cradle of western civilisation, the progess of which is viewed so witheringly by Gibbon, the Diffusionist and Marxist. Gibbon is not the first Scottish writer to attempt to locate for Scotland a pre-Christian Scottish past and in so doing to attempt to reach back beyond the pre-Hellenic-Roman culture, or pre-*biblical* culture (since the *topoi* and philosophy of the Old Testament as well as the New, are couched in Greco-Hebraic ideas). The precedent is to be found in the work of another Scottish Enlightenment figure, James Macpherson, originator of the 'Ossian' phenomenon. Chris's mysticism or her character's selfless communion with the landscape and ancestral memory is something that is pioneered in Macpherson's work. 'Otherness' – the desire for the extinction of the co-ordinates of identity whether these things are related to gender, community or nationality – is an idea powerfully produced prior to the fully-fledged insights of post-colonial and feminist theory in an eighteenth-century European literary context by the Enlightenment-led text of 'Ossian'. In its concerns we find a search for a 'pure' identity that is emptied of the vagaries of the most vulgar historical conflicts of sect and nation (a location prior to the religious and dynastic faction of 'British' experience that came to a head during the 'fanatical' seventeenth century; here we see Macpherson being led by the ideas of the Scottish historians). Notoriously and unsurprisingly, however, Macpherson in his texts cannot slip free from the resonance of his own 'cultured' eighteenth-century perspective, a sin that is made heinous only by the purported authentic translations that he is presenting to the world. We see this perspective writ large in the case of the move away from the eponymous approach of *Fragments of Ancient Poetry* (1760) to the epic-structure of his more extensive Ossianic productions of 1762 and 1763, in which Macpherson veers heavily toward the predilections of the contemporary neo-classical mindset. Gibbon's construction of a notional golden age and, indeed, the whole diffusionist project is similarly 'neoclassical'. One might suggest that the attempt at rounded structure through the three books of *A Scots Quair*, as with the Ossian texts, is an attempt at cyclical epic experience when partial or fragmented form, such as a single open-ended novel might in this case represent, would be much more realistically eloquent of the experience of Gibbon's Chris. Gibbon, like Macpherson, and the Enlightenment generally perhaps, adopts in his trilogy a stadialism, or a sense of teleological progress, by which characters' lives are seen enmeshed in the increasing technological sophistication of physical human community, from farm-town, to rural town to city. He valiantly attempts in *A Scots Quair* to recapture something of 'the pre-modern', but, while largely successful in critiquing the idea of civilised humanity, he is rather too tied in the structure of his trilogy to the modern tropes of development and holism. This is one of the most interesting sites of tension in Gibbon's fiction of which criticism has made too little.

As John MacQueen has flippantly remarked, the 'Caledonian Antisyzygy' – the notion of split and conflicting Scottish cultural (and, indeed, individual personal) character derived as a term from G. Gregory Smith in 1919 – is the 'creation' of the Scottish Enlightenment.[11] More than anything this has to do with the Enlightenment concept of sympathy as a means of objectively reaching out to non-modern mindsets, or those that were previously off-limits for ideological or religious reasons, such as we have seen above. Under the influence of the Enlightenment, the expression of individual Scottish identity becomes commendably less certain and more multifarious than ever. We might cite here the case of a peasant character whose roots, imbued as she is with Thomas Reid's capacity of common sense, are in the Scottish Enlightenment. Chris Guthrie's ancestor, Walter Scott's Jeanie Deans in *The Heart of Mid-Lothian* (1816), is someone who both represents 'the other' in her forays into England (she is another instance of the rehabilitated Presbyterian figure), and goes in search of 'the other' in her attempt to confront a mindset in her own sister alien to Jeanie herself. This turns out, in fact, not to be Effie's wrongly supposed infanticide, but is, however, a dark feminine passion different from her own touchingly pious disposition. Jeanie seeks out her sister-self in an *a priori* act of sympathy and ends up achieving justice for Effie in the face of wrongly brought criminal charges. She does so even as she can never fully countenance the alien cultural predispositions of Effie in her less than pious Presbyterian disregard for the proscription of pre-marital sex and her ultimate marriage to her Catholic lover. Chris Guthrie, as a fictional character of the modernist period rather than the 'age of Scott', has to deal with internalised division, and also, in this situation of 'otherness' within herself has the potential for greater feminine liberation. Even as she observes

that her Aberdeenshire peasant upbringing and her 'English' schooling are
things that do not fit easily together, she is not any less whole a person for
this. Gibbon finds for Chris mystical moments of return to the ancient
Pictish site, and the standing stones allow Gibbon to show the character's
full spectrum of identity: Chris's objectivity is represented (where she
observes herself) but we also see her selfless subjective moments. Such
techniques of characterisation may fit very well with the priorities of
modernism, but in the Scottish context especially, the debates over
individual identity and the difficult relationship of the individual to
modernity or civilisation are strongly rooted in the Enlightenment period
and its apprehension of the extension of sympathy within cultural identity.

Around the time of Chris's growing apprehensions of her 'plurality' she
encounters Cuddieston Andy singing 'Bonny wee thing / Canty wee thing';
following this chance meeting, the sexually aroused Andy chases Chris.
Afterwards we witness Chris's father's intemperate reaction to the event:

> Father raged when he heard the story from Chris, queer raging it was, he
> took her out to the barn and heard the story and his eyes slipped up and
> down her dress as she spoke, she felt sickened and queer. *He shamed you*
> *then?* He whispered; and Chris shook her head and at that father seemed
> to go limp and his eyes grew dull. *Ah well, it's the kind of thing that would*
> *happen in a godless parish like this. It can hardly happen again with the Reverend*
> *Gibbon in charge.* (SS, 52-3)

Civilisation here collides with primitivism, the former quality standing in
judgement upon the latter. We judge differently. We find it the most
reprehensible fact that Chris is the passive female able to be 'shamed'
through no actions of her own. Andy himself, is thoughtlessly, 'innocently'
bestial. It is John Guthrie's behaviour, in fact, which is the most sickening
as his combination of incestuous lust and stern moral voice make him very
obviously a 'Holy Willie' figure (one of the greatest of Enlightenment
inspired utterances of negative sympathy). Guthrie represents another
manifestation of 'the human animal'; this time as a dangerously repressed
and cant-ridden individual. Other characters in *Sunset Song* such as Ewan
Tavendale senior or Chae Strachan are, like John Guthrie, also eventually
sucked into the quagmire of 'civilised' dissolution. Ewan is a very notice-
able example where he leaves the land for the town through being con-
scripted during World War One and becomes brutalised in his personality
(men, generally, tend to be more susceptible to corruption in Gibbon's
fiction than women). Chris, on the other hand, refuses to be traumatised by
the structures of civilisation and their conceit of integrated rationality.

Increasingly, in the *Scots Quair* trilogy, she is not ashamed of the sexual desires and simple physical functions of her body that 'civilisation' finds so morally and aesthetically awkward. We might mention here also the prodigiously fertile Meg Menzies in 'Smeddum' (1934) – refusing to conform to the bourgeois institution of marriage – or, conversely, Rob Galt in 'Clay' (1934) – respectably married, but with the land seeming to suck vampirically at his blood so that he loses his sense of family. In 'Clay' we have an extreme version of the Enlightenment historiographic idea of people as products of their environment. Environment eventually claims Rob, not really because of some mysterious power in the land, but due to his obsessively productive tenancy in the context of organised farming. In this story we have a clever interplay between the supernatural and civilisation. It is the civilisation of the land, however, or farming, which brings about the downfall of Rob, rather than the animistic landscape. Gibbon's technique here is a hallmark of his fiction in that we have the interplay between the discourses of folk-culture and 'civilised' society. He provides a shudder for civilisation in the face of something seemingly supernatural, but the irony is that the shudder really should be reserved for civilisation itself as in Burns's 'To a Louse'. With Gibbon in this mode we have his solution to the exploration of civilisation and primitivism initiated by the Scottish Enlightenment. In a reversal of one strand of modern liberal philosophy (that also stems in part from the Enlightenment), civilisation rather than savagery brings fearfulness and fragmentation; at the same time this viewpoint is a teasing out and logical conclusion of an apprehension found in the Scottish Enlightenment. In his essay 'Religion' (1934), Gibbon sounds remarkably like the 'father' of the Scottish Enlightenment, Francis Hutcheson, when he says: 'Benevolence is as natural to Natural Man as hunger.'[13] Gibbon's diagnosis here is that institutional (socially-conditioned) Christianity corrupts this natural propensity with what amounts to civilised ritual (or regulation) according to certain vested interests of power.

In conclusion, therefore, I would suggest that in much of his fiction, Gibbon continues the cultural tradition of the Scottish Enlightenment in unpicking and worrying away at the supposed bonds of humanity and civilisation. The 'real' characters he creates, such as Chris Guthrie are not so much an antidote to the imagined identities in Scottish history created by the Scottish Enlightenment as they are a continuation of the witness to the subjectivity / objectivity problem, of the collision of civilisation and nature, and of the generous extension of plurality in identity which was begun in the eighteenth-century period of Enlightenment.

Notes

1. Lewis Grassic Gibbon, *A Scots Hairst* (Hutchinson: London, 1967) ed. by Ian S. Munro, pp. 123-24; *Smeddum* ed. by Valentina Bold (Edinburgh: Canongate, 2001), p. 4.

2. For a discussion of William Robertson's influence here, see Alexander Broadie, *The Scottish Enlightenment: the historical age of the historical nation* (Birlinn: Edinburgh, 2001), p. 53. The present essay is heavily indebted to Professor Broadie's incisive account of the Scottish Enlightenment which opens up the period as a more vibrant cultural arena than Scottish literary critics have traditionally perceived.

3. Burns's lines on the Covenanters are interesting as both an act of historical revisionism and in their highly emotional empathy:

> The Solemn League and Covenant
> > Now brings a smile, now brings a tear.
> But sacred Freedom, too, was theirs;
> > If thou'rt a slave, indulge thy sneer.

   Burns: Poems and Songs ed. by James Kinsley (Oxford: Oxford University Press, 1971), poem no. 512.

4. *A Scots Hairst*, pp. 86-87; *Sm*, pp. 101-2. As Colin Kidd writes, 'Mitchell [Gibbon] retreats into elegy and, eventually, despair, in the face of an all-encroaching so-called civilisation' in 'The Ideological Uses of the Picts' in *Scottish History: The Power of the Past* ed. by Edward J. Cowan and Richard J. Finlay (Edinburgh: Edinburgh University Press, 2002), p. 183. Such despair comes into conflict with the more 'positive' modernist agenda being pursued by Gibbon and represents another site of tension in his work as yet inadequately explored by criticism.

5. Over the last dozen years the project of tracing the tradition of Scottish Enlightenment thought through the nineteenth century has begun to receive some serious attention; see, especially, Craig Beveridge and Ronald Turnbull, *The Eclipse of Scottish Culture* (Edinburgh: Polygon, 1989), pp. 77-111.

6. In 'The Land', Gibbon writes: 'Those folk in the byre whose lantern light is a glimmer through the sleet as they muck and bed and tend the kye, and milk the milk into tin pails, in curling froth – they are The Land in as great a measure.' (*A Scots Hairst*, p. 67; *Sm*, p. 83). Even as he attempts a kind of starkly reductive realism, Gibbon simultaneously, and probably quite consciously, finds a mythic (imaginative) *locus* for 'the folk'.

7. Burns was very aware of Smithian discussions of the 'impartial spectator' that provided such an important part of the intellectual fabric in the 'age of sensibility' (see *The Theory of Moral Sentiments* ed. by D. D. Raphael and A. L. Macfie (Indianapolis: Liberty, 1982), especially pp. 15-18 [introduction], 154-56 and 269-70).

8. A good example here is to be found in 'Smeddum' where Meg Menzies finds herself at odds with the doctor's wife: 'There was a fair speak about that at the

time, Meg Menzies and the vulgar words she had used, folk told that she'd even said what was the place where she'd skelp the bit doctor's wife. And faith! that fair must have been a sore shock to the doctor's wife that was that genteel she'd never believe she'd a place like that' (*A Scots Hairst*, pp. 6-7; *Sm,* p. 37).

9. *A Scots Quair,* ed. and intro. by Tom Crawford (Edinburgh: Canongate, 1995), *SS* p. 32

10. 'The Antique Scene' in *A Scots Hairst*, pp. 126-130; *Sm*, pp. 4-8.

11. John MacQueen, *Progress and Poetry: The Enlightenment and Scottish Literature* (Edinburgh: Scottish Academic Press, 1982), p. 122.

12. *Sunset Song*, pp. 52-53.

13. *A Scots Hairst*, p. 171; *Sm*, p. 166. Francis Hutcheson famously advanced the primary importance of the 'moral sense' so that, for instance, heathens might know goodness even though they had no knowledge of the Christian gospels. For proffering such a postulation Hutcheson, a Presbyterian minister, was accused of heresy within the Presbytery of Glasgow (see William Robert Scott, *Francis Hutcheson* (Cambridge: Cambridge University Press, 1900), p. 84).

The Gospels According to Saint Bakunin: Lewis Grassic Gibbon and Libertarian Communism

Keith Dixon

> Burns lived a tormented life in a land which treats poets and genuinely creative artists as criminal lunatics – until they are safely dead. And, when it had safely killed him, Scotland proceeded to mummify Burns's corpse and set it up in a heather shrine for the worship of the dull and the base and the flabbily loquacious. In life he hated and despised such people; in death they hold him captive and cover away his angry pity for the common man under the blether of an annual alcoholic emotionalism.[1]

The Canonisation of Grassic Gibbon

One of the perverse effects of the canonisation of James Leslie Mitchell/ Lewis Grassic Gibbon over the last quarter of a century, within Scottish academia, and subsequently within the secondary school curriculum in Scotland, has been a substantial rewriting of his politics, or the erasure of his politics altogether from academic discussion and educational presentation, which of course amounts more or less to the same thing. The process has gone so far that those whom I would like to describe as his natural allies in contemporary Scottish cultural politics are loath to cite him as an influence or inspiration. Now perceived as an icon of the Scottish literary establishment, Lewis Grassic Gibbon has become bad news for Scotland's cultural radicals. When questioned on the subject, James Kelman, for example, has shown a remarkable lack of interest in Grassic Gibbon's work and has seen no point of comparison between his own work and the political and cultural activities of the black sheep of the Mearns, despite evident similarities in their use of voice, for example. Another contemporary Scottish writer, Christopher Brookmyre, who very much shares Grassic Gibbon's un-Calvinist delight in the pleasures of the flesh, goes even further than this in *One Fine Day in the Middle of the Night*, where he has one of his characters describe Gibbon as one of the major culprits in teenage alienation from literature as taught in contemporary Scottish schools. Meeting up with a former school teacher from the 1980s, the character in question, Ali McQuade, provides a retroactive explanation for the unruliness within the English class:

> Christ what did you expect, inflictin' that Grassic Gibbon damage on us? You'd be up on an abuse charge for that these days. [...] you could have made it easier on yoursel's. I know it was the curriculum, but I mean, if it was up to you and you were tryin' tae get teenagers interested in books, is that what you'd throw at them? Grassic Gibbon? Teuchter farmyard dreichness?[2]

And yet a glance back at the reactions that Grassic Gibbon's *Sunset Song* provoked in the local Scottish press in 1932 only serves as confirmation of his proximity to today's bad boys (and girls) of the cultural scene. The *Paisley Express* was not alone in condemning Grassic Gibbon's first Scottish novel in terms that should have some contemporary resonance for writers like Kelman or Brookmyre. Have they not also been castigated for 'the unredeemed close-packed filth, meanness, spite, brutality, lying squalor and stupidity' of their novels?[3]

As my preliminary quotation about Burns suggests, there is nothing particularly new about this situation: writers of the past, and particularly politically radical writers of the past have often suffered the same fate, wheedled onto the school and university syllabi, once their literary or political wings (or both) have been conveniently clipped (exit the revolutionary poems of Burns or the bawdy poems of Pushkin). As far as Lewis Grassic Gibbon is concerned, the process began in the 1970s, as the strength of cultural and political nationalism began to grow in Scottish society: the predominantly nationalist and accommodative readings of his work date back to this time. Of course, the academics most directly involved in the process of reappropriation and respectabilisation were more at home, for a variety of reasons which I do not have room to deal with here, with nationalist or nationalist/ruralist readings of Lewis Grassic Gibbon than with exploring his revolutionary stand in both the cultural and political fields. At university level, a handful of academics, in particular in Edinburgh and Glasgow, provided alternative but innocuous readings of Grassic Gibbon which the Scottish Education Department could easily do business with. They were to set the mould in Scottish Grassic Gibbon studies for the next quarter of a century. The Longman Modern Classics edition of *Sunset* Song (1971), aimed at secondary school consumption, with commentary and notes by J.T. Low, is noteworthy in this respect: a monument of understatement and polite suppression, not to mention more straightforward misrepresentation. Thus, in the biographical note on James Leslie Mitchell provided by Low, Mitchell's participation in the Aberdeen Soviet in 1918 becomes an interest 'in economic and social problems and in left-wing politics'; his sacking from his job on the *Scottish Farmer* in Glasgow after it was discovered that he'd been fiddling his expense account becomes 'trouble with his editor eventually led to his dismissal'; the crofters of Lewis Grassic Gibbon's Kinraddie who lost their lives during the First World War are described with impeccable Great British political correctness as 'the men who gave their lives for their country (and their way of living)', in flagrant contradiction of the violent critique of British militarism and of the war hysteria that accompanied the 'Great War' which we find not only in the trilogy but throughout Grassic Gibbon's writing; the final sermon at the end of *Cloud Howe* in which the Reverend Colquohoun urges his parishioners to abandon their Christianity, to 'forget the dream of the Christ' and seek out a 'stark, sure creed that will cut like a knife, a surgeon's knife through the doubt and disease' – a creed, communism, that the young Ewan Tavendale is to embody in *Grey Granite*, becomes an 'elegy or requiem by Colquohoun' by means of which 'Grassic Gibbon is placing the theme of this Scottish story in a universal context'. Above all, Low takes up the academically well-worn 'Chris Caledonia' theme to claim that the central character of the trilogy 'is seen to be an allegorical figure who personifies the history of Scotland and the Scot, and perhaps more generally the relationship between Woman and the Land'.[4] It seems to have escaped the author of this presentation that Lewis Grassic Gibbon did not share this 'organic' vision of Scottish history and well knew there was no such thing as 'the Scot', but Scottish rulers and ruled, masters and servants, bosses and workers.[5]

Nevertheless, conveniently shorn of his subversive potentialities, hung, drawn and quartered by academic bad faith, transformed miraculously into the nationalist he never had been, Lewis Grassic Gibbon was, by the mid-1970s seen fit to enter the pantheon of ScotLit.

This could all be seen as the ignominious end of a long tradition of misrepresenting Grassic Gibbon, in which his friend and adversary Hugh MacDiarmid played a not inconsiderable part. It was after all MacDiarmid who invented Grassic Gibbon's Trotskyism (a heinous crime in the eyes of a Stalinist nationalist) and reduced the novelist's public statements on matters political and cultural to so many manifestations of that infantile disorder. It was in MacDiarmid's political interest to play down the importance of Grassic Gibbon's violent critique of exclusive nationalisms and their sombre consequences in interwar Europe and, concerning Scotland more directly, of the cant that accompanied the imaginary reconstruction of the country's past by Celtic nationalists.

What I intend to do here is not so much discuss whether Grassic Gibbon was a political revolutionary or not – I'm afraid I consider that to be self-evident from even a cursory reading of his public pronouncements. What is of interest to me is how he situated himself within the political debates of the revolutionary Left of the 1920s and 1930s, how he walked the narrow and difficult path between communism and anarchism. I will, for convenience's sake, be focusing on his non-fictional prose writing, but am quite willing to argue that there is indeed much more of a continuity than a break between this writing and his fiction. Indeed I would be more than tempted to argue that the fictional work cannot be properly understood if it is not related to the intense political debates of the so-called *hors texte* which, I feel obliged to point out and despite postmodern babblings to the contrary, does very much exist.

A key source for any understanding of Lewis Grassic Gibbon's public positioning in the political and cultural fields of the time is the extraordinary joint literary venture in which he participated with Hugh MacDiamid, published as a collection of articles, poems and short stories in 1934 under the title *Scottish Scene*.[6] One might be tempted to write off the tensions and contradictions expressed on those sulphurous pages, as each of the two writers sets about destroying the arguments put forward by the other, as simply another exercise in public relations for a concept that had been hijacked by MacDiarmid and nailed to the Lion Rampart: the so-called *Caledonian Antisyzygy*, a predisposition for contrariness attributed by the literary historian Gregory Smith (one suspects tongue in cheek) to the Scottish imagination and by MacDiarmid more generally to the Scottish psyche.[7] These visions do, however, deserve more serious consideration, expressing as they do two radical and radically opposing visions of the 'state that Scotland's in the day'[8] in the midst of the Great Depression. That of MacDiamid is well-known and has been the object of many an academic study. Lewis Grassic Gibbon's political vision has, on the other hand, with only one or two notable exceptions, been largely neglected.

The Communism of Grassic Gibbon
Like MacDiarmid, Lewis Grassic Gibbon was a revolutionary socialist, or a communist if you prefer, although he was never a member (to our

knowledge) of the Communist Party of Great Britain. He identified strongly with the labouring classes (although with a special and un-communist predilection for rural workers) and saw these latter as historically in irreconcilable opposition to their masters. His work is littered with positive references to what he sees as the revolutionary movements and revolutionary leaders of the past (among the latter he includes William Wallace, Oliver Cromwell, Abraham Lincoln and Vladimir Illitch Lenin and the somewhat unlikely John Knox); revolutionary insurrection is, indeed, the subject of *Spartacus* (1933), perhaps alone among his 'English' novels to be of any lasting literary importance.

His early English fiction is full of characters who toy with what is alternatively described as communism or anarcho-communism, although it also contains a recurrent, critical representation of middle-class communists. 'Barricades delighted her' says the narrator about Mrs Gayford, a bourgeois left-winger in the early *roman à thème, Stained Radiance* (1930). 'The thought of machine-guns and brave, clean sanitary workers pumping lead into attacking Whites moved her with an extasy that was religious.'[9]

The construction of a radically different, egalitarian future, that would realise the 'brotherhood of the shamed and tortured'[10] – a 'brotherhood' that would provide pride of place to women, it should be pointed out – is nonetheless a recurrent theme in Grassic Gibbon's work, from his early 'Egyptian' short stories to his more mature 'Scottish' work. Nowhere, however, is Grassic Gibbon's approval of the revolutionary socialist cause, and his rejection of the compromises of home-grown Labourism, more openly expressed than in his political essays in *Scottish Scene*. Ramsay Macdonald provides a pretext for a sarcastic rejection of Labourite reformism:

> So with that philosophy of Socialism which Mr. MacDonald was wont to exfoliate in the days before, glancing downwards and backwards, he caught sight of the seemly shape his calves occupied inside the silk stockings of Court dress. Perhaps this Socialism had once a logic, as certainly it had once a fine, if anaemic, sincerity, a passionate pity if also an impassioned patience. In the mazes of Mr. MacDonald's vocabulary it behaves like a calf in an amateurish slaughter shed, dodging with frightened moos the impact of innumerable padded bludgeons. (*Sm*, 138)

As Lenin had done before him, Grassic Gibbon points to the strength of the British trades unions and the relative prosperity that the British imperium could provide for its workers as the main determining causes of the reformism of Labour:

From 1906 until 1914 there were strikes and disputes and wage-cuts: there were folk who starved to death, folk who lived mean and desperate lives, pthisitic children who gasped out their last breaths in the slums of the Duke of Westminster – but the great trade unions were powerful and comparatively rich. Conditions pressed not too bitterly on the great mass of labouring men and women. There was no direct and brutal tyranny, and this philosophy of slow and gradual and easy change, when no blood would be shed and little exertion would be required and the repentant lion would turn to a lamb, suited admirably the temper of the padded times. (*Sm*, 144-45)

Gradualism is, however, doomed in the eyes of Grassic Gibbon. The crisis has made sure of that. Rejecting the illusions of what he calls 'evolutionary Socialism', he ends this particular essay on a distanced and sombre note, that gives no direct clue as to his own positioning in what he sees as henceforth a bi-polar world:

Time, impatient, has turned its back on new re-echoings of those thunderous platitudes which once seemed to ring prophet-inspired from a MacDonald platform. New armies are rising, brutal and quick, determined, desperate, mutually destructive, communist and fascist. (*Sm*, 151)

It is not until a later essay in the same collection that Grassic Gibbon makes explicit where his own, albeit ambivalent, sympathies lie: Glasgow is to be the location for this *profession de foi*. The tone is set early in the essay titled 'Glasgow': 'There is nothing in culture or art that is worth the life and elementary happiness of one of those thousands who rot in the Glasgow slums' (*Sm*, 102). This inaugurates what is not only a critical review of the political solutions on offer during the Depression years, but also a hymn to revolutionary action. Returning to the metaphor he has already employed in *Cloud Howe*, Grassic Gibbon calls for the communist scalpel:

The shipyards are still, with rusting cranes and unbefouled waters nearby, in Springburn the empty factories increase and multiply, there are dead windows and barred factory-gates in Bridgeton and Mile End. Commercialism has returned to its own vomit too often and too long to find sustenance therein. Determinedly in Glasgow (as elsewhere) they call this condition 'The Crisis' and [...] invoke Optimism for its cure. But here, as nowhere else in the modern world of capitalism does the impartial observer realize that the remedy lies neither in medicine nor massage, but in surgery. (*Sm*, 104)

A self-taught historian of sorts, Grassic Gibbon has a keen sense of
what he calls 'the direction of historic forces', which at times leads him,
like so many other revolutionary writers of the time, into a mechanistic
historical determinism. This is omnipresent throughout the third volume
of his Scottish trilogy in which Ewan Tavendale opts for what the narrator
calls 'the workers' road': '*You don't quarrel with History and its pace of change*',
Ewan explains, '*any more than you quarrel with the law of gravitation. History's
instruments, the workers, 'll turn to us some time*' (*GG*, 83).

A feeling of 'final crisis' haunts his writing – something he had in
common with MacDiarmid and many other writers of his generation – and
gives it an apocalyptic, sometimes hysterical tone. This is particularly the
case in his less successful 'English writing' where the balm of his Scottish
humour is lacking. Thus we find Gershom, one of the central characters of
Image and Superscription reflecting dramatically on the imminence of radical
change:

> And it came on him that this indeed was the evening of the world, the
> sunset of mankind that he sat and watched. Some other life-form might yet
> arise and essay the adventure, some beast or bird or insect, life in a form
> unguessable, but one with a steadfast beacon of surety in mind and heart,
> not a torn, tormented thing, dragging, clanking the chains of its ancestry.[11]

That Grassic Gibbon had his qualms about the destructive dimension of
the social upheaval that he called for and the alienating effects of
revolutionary discipline on those most directly involved in bringing it
about is evident from his ambivalent portayal of Ewan in *Grey Granite*. He
nonetheless remained convinced of their historical necessity.

Although Grassic Gibbon's writing is inspired by a radical communist
critique of the functioning of capitalist society in times of crisis and its
dramatic social consequences, there are nonetheless tensions and
contradictions that make him very much of a heterodox thinker and writer,
at a far remove from the dogma of socialist realism that was to fall like a
shroud on communist literature from the 1930s onwards, or the platitudes
of proletarian puritanism that, in the Scottish context, had resulted from
the unholy alliance in radical labour politics between demands for social
justice and transformation and a stern prebyterianism (and, in the West of
Scotland, an equally stern Roman Catholicism). Despite his rhetorical
proclamations to the contrary, he is very much of a heterodox communist,
in the final instance unwilling to toe the party line if that line differs
significantly from his own idiosyncratic representation of social change, and
open to other influences than Marxism, no matter how extensive our

definition of the Marxist tradition may be. This is most clearly expressed in his provocative treatment of the 'national question' and in his libertarian distrust of hierarchy and authority.

The Cosmopolitanism of Lewis Grassic Gibbon

Unlike MacDiarmid, Lewis Grassic Gibbon was a cosmopolitan (not, he says, an internationalist), who railed against the nationalism of small nations that was championed by MacDiarmid throughout his political life. In his violent diatribe in 'Glasgow' against small-nation nationalism he pinpoints what he sees as its fatal weaknesses, exclusiveness and a tendency towards ethnic violence:

> What a curse to the earth are small nations! [...] there is an appalling number of disgusting little stretches of the globe claimed, occupied and infected by groups of babbling little morons – babbling militant on the subjects (unendingly) of their *exclusive* cultures, their *exclusive* languages, their *national* souls, their *national* genius, their unique achievements in throat-cutting in this and that abominable little squabble in the past. (*Sm*, 106)

This, of course, is a direct attack on MacDiarmid and the poet's ambition to put 'little Scotland' back on the cultural and political map of Europe. It is also, as Grassic Gibbon makes clear in the same essay, a refusal to rally to the banner of the 'liberated' Irish Free State.

Indeed, the foregrounding of the Celt and the imaginary reconstruction of the Celtic contribution to Scottish history, largely borrowed from the theorisations of Irish Irelanders such as Douglas Hyde, were anathema to Lewis Grassic Gibbon. In his angry, polemical rejection of Celtic nationalism, Gibbon was not averse to employing a counter-chauvinism of his own, with more than a tinge of anti-Irish xenophobia:

> It is doubtful if the Kelts ever contributed a single item to the national cultures of the countries miscalled Keltic. [...] They were, and remain, one of the greatest curses of the Scottish scene, quick, avaricious, unintelligent, quarrelsome, cultureless, and uncivilizable. (*Sm*, 7-8)

Grassic Gibbon's cosmopolitanism is indeed marred by these recurrent, violent attacks on those whom he sees as standing in the way of cosmopolitan fraternity. We find the same tone of radical intolerance that permeates his anti-Celticist outburts in his treatment, elsewhere in his work, of Muslim nationalists, whom, as a member of His Majesty's armed forces, he had confronted in the Middle East, where he was posted in the late 1920s. In *Hanno: or The Future of Exploration*, we find him condemning the 'insanitary, Moslem bigotry'[12] of the Wahabis in Jordan; and again in *Niger: The Life of Mungo Park*, denouncing the Muslims of North Africa and the 'rule of life led under the green flag of their bestial faith'.[13]

Nonetheless, the writing of Lewis Grassic Gibbon on the national question stands in stark contrast to much of what was written in Scotland in the thirties on this issue. MacDiarmid had by that time erected an intellectual barricade around his eccentric (and ethno-centric) vision of the Scottish cultural heritage and won over innumerable converts in the cultural field to the nationalist camp (writers as different as Neil Gunn, Compton Mackenzie and Eric Linklater had rallied to the cause of both cultural and political nationalism). Grassic Gibbon, on the other hand, saw the demands of nationalism and social revolution as incompatible and denounced the ambiguities of the nationalists concerning what he believed to be the key issues of the age: social oppression, exploitation, unemployment. There is in Gibbon's analysis of the political situation in the 1930s something of the 'tartan Tory' vision of Scottish nationalism: he saw the nascent nationalist movement essentially as social and political conservatism dressed up in national costume. Of course, in many ways he was not far off the mark. The writings of influential nationalists like Andrew Dewar Gibb, who was to become chairman of the Scottish National Party in 1936, or of his friend in the publishing world, George Malcolm Thomson, testify to this strongly conservative, even reactionary strain among the Scottish nationalists of the time. Hence, Grassic Gibbon's ironic affirmation about a possible Scottish future under the colours of nationalism in the 'Glasgow' essay already referred to:

> It will profit Glasgow's hundred and fifty thousand slum-dwellers so much to know that they are being starved and brutalized by Labour Exchanges and Public Assistance Committees staffed exclusively by Gaelic-speaking, haggis-eating Scots in saffron kilts and tongued brogues full of such typical Scottish ideals as those that kept men chained as slaves in Fifeshire mines a century or so ago. (*Sm*, 108)

There is in Grassic Gibbon's vision of these issues of national, linguistic and cultural identity a strongly utopian strain. Occupying a position that few envied him, he pilloried MacDiarmidian nationalist intransigence. In so doing, he also strayed far from what was becoming, within the Third International, the official communist position on the national question. On the language issue he rejected the dogmatic Anglophobia of MacDiarmid and the Gaelic revivalists, provocatively singing the praise, in his essay 'Literary Lights', of the *English* language. Beyond the defence of his own experimental attempt to 'mould the English language into the rhythms and cadences of Scots spoken speech', Gibbon called for the creation of a synthetic Esperanto-type world language, what he calls 'the perfected speech of Cosmopolitan man' (*Sm*, 108), that would combine the best of national traditions. It is here that we find the millenarian dimension of his writing, at a far remove from the hard-nosed communist who only a few lines earlier had been calling for the surgeon's scalpel to hasten the outcome of the class struggle.

The Libertarian Impulse: religion, hierarchy and sexuality in the work of Grassic Gibbon

It was indeed in a millenarian interpretation of a contemporary school of historical thought that Grassic Gibbon found the societal myth that under-pins so much of his writing. Although there are some sparse references to the orthodox anarchist traditions in the writing of Grassic Gibbon and he was evidently aware of anarchist doctrine (he was a journalist in Glasgow at a time when the English anarchist, Guy Aldred, was active there), he found his inspiration not so much in the work of Proudhon, Kropotkin or Bakunin, although he refers to the last intermittently without revealing any intimate knowledge of his writing, but rather in the pseudo-scientific speculations of Professor Grafton Elliot Smith, principal academic protag-onist in the 1930s of the Diffusionist school of historical anthropology. The Diffusionists saw 'civilisation' as emerging in the Nile basin and being diffused throughout the world from that early base. It was however the phase that *preceded* the predominantly agricultural civilisation of the Diffusionists that fascinated Grassic Gibbon: a primitive communistic society based on nomadic hunting, a 'Golden Age' when men and women lived free from the constraints of religion, hierarchy and authority.

Grassic Gibbon presents this phase, which he apparently believed to be a historical reality, as an early Arcadia, and references to it are numerous throughout his fictional and non-fictional writing. Indeed, his study entitled *The Conquest of the Maya* is written from the point of view of an orthodox Diffusionist, and his writing on exploration is littered with references to the 'Golden Age'. Returning to his home country, he says of the first Scots in his historical essay 'The Antique Scene': 'They were men naked, cultureless, without religion or social organization, shy hunters, courageous, happy, kindly, who stared at the advent of the first great boats that brought the miners and explorers of the Archaic civilization from

Crete or Southern Spain.' (*Sm*, 5) (Those who know something of the climate of Scotland might doubt the advisability, or the repeatability, of this primitive nakedness.)

This anarchistic myth is to be used recurrently in the writing of Grassic Gibbon, and provides one of the sources of the salutary tension in the writer's political vision. For Grassic Gibbon was both a revolutionary socialist, who resolutely believed in the iron discipline of communist action ('the weakness of even heroic peasants without a definite creed or code of revolt destroys them', he points out, rather sententiously, to the communist James Barke in a review article in early 1934),[14] and a libertarian with a solid distrust not only of all forms of organised religion (within the Bakunian tradition here) but also of hierarchy and social norms. He takes very seriously the notion of a post-revolutionary society constructed along anti-authoritarian lines and explores this in several of his (mainly unsuccessful) utopian science-fiction novels. His thinking and writing thus attempts to bridge what had by the interwar period become a perhaps unbridgeable gap between two traditions within the radical European and British labour movement, 'libertarian communism' (or anarchism) and 'authoritarian communism' (or 'orthodox' Marxism) – to use the terms that Bakunin himself employed.[15] Uncomfortably, of course.

History has moved on since the untimely death of Grassic Gibbon in 1935. Paradoxically, however, the final collapse of 'really existing socialism' in its most authoritarian of expressions has opened up a new space to take up once again, in the political and cultural fields, that internal dialogue within Grassic Gibbon's political writing that I have alluded to here. Grassic Gibbon dreamt of an altogether better future freed from the 'base shames and tabus of civilization'.[16] We could perhaps more modestly dream of new interpretations of the work of one of Scotland's rare libertarian revolutionaries once the 'base shames and tabus' in Grassic Gibbon studies have been put to rest.

Notes

1. Lewis Grassic Gibbon, Letter to the Editor, *Mearns Leader* 8 February, 1934.
2. Christopher Brookmyre, *One Fine Day in the Middle of the Night* (London: Little, Brown and Company, 1999), p. 67.
3. Quotation from *Paisley Express* in 'Newsreel' in Lewis Grassic Gibbon and Hugh MacDiarmid, *Scottish Scene or the Intelligent Man's Guide to Albyn* (London: Jarrolds, 1934), p. 209.
4. J. T. Low, Commentary and Notes, *Sunset Song* (London: Longman, 1971), pp. 259, 267, 270, 272.

5. He made this point quite explicitly in his attack on the 'conception of a community sharing a common tradition in the past and bound by ties of language' propagated by the nationalists of his time, in an article published in *The Free Man* in February, 1934: ' But what ties of language and kinship bind together a Glasgow-domiciled Irish labourer from County Cork, an inadequately Celticized fisherman in the Western Islands, a Harrow-educated brewer in Inverness, a Mearns ploughman and a Polish miner in Fifeshire?'

6. For convenience, quotations from Gibbon's essays in *Scottish Scene*, will be referenced where possible from *Smeddum: A Grassic Gibbon Anthology*, ed. by Valentina Bold (Edinburgh: Canongate, 2001), with page numbers given in the text, prefaced by *Sm*.

7. G. Gregory Smith, *Scottish Literature: Character and Influence* (London: Macmillan, 1919), p. 4.

8. Hugh MacDiarmid, 'Lourd on My Hert', *Selected Poems*, ed. by Alan Riach and Michael Grieve (Harmondsworth: Penguin Books, 1994), p. 125.

9. James Leslie Mitchell, *Stained Radiance* (London: Jarrolds, 1930), p. 55.

10. *Stained Radiance*, p. 283.

11. James Leslie Mitchell, *Image and Superscription* (London: Jarrolds, 1933), p. 193.

12. James Leslie Mitchell, *Hanno: or The Future of Exploration* (London: Kegan Paul, 1928), p. 43.

13. Lewis Grassic Gibbon, *Niger: The Life of Mungo Park* (Edinburgh: The Porpoise Press, 1934), p. 116.

14. Lewis Grassic Gibbon, Review of *The Wild Macraes* by James Barke, *The Free Man*, 24 February, 1934.

15. An introduction to the writings of Mikhail Bakunin can be found in *From Out of the Dustbin: Bakunin's Basic Writings 1869-1871*, trans. and ed. by Robert M. Cutler (Ann Arbor: Ardis, 1985); and in *Michael Bakunin: Selected Writings* ed. and introd. by Arthur Lehning (London: Cape, 1973).

16. J. Leslie Mitchell, *The Thirteenth Disciple* (Edinburgh: Paul Harris Publishing, 1981), p. 47.

A version of this essay previously appeared in *Études Écossaises* 8 (2002).

The Kindness of Friends:
The Grassic Gibbon Centre

Isabella M. Williamson

The Past

We need to go back to early 1988 to find the catalyst for what was eventually to become The Grassic Gibbon Centre of today. Looking back, I have difficulty remembering exactly what happened to set the whole thing in motion, and perhaps the memories of others involved at the time will vary a little, but for me it was not just one single event but a series of factors that set things in motion.

Firstly, Mrs Karpinski the local postmistress was due to retire. Everyone who visited Arbuthnott before her retirement will remember her as from 'Arbuthnott shoppie'. In addition to dispensing everything from groceries and sweets to stamps and shoelaces, she acted as an unofficial Lewis Grassic Gibbon tourist guide. For over twenty years she gave information on and directed interested visitors to Grassic Gibbon-related sites of interest in the community. Everyone knew her retirement was going to leave an enormous gap.

Secondly, the Parish Hall was badly in need of upgrading. Little had been done to the building over the years and the toilets and kitchen were in an appalling state. With rumblings about the licensing of public buildings and the growing attention to health and hygiene issues, we knew it was only a matter of time before someone would insist on the closure of the building when our corrugated lean-to kitchen with connecting toilets was noticed!

Thirdly, the District Council had attempted but failed to buy 'Bloomfield', James Leslie Mitchell's former home in Arbuthnott. Shortly after that disappointment, the local newspaper ran a story which suggested that the District Council, having failed to purchase 'Bloomfield', was planning to include an exhibition on Lewis Grassic Gibbon in a disused mill scheduled for renovation at Benholm, a village down the coast. The only connection Benholm Mill had with Lewis Grassic Gibbon was that the BBC had filmed the mill scenes there for their television dramatisation of *Sunset Song* in the early 1970s.

Now the folk of Arbuthnott today are exactly as Lewis Grassic Gibbon portrayed them in *Sunset Song*, and tongues began to wag. Folk did not take kindly to the idea of a Grassic Gibbon exhibition at Benholm. The main question being asked was, why Benholm Mill? If the Council was interested in a Grassic Gibbon exhibition, then this should be situated in Arbuthnott and nowhere else (well, perhaps Auchterless could be seen to have a little bit of a claim as well). Many local folk were actually fiercely protective of what they saw as Lewis Grassic Gibbon's legacy to Arbuthnott. One person talked to another and eventually a meeting of the local Community Association was arranged. The outcome of the meeting was the agreement that Arbuthnott should make an attempt to raise money to have its own Lewis Grassic Gibbon exhibition. Plans were drawn up and the three folk doing the most talking – Keith Arbuthnott, John Briggs and myself – formed a small steering group and began the job of looking for funding.

Arbuthnott Community Association is a registered charity and the voluntary management body of Arbuthnott Hall. I was then and still am its secretary and treasurer. Arbuthnott School was closed in 1973 and the Hall is the only public building in Arbuthnott where community activities can take place. The Hall itself was built in 1908, just around the time the Mitchell family moved to Arbuthnott, and it belongs to the community through an ancient Deed of Trust. It was therefore agreed that it would be in the community's best interest to build an extension onto the Hall to accommodate our exhibition. We would then be able to upgrade the facilities of the Hall at the same time, and we would have only one building to manage in the future. In addition, we felt that providing modern facilities for the community was a much more acceptable and fitting memorial to James Leslie Mitchell than a separate stand-alone building; and if it were seen that local people were benefiting, then it would help persuade any negative voices in the community that it was a worthwhile cause. There was, of course, a small degree of negativity, as one would expect; folk have very long memories and a number of people around still knew people or had relatives who were 'recognised' in *Sunset Song*.

In the beginning, my motivation was entirely to promote the interests of the community and in many ways that is the same today. However, the road I've journeyed down to reach where we are today has certainly changed my views on Lewis Grassic Gibbon. Or perhaps not changed them, but formed them, because in the beginning, just like the vast majority of people I meet, I had little knowledge about the man himself or his work, except that he wrote *Sunset Song*.

Although we had drawn up plans for the building early on, in the beginning we had no real strategy for what we were doing. You could say that initially we were motivated by pure thrawn-ness at the thought of someone else having something that we felt was ours – just like a spoilt child. However, as we launched our appeal and folk started to contact us, we – or certainly I – realised that we had embarked upon something that had captured people's imagination and would be impossible to stop.

The defining moment for me was the day I received a letter from a certain Mr Robertson. Mr Robertson was, and may well still be, a pensioner living in Elgin. He wrote to say how wonderful he felt our endeavours were and that he would like to make a donation towards our appeal. However, he only had his pension to live on and therefore he could not afford to send anything that week but if he could afford it he would send something the following week. I was very touched by his letter but never expected to hear from him again (lots of people said they admired what we were trying to do but few parted with their money). However, just as he had promised, the following week a ten-pound note arrived in the post from Mr Robertson.

Receiving Mr Robertson's ten pounds meant much more to me than two or three hundred pounds from a bank or one thousand pounds from an oil company. And it was at that moment that I realised that what we were doing, raising money to build the Grassic Gibbon Centre, was about much, much more than just the community of Arbuthnott; and that even if we were unsuccessful with our current plans and were unable to secure Scottish Tourist Board funding, as we were attempting to do, we would still, eventually, create a memorial to James Leslie Mitchell of some description. We owed it to all the people who were supporting us and in no small part to Mr Robertson. So if you happen to be reading this, Mr Robertson, you have my very grateful thanks; without the inspiration of your unselfish generosity things may not have turned out the way they did.

It was also around this time that I decided that I'd better start finding out a bit more about this chap Gibbon, and decide for myself whether I actually liked him or not. After all, I was spending an extraordinary amount of time talking about him and writing letters about him and everyone I met hung a different label on him. I found it quite difficult to decide which were accurate and which were not. I had to make up my own mind, so I began reading everything written by him and about him that I could find.

It took nearly four years before the Centre was eventually built and this only after a great deal of hard work. We managed to secure Scottish Tourist

Board and local authority funding but not without fighting for it every inch of the way. Luckily, as well as those opposed to the project, there were enough people in the right places that wished to support us. The community alone raised somewhere in the region of £50,000 – not through the usual community fund-raising initiatives such as coffee mornings, but through grants, donations and corporate sponsorship. This was in the days before lottery funding and also before computers were everyday household items. I often think how much easier life would have been if I had had a computer instead of my battered old portable typewriter to produce the endless begging letters and also, thank goodness, the thank-you letters as well.

During the fund-raising period we came across an organisation called Community Business Grampian which gave us money to produce a feasibility study. Our study was not the usual type of study which costs thousands of pounds, but it did the job equally as well as the more expensive kind: an important difference being that we ourselves were in control of the content and quality and we were not inclined to waste money which could be better used for bricks and mortar. Undertaking the study helped focus our minds on what we saw happening with the Centre in the future and set in place one of our main values: that of being in control and undertaking things ourselves.

We met with a variety of people and embarked upon various activities along the way, including the commissioning of students from Gray's School of Art in Aberdeen to undertake some design work for us – some of which we still use today. Everyone we met and the advice given to us helped shape what was to come. We had still not decided on a management structure but once the building was in place (the name was agreed early on) we remembered our conversations with Community Business Grampian and agreed that that was what we had become – a community business. With the support of Community Business Grampian, we went ahead and registered ourselves as a company limited by shares. Directors were appointed and I had to decide where I fitted into the structure. I had the choice of applying for the manager's job or stepping back and leaving the Centre's future to others. However, I found that after spending four years actively helping to develop the project, I wanted to continue in the driver's seat so I posted my application form and the rest is history.

Eventually, we had a building but no money. Our fund-raising had been all about bricks and mortar; no one was interested in giving money to buy stock or for wages, and we did not want to borrow from the bank. We were also just emerging from an unfortunate experience with the exhibition design, from which the lessons learned have endured over the years. The local authority had provided funding for the planning and designing of the exhibition. However, due to circumstances outwith their and our control, the story panels had to be replaced immediately after the Centre's opening in May 1992 because of poor quality and inaccuracies. We did not have the financial resources to meet the cost of replacing the panels, but luckily help was at hand, and through the voluntary support of 'friends' we were able to produce a new set of boards, which were accurate and well designed. In addition, we were fortunate that enough visitors came in the first month to cover staff wages and allow us to buy some stock; and so we continued from there. Little by little, building on our achievements, we grew stronger day by day.

The Present

Today the Centre is a multifaceted thing. Its two main objectives are very simple: to promote the life and work of Lewis Grassic Gibbon; and to create local employment.

These objectives are achieved in the main through the visitors who come to the Centre and who purchase goods in the gift and coffee shop or visit the exhibition. The Centre is completely self-financing. We attract between 6,000 and 7,000 visitors a year, which just about allows us to survive – but only just – and only through carefully managed finances and our ability to attract the help and support from our many 'friends'.

We were determined from the beginning that the Centre should not become just a static, musty exhibition, but that it should be a living, changing place. To achieve this, we initially attempted to have a different theme each year, beginning with the short story 'Clay' followed by 'Smeddum' in the next year. As well as story boards, we printed our own version of the short stories with illustrations and photographs. At that time the short stories were not in print in any other format and we intended continuing over the next few years with 'Sim', 'Greenden' and 'Forsaken'. However, we soon discovered that this was not a sustainable objective. It was far too time-consuming and expensive. In addition, the short stories came back into print in other publications, so the pressure was taken off from that direction as well.

When we first set up the exhibition, what was then the North of Scotland Museums Service provided hand-tools and artefacts for us to display. Therefore when we were developing the exhibition associated with the story 'Clay', we approached them and asked if they could provide us with a replica burial kist. They agreed and we waited in anticipation. True to their word, a short time later in walked their representative carrying the replica – approximately 2-foot square and made of polystyrene! This was not quite what we had envisaged and we were therefore left with no option but to make one ourselves. One of our directors at that time was a carpenter and he made a frame for the kist. Another provided the soil – red Kinraddie clay – and stone slabs. Yet another modelled clay pots as a hobby and he provided those. Some broom and bits of flint were found around the community, and we were just about there. The only thing now required was a skeleton. Where would we find that?

I phoned the local newspaper and they ran a story appealing to anyone with a spare skeleton to contact us and a short time later we had our skeleton. We actually ended up with two and had to return one. The one we accepted remains with us to this day, carefully and accurately laid out in our replica kist by yet another friend. We were so proud of what we had been able to achieve – once again from knowing what we wanted and not being prepared to accept anything less – that we've not had the heart to dismantle the burial kist since. The skeleton, apparently, was surplus to requirements at Aberdeen University and at the time we were reliably told that it had originated from Egypt, having been washed up on the banks of the Nile and the bones bleached in the hot baking sun. This was perhaps not quite the bones of Lewis Grassic Gibbon's antique man of Kinraddie, but considering Gibbon's diffusionist views, it was possibly more fitting than we realised at the time.

So what else happens at the Centre today? Visitors come seeking many things, yes, including on occasions, monkeys! Some visitors relate to Gibbon's writings, some to the land; some seek information about relatives who once lived in the community and some simply want a cup of tea. We also have visits from students and academics from all over the world. We have a growing archive of Gibbon material, much of which is of a personal nature rather than a literary one. And it is with great delight that we accept that we are now acknowledged as *the* place for depositing Gibbon-related material. We have a unique collection of signed first editions, replica first edition dust jackets and photographs of the man himself. We have also an enormous collection of photographs, through our reminiscence group, of the folk and places of Arbuthnott spanning from the turn of the century, including photographs of people Gibbon knew and wrote about. And we are currently in the process of having these published along with stories, factual information and anecdotes of the period.

We also have unique Arbuthnott Church and Parish records, which are invaluable, along with the original School register, when helping folk trace their relatives. Last year the Church Session entrusted its ancient communion pewter to us – not a deposit of any real monetary value, but having it with us does ensure that it stays in the community for the folk of Arbuthnott to enjoy today and in the future. Receiving the communion pewter also says a great deal about the Centre's relationship with the Church today. We also endeavour to support local people and businesses by selling local crafts and products in the gift shop and whenever possible we use local tradesmen. The Centre additionally supports local groups and activities through free photocopying and secretarial services and by producing items such as their posters and tickets . We are also able to sell articles in the shop for their fund-raising activities. We produce a monthly newsletter, *The Arbuthnott Times*, which is circulated around the whole community and contains information about activities happening in the area. And we are just about to install an Internet-accessible computer in the Centre for local people and visitors to use. Yes, amongst all our other functions, we are just about to become a Cyber Café!

The Centenary year of 2001 saw the Centre host many well-supported activities relating to Grassic Gibbon and his work, including three sell-out performances of the adaptation of *Sunset Song* by Prime Productions theatre company. In March we hosted the 'Friends' supper, again a sell-out, and we were delighted that Buff Hardie and Tich Frier gave their time to support us, with Buff's after-dinner speech showing connections between Grassic Gibbon and Shakespeare being considered 'brilliant' by his audience. In May, we held a two-week art exhibition called *Under the Influence*. This also proved to be a great success, with over eighty art exhibits on show, ranging from ceramics to weaving, music, poetry and photographs as well as the expected paintings in every conceivable medium – a truly fantastic tribute to Lewis Grassic Gibbon. We were the venue for our first book launch on Friday 1st June 2001 – an experience we felt we would like to repeat. The local Council held their 'area meeting' with us on the following Tuesday and we were the polling station for the General Election on the Thursday of the same week. These are all small things in themselves but all add to our income in addition to spreading awareness of Grassic Gibbon and his significance in the community.

The Centre, in fact, will adapt to whatever anyone wants – within reason, of course. We can be a training venue, a conference centre or an arts venue. And all take place within our traditional hall which we also use for group teas and which still manages to house the Women's Rural Institute, Women's Guild, Youth Club, Bowling club, meetings, private parties, weddings and funeral teas. As you can see, the Grassic Gibbon Centre is a busy place. But it doesn't operate on its own.

Over the years we have met and made friends with numerous people who have been willing and able to help us in a variety of ways by voluntarily donating their time and skills. This continues to happen today and has become another fundamental principle of the Centre. We could not function without the voluntary help we receive from our directors and others; and I would like to take this public opportunity to thank them for their support, friendship and companionship shown over the years, without which I could not do what I do and the Centre would be a much poorer place.

In January 1998, we set up the 'Friends of the Grassic Gibbon Centre' association. This is a support group for the Centre and a means by which Grassic Gibbon enthusiasts can share and exchange views. In return for a minimum annual fee of ten pounds, 'Friends' receive a bi-annual copy of the newsletter *Speak of the Place,* edited by Dr William Malcolm, as well as free entry to the exhibition, reduced price books, advance warning of activities and a unique car sticker. Joining the 'Friends' is the principal way (apart from making a direct donation, grant or bequest) you can financially support the work of the Centre without actually visiting yourself – and we do need your help.

As previously mentioned, we are a totally not-for-profit organisation and do not receive grant aid or core funding for day-to-day activities from anywhere. In many ways we don't mind this because we are fiercely independent, and when I see other activities closing because of Council budget cuts, I realise how lucky we are to be independent. I do, however, spend a lot of time juggling with accounts and applying for project grants and luckily we have been successful on a number of occasions. Nevertheless, it is still a struggle.

The Future

My vision of the future is that the Centre will continue to go from strength to strength. I feel this because throughout the past thirteen or so years, since the idea for the Centre was first mooted, I have never ceased to be amazed at the extent to which Grassic Gibbon's work inspires people. I know I probably shouldn't be amazed; I accept without reservation that he is a brilliant writer, even when his work is dissected and criticised. But he does inspire. He inspires people to take action just as he has with me. I'm often asked how I manage to sustain my energy and enthusiasm for the Centre and I'm never quite sure what to say. I feel, however, that I'm in a unique and very fortunate position, and I do it because I can. I live and work in Gibbon's Kinraddie. I see the same views (albeit with fewer trees and with telegraph poles and pylons) as he did, and I meet and work on a daily basis with the same kind of folk that he knew. He is the catalyst for me as he is for many people. I have never regretted for one minute being part of the gang of three who worked to build the Centre and I hope I'm around it for a good number of years to come. Mainly I'm interested in the man himself, what he was like and what he believed. Most of all, I admire his humanitarianism, his championing and caring for his fellow man. I like to think that that is the hallmark of the Centre also. I like to think too that the determination and struggle to survive which the Centre has experienced equates in some small way with James Leslie Mitchell's own struggle and determination to fulfil his ambition as a professional writer. However, despite my personal feelings about the man, he is not placed on a pedestal in the Centre; visitors are given information about him and then they make up their own minds.

I could speak at length about my long-term view or dream of expanding the Centre but that, I think, will keep for another day. And I've not yet mentioned the quiet unassuming staff who work there. It is their traditional cooking and baking skills and their knowledge of the local area that make the Centre the warm inviting place it is. They are our greatest asset.

I'll finish with Gibbon himself and with the inscription on his gravestone which he originally wrote in *Sunset Song*:

> The kindness of friends
> The warmth of toil
> The peace of rest

This is exactly what I have found during my time with the Centre. Although there may not be too many occasions for rest at the moment, there is plenty work made all the more pleasant through sharing it with friends.

Lewis Grassic Gibbon:
A Bibliographical Checklist

Hamish Whyte

Introduction

This checklist is very rough and *pro tempore*. Time has not allowed detailed searching and checking. It is basically a recension of some of the pioneering bibliographical work done previously by Geoffrey Wagner, W.R. Aitken, Douglas F. Young, James Kidd and William K. Malcolm – to all of whom I am most grateful – plus some additional research. It is worth doing at this stage in Lewis Grassic Gibbon studies simply as a record of an extraordinary output in such a short span of time. I hope it will prove useful to students and readers of LGG and perhaps serve as a basis for a full bibliography at some point in the not too distant future. Needless to say, errors and omissions are my own.

The checklist is divided into sections as follows:

A   Books by James Leslie Mitchell/Lewis Grassic Gibbon. Arranged chronologically by date of first edition. Place, publisher, date and contents of each book are given, with occasional notes and listing of some reviews.

B   Books containing contributions by LGG. Arranged chronologically. Page numbers are given where known.

C   Periodicals containing contributions by LGG. Arranged chronologically. As much detail given as possible.

D   Manuscripts – brief listing of main depositories.

E   Selected critical and biographical works. Arranged by author. Very selective. See comprehensive listing by William K. Malcolm on LGG website: www.grassicgibbon.com

F   Bibliography. Arranged chronologically – in the lists cited there is often more detail than given here, and useful introductory matter.

I have excluded books dedicated to LGG (listed in W.R. Aitken's article), stage and television versions of LGG's work (such as the famous BBC TV dramatisation of the *A Scots Quair* trilogy 1971-83), radio broadcasts and translations of his work into other languages.

Finally, I would like to thank Ian Campbell, Sarah Dunnigan, Margery Palmer McCulloch, Edwin Morgan, Richard Price and Alan Riach for their help in compiling this checklist.

A: BOOKS BY JAMES LESLIE MITCHELL/LEWIS GRASSIC GIBBON

A1
(a)   *Hanno: or the Future of Exploration: an Essay in Prophecy.* By J. Leslie Mitchell. London: Kegan Paul, Trench, Trubner and Co. Ltd, 1928.
(b)   American edition. New York: E. P. Dutton and Co. Inc., 1928.

A2
(a)   *Stained Radiance: A Fictionist's Prelude.* By J. Leslie Mitchell. London: Jarrolds Publishers (London) Ltd, 1930.
(b)   New edition with introduction by Brian Morton. Edinburgh: Polygon, 1993.
      Reviews: John Sutherland, *London Review of Books* 18 August 1994, p. 12.

A3
(a)   *The Thirteenth Disciple, being Portrait and Saga of Malcolm Maudslay in his Adventures Through the Dark Corridor.* By J. Leslie Mitchell. London: Jarrolds Publishers (London) Ltd, 1931.
(b)   New edition with introduction by Douglas F. Young. Edinburgh: Paul Harris Publishing, 1981. (Scottish Fiction Reprint Library)
      Reviews: Alan Bold, *TLS* 24 July 1981; John Linklater, *Glasgow Herald* 7 July 1981.

A4
(a)   *The Calends of Cairo.* By J. Leslie Mitchell. With an introduction by H.G. Wells and Leonard Huxley. London: Jarrolds Publishers (London) Ltd, 1931.
      Contents: 'For Ten's Sake'; 'He Who Seeks'; 'The Epic'; 'A Volcano in the Moon'; 'The Life and Death of Elia Constantinidos';

'Cockcrow'; 'Gift of the River'; 'East is West'; 'Vernal'; 'Daybreak'; 'It is Written'; 'The Passage of the Dawn'.

(b)   American edition as *Cairo Dawns: A Story Cycle with a Proem*. Indianapolis: Bobbs-Merrill Company, 1931.

A5

(a)   *Three Go Back*. By James Leslie Mitchell. London: Jarrolds Publishers (London) Ltd, 1932.

(b)   Reprint. With Afterword by Brian Stableford. London: Greenhill Books, 1986. (Greenhill Science Fiction & Fantasy series)

(c)   Reprint. With Introduction by Ian Campbell. Edinburgh: Polygon, 1995.
Reviews: Ann Donald, *The List* 269, 15 December 1995 - 11 January 1996.

A6

(a)   *The Lost Trumpet*. By J. Leslie Mitchell. London: Jarrolds Publishers (London) Ltd, 1932.

(b)   American edition. Indianapolis: Bobbs-Merrill Company, 1932.

A7

(a)   *Sunset Song*. By Lewis Grassic Gibbon. London: Jarrolds Publishers (London) Ltd, 1932.

(b)   Cheap reprint, 1933, without endpaper maps.

(c)   American edition. New York: The Century Co., 1933.
(Note – includes 'Note the Reader is Advised to Read' which is different from the 'Note' in the British edition and also a glossary compiled by LGG)

(d)   As No. 16 in Jarrolds Jackdaw Library, 1937.

(e)   New edition, with commentary and notes by J.T. Low. London: Longman, 1971. (The Heritage of Literature Series, modern classics)

(f)   Paperback edition. Foreword by Ivor Brown. London: Pan, 1973.

(g)   New edition, edited with an introduction by Tom Crawford. Edinburgh: Canongate, 1988. (Canongate Classics 12)

A8

(a)   *Persian Dawns, Egyptian Nights*. By J. Leslie Mitchell. With Foreword ('Good Wine') by J.D. Beresford. London: Jarrolds Publishers (London), 1932.
Contents: Persian Dawns: 'The Lost Continent'; 'The Lovers'; 'The

Floods of Spring'; 'The Last Ogre'; 'Cartaphilus'; 'Dawn in Alarlu';
Egyptian Nights: 'Amber in Cold Sea'; 'Revolt'; 'Camelia Comes to
Cairo'; 'Dienekes' Dream'; 'Siwa Plays the Game'; 'The Children of
Ceres'.
(Note – Dedicated to H.G. Wells)

(b)   Reprint, with introduction by Ian Campbell. Edinburgh: Polygon,
      1997.

A9   *Image and Superscription: a novel.* By J. Leslie Mitchell. London: Jarrolds
      Publishers (London) Ltd, 1933.

A10

(a)   *Cloud Howe.* By Lewis Grassic Gibbon. London: Jarrolds Publishers
      (London) Ltd, 1933.
(b)   Cheap reprint, 1934.
(c)   As No. 19 in Jarrolds Jackdaw Library, 1937.
(d)   Paperback edition. London: Pan, 1973.
(e)   New edition, edited with an introduction by Tom Crawford.
      Edinburgh: Canongate, 1989. (Canongate Classics)

A11

(a)   *Spartacus.* By J. Leslie Mitchell. London: Jarrolds Publishers (London)
      Ltd, 1933.
(b)   As No. 11 in Jarrolds Jackdaw Library, 1937.
(c)   Reprint, with introduction by Ian S. Munro. London: Hutchinson,
      1970.
(d)   New edition, edited by Ian Campbell. Edinburgh: Scottish
      Academic Press in conjunction with the Association for Scottish
      Literary Studies, 1990.
      (Note – text based on surviving typescript)
(e)   Reprinted with introduction by Edwin Morgan. Edinburgh: B&W
      Publishing, 1996.
(f)   Edited by Ian Campbell. Edinburgh: Polygon, 2001.

A12

(a)   *Niger: The Life of Mungo Park.* By Lewis Grassic Gibbon. Edinburgh:
      The Porpoise Press / London: Faber and Faber, 1934. Portrait, maps.
      (Notes – 'Preliminary Note' dated 1933. Book dedicated to Compton
      Mackenzie)
(b)   American edition. New York: Ryerson Press, 1934.

A13

(a) *The Conquest of the Maya.* By J. Leslie Mitchell. With a Foreword by G. Elliot Smith. London: Jarrolds Publishers (London) Ltd, 1934. Illustrated.
(Note – dedicated to Alexander Gray)

(b) American edition. New York: E. P. Dutton and Co., 1935.

A14

(a) *Gay Hunter.* By J. Leslie Mitchell. London: William Heinemann, 1934.

(b) Cheap reprint, 1935.

(c) New edition. With an introduction 'Lewis Grassic Gibbon and Science Fiction' by Edwin Morgan. Edinburgh: Polygon, 1989.
Reviews: John Clute, *TLS* 23 February-1 March 1990; Isobel Murray, *Scotsman* 23 December 1989.

A15

(a) *Nine Against the Unknown: a Record of Geographical Exploration.* By J. Leslie Mitchell and Lewis Grassic Gibbon. London: Jarrolds Publishers (London) Ltd, 1934. Illustrated.
Contents: Leif Ericson, Marco Polo, Christopher Columbus, Alvar Nunez Cabeza de Vaca, Ferdinand Magellan, Vitus Bering, Mungo Park, Richard Burton, Fridtjof Nansen.
(Note – dedication 'For Ivor Brown')

(b) American edition as *Earth Conquerors: The Lives and Achievements of the Great Explorers.* By J. Leslie Mitchell. New York: Simon and Schuster Inc., 1934.

(c) American reprint. New York: Garden City Press, 1936.

(d) New edition, with introduction by Ian Campbell. Edinburgh: Polygon, 2000.

A16

(a) *Grey Granite.* By Lewis Grassic Gibbon. London: Jarrolds Publishers (London) Ltd, 1934.

(b) American edition. New York: Doubleday Doran and Co., 1935.

(c) Cheap reprint of first edition, 1936.

(d) As No. 2 in Jarrolds Jackdaw Library, 1937.

(e) Paperback edition. London: Pan, 1973.

(f) New edition, edited with an introduction by Tom Crawford. Edinburgh: Canongate, 1990. (Canongate Classics)

A17
(a) *A Scots Quair: a trilogy of novels: Sunset Song, Cloud Howe, Grey Granite.*
     By Lewis Grassic Gibbon. With a Foreword by Ivor Brown. London:
     Jarrolds Publishers (London) Ltd, [1946].
(b) New edition, 1950. (Reprinted 1952, 1959, 1963)
(c) Reprint. London: Hutchinson, 1966. (Reprinted 1967, 1969, 1971,
     1973, etc.)
     (Note: Jarrolds was taken over by Hutchinson in 1966)
     Reviews: David Macaree, *Studies in Scottish Literature* 4:2, October
     1966, pp. 121-2.
(d) American edition. New York: Schocken Books, 1977.
(e) American paperback edition. New York: Pocket Books, 1979.
(f) Paperback edition. London: Pan, 1982.
(g) New edition, with introduction by David Kerr Cameron. London:
     Penguin, 1986. (Penguin twentieth-century classics)
     (Note: reprinted for Lomond Books, 1998)
(h) New edition, edited and introduced by Tom Crawford. Edinburgh:
     Canongate Books, 1995. (Canongate Classics 59)
     (Note: pp. 125-33 [extract from *Cloud Howe*] reprinted in *Canongate
     Classics: An Anthology.* Chosen and introduced by J.B. Pick.
     Edinburgh: Canongate Books, 1997)

A18 *A Scots Hairst: Essays and Short Stories.* By Lewis Grassic Gibbon.
     Edited and introduced by Ian S. Munro. London: Hutchinson, 1967.
     Contents: Short Stories (Gibbon): 'Smeddum'; 'Clay'; 'Greenden';
     'Sim'; 'Forsaken'; Essays (Gibbon): 'The Land'; 'Glasgow'; 'Aberdeen';
     'The Wrecker – James Ramsay MacDonald'; 'The Antique Scene';
     'Literary Lights'; 'Religion'; Arbuthnott School Essay Book (Mitchell):
     'Arbuthnott'; 'The Harvest'; 'Bervie'; 'Autobiography of a River';
     'Power'; 'Arbuthnott Church'; Unpublished Poems (Mitchell): 'In
     Exile'; 'The Lovers'; 'Rondel'; 'Vignette'; 'Vision'; 'A Last Nightfall';
     'Dust'; 'Spartacus'; Short Stories (Mitchell): 'Siva Plays the Game'; 'For
     Ten's Sake'; 'Daybreak'; 'Cockcrow'; Fragments from unfinished
     manuscript (Gibbon). (Reprinted 1967, 1969, 1972, 1974)
     Reviews: Malcolm J. McDougall, *New North* (Aberdeen University)
     3, May 1968, pp. 43-44.

A19 *Smeddum: Stories and Essays.* By Lewis Grassic Gibbon. With commen-
     tary and notes by D.M. Budge. London: Longman, 1980. (Heritage
     of Literature Series)

Contents: Stories: 'Greenden'; 'Smeddum'; 'Forsaken'; 'Sim'; 'Clay';
Essays: 'The Antique Scene'; 'Glasgow'; 'Literary Lights'; 'The Land'.

A20 *The Speak of the Mearns.* By Lewis Grassic Gibbon. With introduction
and postcript by Ian Campbell. Edinburgh: Ramsay Head Press,
1982.
(Note – first publication of typescript of unfinished novel)
Reviews: Douglas Gifford, *Glasgow Herald* 29 January 1983; James
Hunter, *TLS*, 18 March 1983; Edwin Morgan, *Glasgow Magazine* 2,
Spring 1983, pp. 21-23; Isobel Murray, *Scotsman* 15 January 1983.

A21 *The Speak of the Mearns, with selected short stories and essays.* By Lewis
Grassic Gibbon. Introduced by Ian Campbell and Jeremy Idle.
Edinburgh: Polygon, 1994.
Contents: *The Speak of the Mearns*; essays from *Scottish Scene* ('The
Antique Scene'; 'The Wrecker: James Ramsay MacDonald'; 'Glasgow';
'Literary Lights'; 'Aberdeen'; 'The Land'; 'Religion'); short stories
('Smeddum'; 'Greenden'; 'Sim'; 'Clay'); three JLM stories ('The Epic';
'Dienekes' Dream'; 'Revolt').
Reviews: Ian Bell, *Herald* 23 July 1994.

A22 *Smeddum: A Lewis Grassic Gibbon Anthology.* Edited and introduced by
Valentina Bold. Edinburgh: Canongate Books, 2001. (Canongate
Classics 97)
Contents: I *Scottish Scene*: 'Curtain Raiser'; 'The Antique Scene';
'Greenden'; 'Smeddum'; 'Forsaken'; 'Sim'; 'Clay'; 'The Land';
'Glasgow'; 'Aberdeen'; 'Literary Lights'; 'The Wrecker – James
Ramsay MacDonald'; 'Religion'; 'Postlude by Hugh MacDiarmid'; II
Songs of Limbo: 'In Exile'; 'Lines Written in a Happy-Thoughts
Album'; 'Six Sonnets for Six Months'; 'Her Birthday, 1928'; 'Rhea,
Remembered Suddenly'; 'Vision'; 'Dear Invalid'; 'Vimy Ridge: Seven
Years After'; 'Renunciation'; 'Her Birthday'; 'Spartacus'; 'A Last
Nightfall'; 'Lost'; 'Vignette'; 'Nostalgia: A Parody'; 'A Song of
Limbo'; 'Rupert Brooke'; 'Dawn Death'; 'Christ'; 'Song'; 'Lenin:
1919'; 'The Unbeloved'; 'At the Last'; 'Réponse'; 'Peace: To the Irene
of Kramelis'; 'The Communards of Paris'; 'The Romanticist'; 'On the
Murder of Karl Liebknecht and Rosa Luxembourg'; 'When God
Died'; 'Nox Noctes'; 'A Communist's Credo'; 'Dead Love'; 'Verses
Towards "Knowles' Last Watch"'; 'To Billie on her Birthday'; 'Dust';
'Song of a Going Forth'; 'Morven'; 'The Photograph'; 'Tearless'; 'At

Dusk'; 'Rondel'; 'La vie est breve'; 'On a Vernacular Society'; III
Polychromata: 'He Who Seeks'; 'The Epic'; 'The Road'; 'A Volcano in
the Moon'; 'The Life and Death of Elia Constantinidos'; 'Cockcrow';
'Gift of the River'; 'East is West'; 'Vernal'; 'Daybreak'; 'It is Written';
'The Passage of the Dawn'; IV *The Glamour of Gold*: 'The Glamour of
Gold and the Givers of Life'; 'Mungo Park Attains the Niger and
Passes Timbuctoo'; 'Don Christobal Colon and the Earthly Paradise';
'The End of the Maya Old Empire'; 'Yucatan: New Empire Tribes and
Culture Waves'; 'The Buddha of America'; 'William James Perry: A
Revolutionary Anthropologist'; VI *In Brief*: 'Controversy: Writers'
International (British Section)'; 'A Novelist Looks at the Cinema';
'Synopsis of America before Columbus'; 'History of the Continents of
America before Columbus'; 'Preliminary Precis of a Still Untitled
History of the Conquest of the Maya'; 'Brief Synopsis of A History of
Mankind'; 'Synopsis of Memoirs of a Materialist'; 'Synopsis of The
Story of Religion'; 'Notes for a Stained Radiance Sequel'; 'Notes for
Domina'; 'Notes for Three Stories'; 'Notes for The Rooftree'; 'Notes
for Men of the Mearns'; VII *Speak of the Mearns.*
(Note – includes notes and a glossary)

B: BOOKS CONTAINING CONTRIBUTIONS BY JAMES
LESLIE MITCHELL/LEWIS GRASSIC GIBBON

B1   *Grim Death.* Edited by Christine Campbell Thomson. London:
     Selwyn and Blount, 1928.
     'If you sleep in the moonlight'. Story by J. Leslie Mitchell.

B2   Heinrich Mann, *The Blue Angel.* London: Jarrolds Publishers
     (London) Ltd, [1932].
     'Introduction'. By J. Leslie Mitchell. (pp. 5-7)

B3   Peter Freuchen, *Eskimo: a novel.* London: Jarrolds Publishers (London)
     Ltd, 1932.
     'Introduction'. By JLM.

B4   Peter Freuchen, *Mala the Magnificent.* London: Jarrolds Publishers
     (London) Ltd, 1932.
     'Introduction'. By J. Leslie Mitchell. (p. 5)

B5

(a)   Lewis Grassic Gibbon & Hugh MacDiarmid, *Scottish Scene or The Intelligent Man's Guide to Albyn*. London: Jarrolds Publishers (London) Ltd, 1934.
'The Antique Scene' (pp. 19-36); 'Greenden' (pp. 69-79); 'Representative Scots (1) The Wrecker: James Ramsay MacDonald' (pp. 95-108); 'Smeddum' (pp. 117-27); 'Glasgow' (pp. 136-47); 'Forsaken' (pp. 178-88); 'Literary Lights' (pp. 194-207); 'Sim' (pp. 215-25); 'Aberdeen' (pp. 239-51); 'Clay' (pp. 268-79); 'The Land' (pp. 292-306); 'Religion' (pp. 313-27).

(b)   Reprint. London: Hutchinson (for National Book Association), [*c.*1940].

(c)   Reprint. Bath: Chivers, 1974.

B6   *The Fife and Angus Annual*. 1935.
[extract from] 'Clay' by LGG. (pp. 105-7)

B7   *Masterpiece of Thrills*. Edited by John Gawsworth [Terence I.F. Armstrong]. London: Daily Express Publications, [1936].
'Busman's Holiday' by J. Leslie Mitchell (pp. 37-52); 'Kametis and Evelpis' by J. Leslie Mitchell and Fytton Armstrong (pp. 193-238); 'A Stele from Atlantis' by Lewis Grassic Gibbon (pp. 271-6); 'The Road to Freedom' by J. Leslie Mitchell (pp. 463-71); 'The Woman of Leadenhall Street' by Lewis Grassic Gibbon (pp. 567-86); 'Lost Tribes' by J. Leslie Mitchell (pp. 623-30); 'First and Last Woman' by Lewis Grassic Gibbon (pp. 729-35).

B8   *A Book of Scotland*. Edited by G.F. Maine. London: Collins, 1950.
'Loch Lomond' (extract from *Scottish Scene*); 'Snip the Willow' (extract from *Sunset Song*); 'An Aberdeen High Tea' (extract from *Scottish Scene*) by LGG. (pp. 49, 172-3, 309-10).

B9   *Scottish Short Stories*. Edited by Fred Urquhart. 3rd revised edition. London: Faber and Faber, 1956.
'Smeddum'. (pp. 127-37)

B10   *Scottish Short Stories*. Edited by J.M. Reid. London: Oxford University Press, 1963. (World's Classics)
'Smeddum'. (pp. 226-37)

C: CONTRIBUTIONS TO PERIODICALS AND NEWSPAPERS

1924

C1 'Siva Plays the Game' (JLM story). *T.P.'s and Cassell's Weekly* 18 October 1924, pp. 849-50.

1929

C2 'For Ten's Sake'(JLM story). *The Cornhill* 66, January 1929, pp. 38-51.

C3 'One Man with a Dream' (JLM story). *The Cornhill* 66, May 1929, pp. 589-600. (As 'Revolt' in *Persian Dawns, Egyptian Nights.*)

C4 'I: He Who Seeks' (JLM story). *The Cornhill* 67, July 1929, pp. 97-107.

C5 'II: The Epic' (JLM story). *The Cornhill* 67, August 1929, pp. 160-70.

C6 'III: The Road' (JLM story). *The Cornhill* 67, September 1929, pp. 341-52. (As 'The Lost Prophetess' in *The Calends of Cairo.*)

C7 'IV: A Volcano in the Moon' (JLM story). *The Cornhill* 67, October 1929, pp. 463-76.

C8 'V: The Life and Death of Elia Constantinidos' (JLM story). *The Cornhill* 67, November 1929, pp. 513-26.

C9 'VI: Cockcrow' (JLM story). *The Cornhill* 67, December 1929, pp. 641-54.

1930

C10 'VII: Gift of the River' (JLM story). *The Cornhill* 68, January 1930, pp. 17-30.

C11 'VIII: East is West' (JLM story). *The Cornhill* 68, February 1930, pp. 129-43.

C12 'IX: Vernal' (JLM story). *The Cornhill* 68, March 1930, pp. 257-70.

C13 'X: Daybreak' (JLM story). *The Cornhill* 68, April 1930, pp. 385-96.

C14 'XI: It is Written' (JLM story). *The Cornhill* 68, May 1930, pp. 513-26.

C15 'XII: The Passage of the Dawn' (JLM story). *The Cornhill* 68, June 1930, pp. 641-55.
(Note: the roman numerals indicate the story sequence which JLM called *Polychromata*)

C16 'The End of the Maya Old Empire' (JLM article). *Antiquity* 4:15, September 1930, pp. 285-302.

C17 'Yucatan: New Empire Tribes and Culture Waves' (JLM article). *Antiquity* 4:16, December 1930, pp. 438-53.

1931

C18 'The Diffusionist Heresy' (JLM article). *Twentieth Century* 1:1, March 1931, pp. 14-18.

C19 'If You Sleep in the Moonlight' (JLM story). *Reynolds Illustrated News* 15 March 1931, p. 10.

C20 'Siva Plays the Game' (JLM story). *The Millgate* 26:2, April 1931, pp. 405-7.

C21 'Inka and pre-Inka' (JLM article). *Antiquity* 5:18, June 1931, pp. 172-84.

C22 'Roads to Freedom' (JLM story). *The Millgate* 26:2, June 1931, pp. 547-50. (As 'The Road to Freedom' in *Masterpiece of Thrills*.)

C23 'Near Farnboru' (JLM story). *Reynolds Illustrated News* 12 July 1931, pp. 10, 18. (As 'First and Last Woman' by LGG in *Masterpiece of Thrills*.)

C24 'A Footnote to History' (JLM story). *The Cornhill* 71, August 1931, pp. 195-212. (As 'The Lovers' in *Persian Dawns, Egyptian Nights*.)

C25 'The Lost Constituent' (JLM story). *The Cornhill* 71, September 1931, pp. 355-64.

C26 'The Refugees' (JLM story). *The Millgate* 27:1, October 1931, pp. 33-8. (As 'Amber in Cold Sea' in *Persian Dawns, Egyptian Nights*.)

C27 'The Floods of Spring' (JLM story). *The Cornhill* 71, November 1931, pp. 623-38.

C28 'Thermopylae' (JLM story). *The Cornhill* 71, December 1931, pp. 684-703. (As 'Dienekes' Dream' in *Persian Dawns, Egyptian Nights*.)

1932

C29 'The Prince's Placenta and Prometheus as God' (JLM article). *Twentieth Century* 2:12, February 1932, pp. 16-18.

C30 'William James Perry: A Revolutionary Anthropologist' (JLM article). *The Millgate* 27, 1932, pp. 323-6.

C31 'O Mistress Mine!' (JLM story). *The Millgate* 27:2, May 1932, pp. 491-4.

C32 'The Buddha of America' (JLM article). *The Cornhill* 72, May 1932, pp. 595-604.

C33 'The Last Ogre' (JLM story). *The Cornhill* 72, June 1932, pp. 699-711.

C34 'Cartaphilus' (JLM story). *The Cornhill* 73, September 1932, pp. 344-57.

C35 '*Sunset Song*: Author's Reply to the Editor' (LGG). *Fife Herald and Journal* 28 September 1932, p. 2.

C36 'Greenden' (LGG story). *Scots Magazine* December 1932, pp. 168-76.

1933

C37 'Smeddum' (LGG story). *Scots Magazine* January 1933, pp. 248-56.

C38 'Dawn in Alarlu' (JLM story). *The Cornhill* 74, February 1933, pp. 185-97.

C39 'Clay' (LGG story). *Scots Magazine* February 1933, pp. 329-39.

C40 'Sim' (LGG story). *The Free Man* 2:19, 10 June 1933, pp. 5-7.

C41 'Book Reviews: Fiction – Scots Novels of the Half-Year' (LGG). *The Free Man* 2:21, 24 June 1933, p. 7.

C42 'Segget: A Scots Village' (LGG article). *The Free Man* 2:23, 8 July 1933, pp. 6-7.

C43 'Grieve – Scotsman' (JLM article). *The Free Man* 2, 9 September 1933, p. 7.

C44 'Book Reviews – Man and the Universe' (JLM) [and] 'In Oor Kailyard' (LGG). *The Free Man* 2:36, 7 October 1933, p. 9.

1934

C45 *Cloud Howe* (LGG). *Aberdeen Bon Accord and Northern Pictorial* 2 February - 27 April 1934.
     (Note: serialisation of condensed version of novel)

C46 '"Canting Humbug!" Mearns Author's Reply to Burns Orator' (LGG). *Mearns Leader and Kincardineshire Mail* 8 February 1934, p. 1.

C47 *Cloud Howe* (LGG). *Mearns Leader and Kincardineshire Mail* 8 February - 26 April 1934.
     (Note: serialisation of condensed version of novel)

C48 'Lost Tribe' (JLM story). *The Millgate* 29:1, January 1934, pp. 199-202. (As 'Lost Tribes' in *Masterpiece of Thrills*.)

C49 'New Novels: Mr Barke and Others' (LGG). *The Free Man* 3, 24 February 1934, p. 6.

C50 '"I Kent his Faither!" A Scots Writer Reviews His Reviewers' (LGG). *Glasgow Evening News* (Saturday Supplement) 24 February 1934, p. 1.

C51 'News of Battle: Queries for Mr Whyte' (LGG). *The Free Man* 3, 17 March 1934, p. 9.

1935

C52 'Controversy: Writers' International (British Section)' (LGG article). *Left Review* 1, February 1935, pp. 179-80.

C53 'Religions of Ancient Mexico' (JLM article). *Religions* no. 13, October 1935, pp. 11-20.

C54 'A Novelist Looks at the Cinema' (LGG article) *Cinema Quarterly* 3:2, Winter 1935, pp. 81-5.

D: MANUSCRIPTS

D1   National Library of Scotland
      Acc. 7900

D2   Edinburgh University Library
      MS 2955-11
      MS Gen 1929

D3   Mitchell Library, Glasgow
      Barke Papers, Box 4

D4   Aberdeen University Library
      MS 2337
      (There is also material in Stirling University Library and the University
      of Illinois at Urbana)

E: SELECTED CRITICAL AND BIOGRAPHICAL WORKS

Books
Campbell, Ian, *Lewis Grassic Gibbon.* Edinburgh: Scottish Academic Press,
      1985.
Gifford, Douglas, *Neil M. Gunn & Lewis Grassic Gibbon.* Edinburgh: Oliver
      & Boyd, 1983.
Malcolm, William K., *A Blasphemer and Reformer: A Study of James Leslie
      Mitchell/Lewis Grassic Gibbon.* Aberdeen: Aberdeen University Press,
      1984.
Munro, Ian S., *Leslie Mitchell: Lewis Grassic Gibbon.* Edinburgh: Oliver &
      Boyd, 1966.
Whitfield, Peter, *Grassic Gibbon and his World.* Aberdeen: Aberdeen Journals,
      1994.
Young, Douglas F., *Beyond the Sunset: A Study of James Leslie Mitchell (Lewis
      Grassic Gibbon).* Aberdeen: Impulse Publications, 1973.
Young, Douglas F., *Lewis Grassic Gibbon's Sunset Song.* Aberdeen: ASLS,
      1986. (Scotnotes No. 1)
Zagratzki, Uwe, *Libertare und utopische Tendenzen im Erzahlwerk James Leslie
      Mitchells (Lewis Grassic Gibbons).* Frankurt a.M.: Peter Lang 1991.

University Theses

Figueroa, Ricardo A., *The Model of Society in Lewis Grassic Gibbon's Writings.*
    Glasgow, 1984.

Idle, Jeremy, *Race and Nationality in the Work of James Leslie Mitchell/Lewis
    Grassic Gibbon.* Edinburgh, 1994.

Kerr, Christine, *Lewis Grassic Gibbon: Gender, Sex and Sexualities.* Sussex,
    2002.

McGrath, Michael J., *James Leslie Mitchell (Lewis Grassic Gibbon): A Study
    in Politics and Ideas in Relation to his Life and Work.* Edinburgh, 1983.

Malcolm, William K., *The Novels and Stories of James Leslie Mitchell (Lewis
    Grassic Gibbon) in the Light of his Political and Philosophical Thinking.*
    Aberdeen, 1982.

Watt, Gordon A.J., *Paths to Utopia – A Study of the Fiction of James Leslie
    Mitchell (Lewis Grassic Gibbon).* Exeter, 1977.

Young, Douglas F., *The Relevance of the Non-Fiction Works to the Novels of
    Lewis Grassic Gibbon.* Aberdeen, 1969.

Articles

Aitken, W.R., 'The Inscriptions in *Sunset Song'. The Bibliotheck* 8, 1976,
    pp. 1-6.

Barke, James, 'Lewis Grassic Gibbon'. *Left Review* 2:5, February 1936,
    pp. 220-5.

Bell, Ian, 'Lewis Grassic Gibbon's Revolutionary Romanticism'. *Scottish
    Studies* 10, 1990, pp. 257-69.

Brown, Ivor, 'Lewis Grassic Gibbon: Tragic Loss to Literature'. *Observer* 10
    February 1935, p. 13.

Brown, Oliver, 'Sunset Song, sunset echo'. *New Saltire* December 1962,
    pp. 26-32.

Burns, John, 'Lewis Grassic Gibbon and *A Scots Quair. Chapman* 23-24,
    Spring 1979, pp. 22-27.

Burton, Deirdre, 'A Feminist Reading of Lewis Grassic Gibbon's *A Scots
    Quair*' in *The British Working-Class Novel in the Twentieth Century*,
    edited by Jeremy Hawthorn (London: Edward Arnold).

Caird, James B., 'Lewis Grassic Gibbon and his Contribution to the
    Scottish Novel' in *Essays in Literature*, edited by John Murray
    (Edinburgh: Oliver & Boyd, 1936), pp. 139-53.

Calder, Angus, 'A Mania for Self-Reliance: Grassic Gibbon's *Scots Quair*' in
    The Uses of Fiction, edited by Douglas Jefferson and Graham Martin
    (Milton Keynes: Open University, 1982), pp. 99-113.

Campbell, Ian, 'The Science Fiction of John [sic] Leslie Mitchell'.

Extrapolation 16, 1974, pp. 53-63.

Campbell, Ian, 'Chris Caledonia: The Search for an Identity'. *Scottish Literary Journal* 1:2, December 1974, pp. 45-57.

Campbell, Ian, 'James Leslie Mitchell's *Spartacus*: A Novel of Rebellion'. *Scottish Literary Journal* 5:1, May 1978, pp. 53-60.

Campbell, Ian, 'Gibbon and MacDiarmid in the German Democratic Republic'. *Books in Scotland* 6, Winter 1979-80, pp. 6-7.

Campbell, Ian, 'Lewis Grassic Gibbon'. *Books in Scotland* 11, Winter 1982-3, pp. 8-10.

Campbell, Ian, 'Lewis Grassic Gibbon Correspondence: The Background and a Checklist'. *The Bibliotheck* 12:2, 1984, pp. 46-57.

Campbell, Ian, 'A Tribute that Never Was: The Plan for a Lewis Grassic Gibbon Festschrift'. *Studies in Scottish Literature* 20, 1985, pp. 219-30.

Campbell, Ian, 'Gibbon and MacDiarmid at Play: The Evolution of *Scottish Scene*'. *The Bibliotheck* 13:2, 1986, pp. 46-55.

Campbell, Ian, 'Lewis Grassic Gibbon and the Mearns' in *A Sense of Place: Studies in Scottish Local History*, edited by Graeme Cruikshank (Edinburgh, 1988), pp. 15-26.

Campbell, Ian, 'The Grassic Gibbon Style'. *Scottish Studies* 10, 1990, pp. 271-87.

Campbell, Ian, 'Son of the Mearns'. *Books in Scotland* 40, Winter 1991, pp. 5-6.

Campbell, Ian, 'The Grassic Gibbon Centre'. *Education in the North* NS 1, Winter 1993, pp. 76-84.

Campbell, Ian, 'Lewis Grassic Gibbon: Novelist, social historian and critic' in *Discovering Scottish Writers*, edited by Alan Reid and Brian Osborne (Edinburgh: Scottish Cultural Press and Scottish Library Association, 1997), pp. 38-39.

Clough, R.F., '*A Scots Quair*: Ewan's Rejection of Ellen'. *Scottish Literary Journal* 20:2, November 1993, pp. 41-48.

Crossland, J. Brian, 'Lewis Grassic Gibbon'. *Glasgow Herald* 20 April 1968.

Cruikshank, Helen B., 'Lewis Grassic Gibbon: A Personal Note'. *British Weekly* 14 February 1935, p. 405.

Cruikshank, Helen B., 'Mearns Memory: A Fellow-countryman's View of Lewis Grassic Gibbon'. *Scots Magazine* February 1939, pp. 350-4.

D'Arcy, Julian Meldon, 'Chris Guthrie, Ellen Johns and the Two Ewan Tavendales: Significant Parallels in *A Scots Quair*'. *Scottish Literary Journal* 23:1, May 1996, pp. 42-49.

Dixon, Keith, 'Lewis Grassic Gibbon, Scotland and Nationalism'. *Scottish Studies* 8, 1989, pp. 201-11.

Dixon, Keith, 'Rough Edges: The Feminist Representation of Women in the Writing of Lewis Grassic Gibbon'. *Scottish Studies* 10, 1990, pp. 289-301.

Dixon, Keith, 'Letting the Side Down: some remarks on James Leslie Mitchell's vision of history'. *Études Écossaises Grenoble* 1, pp. 273-81.

Everill, Elizabeth, 'Literary Landscapes'. *Scottish Field* November 1998, pp. 38-42.

Graham, Cuthbert, 'Lewis Grassic Gibbon'. *Aberdeen University Review* 29:85, Winter 1941, pp. 4-16.

Graham, Cuthbert, The Man who Wrote *Cloud Howe*: Lewis Grassic Gibbon – An Intimate Sketch'. *Aberdeen Bon-Accord* 2 February 1934, p. 9.

Graham, Cuthbert, 'Scotland Mourns Lewis Grassic Gibbon'. *The Mearns Leader* 14 February 1935, p. 3.

Graham, Cuthbert, 'The Man who Saw the Morning Star'. *Scots Magazine* August 1966, pp. 417-20.

Gray, Alexander, 'His School Essays Even Baffled the Rector'. *People's Journal* 16 May 1964, p. 13.

Grieve, C.M., 'Contemporary Scottish Studies I: Lewis Grassic Gibbon'. *The Free Man* 29 July 1933, p. 7.

Grieve, C.M. (as Hugh MacDiarmid), 'Lewis Grassic Gibbon: 1901-1935'. *Our Time* 2:2, September 1948, pp. 307-8.

Grieve, C.M. (as Hugh MacDiarmid), 'Lewis Grassic Gibbon: James Leslie Mitchell'. *Scottish Art and Letters* 2, Spring 1946, pp. 39-44. (Reprinted in *The Uncanny Scot: A Selection of Prose*, edited by Kenneth Buthlay [London: MacGibbon & Kee, 1968], pp. 154-63)

Grieve, C.M. (as Hugh MacDiarmid), 'Lewis Grassic Gibbon' in *Selected Essays of Hugh MacDiarmid*, edited by Duncan Glen (London: Cape, 1969), pp. 188-96.

Idle, Jeremy, 'The Bowdlerisation of Lewis Grassic Gibbon's *A Scots Quair*'. *The Bibliotheck* 17:1-3, 1990-1, pp. 63-69.

Johnson, Roy, 'Lewis Grassic Gibbon and *A Scots Quair*: Politics in the Novel'. *Renaissance and Modern Studies* 20, 1976, pp. 39-53.

Katin, Louis, 'Author of *Sunset Song*'. *Glasgow Evening News* 16 February 1933, p. 6.

Kocmanova, Jessie, '*A Scots Quair* and its Relevance to the Scottish Proletarian Struggle of the 1930s' in *English Literature and the Working Class*, edited by Francisco Garcia Tortosa and Ramon Lopez Ortega (Seville, 1980), pp. 77-93.

Lindsay, Jack, 'A Great Scots Novelist: The Cycle of Industrialisation'. *Our Time* 5:12, July 1946, pp. 257-8.

Low, Donald A., 'A Possible Source for Lewis Grassic Gibbon's *Sunset Song*'. *Studies in Scottish Literature* 8, 1970-1, p.272.

Macaree, David, 'Myth and Allegory in Lewis Grassic Gibbon's *A Scots Quair*'. *Studies in Scottish Literature* 2:1, 1964, pp.45-55.

MacGillivray, Alan, 'Obituary: Christine (Chris) Guthrie: (1896-1999)'. *ScotLit* 21, Winter 1999/2000, pp.1-3.

McGrath, Michael J., 'Hugh MacDiarmid and Lewis Grassic Gibbon: A Comparison of Political and Cultural Attitudes'. *New Edinburgh Review* 40, February 1978, pp.8-12.

Maitland, Frank, 'Lewis Grassic Gibbon'. *The Adelphi* 10:1, April 1935, pp.53-55.

Manson, John, 'Hugh MacDiarmid and Lewis Grassic Gibbon's Politics'. *Cencrastus* 50, Winter 1994/5, pp.39-42.

Manson, John, 'Grassic Gibbon's Glasgow'. *Scottish Labour History Review* 10, Winter 1996/Spring 1997, pp.12-13.

Milner, Ian, 'An Estimation of Lewis Grassic Gibbon's *A Scots Quair*'. *Marxist Quarterly* 1:4, October 1954, pp.207-18.

Mitchell, Mrs J. Leslie, 'Lewis Grassic Gibbon: By His Wife'. *New Scot* 4:6, June 1948, pp.16-17.

Montgomerie, William, 'The Brown God: L.G. Gibbon's Trilogy *A Scots Quair*'. *Scots Magazine* December 1945, pp.213-23.

Morton, Brian, 'Lewis Grassic Gibbon and the Heroine of *A Scots Quair*'. *Edda* 80:4, 1980, pp.193-203.

Muir, Edwin, 'Lewis Grassic Gibbon (J. Leslie Mitchell): an appreciation'. *Scottish Standard* March 1935, pp.23-24.

Munro, Ian S., 'James Leslie Mitchell: Lewis Grassic Gibbon' in *Two Essays* (Edinburgh: National Library of Scotland, 1971), pp.8-15.

Murray, Isobel, 'Action and Narrative Stance in *A Scots Quair*' in *Literature of the North*, edited by David Hewitt and Michael Spiller (Aberdeen: AUP, 1983), pp.109-20.

Murray, Isobel and Tait, Bob, 'Lewis Grassic Gibbon: *A Scots Quair*' in *Ten Modern Scottish Novels*, (Aberdeen: AUP, 1984), pp.10-31.

Murray, Isobel, 'Selves, Names and Roles: Willa Muir's *Imagined Corners* offers some inspiration for *A Scots Quair*'. *Scottish Literary Journal* 21:1, May 1994, pp.56-64.

Norquay, Glenda, 'Voices in Time: *A Scots Quair*'. *Scottish Literary Journal* 11:1, May 1984, pp.57-68.

Ortega, Ramon Lopez, 'Language and Point of View in Lewis Grassic Gibbon's *A Scots Quair*'. *Studies in Scottish Literature* 16, 1981, pp.148-59.

Rob, Enid, 'A Scottish Humanist: A Profile of Lewis Grassic Gibbon'. *The Humanist* 75:7, July 1960, pp. 208-11.

Romanova, Titiana, 'The Images of *A Scots Quair*'. Perm University Press, 1997, pp. 45-54.

Romanova, Titiana, 'Irony of the Narrator in *Cloud Howe*'. Perm University Press, 1999, pp. 129-39.

Roskies, D.M.E., 'Language, Class and Radical Perspective in *A Scots Quair*'. *Zeitschrift fur Anglistik und Amerikanistik* 29:2, 1981, pp. 142-53.

Roskies, D.M.E., 'Lewis Grassic Gibbon and *A Scots Quair*: Ideology, Literary Form and Social History'. *Southern Review* 15:2, pp. 178-204.

Scobie, Brian, 'Lewis Grassic Gibbon' in *1936: The Sociology of Literature – Practices of Literature and Politics*, vol. 2, edited by F. Barker et al (Colchester: University of Essex Press, 1979), pp. 134-42.

Sharma, K.N., 'Spartacus: Variations on a Theme' in *Modern Studies and Other Essays*, edited by R.C. Prasad and A.K. Sharma (New Delhi: Vikas Publishing, 1987).

Simpson, Ian J., 'Lewis Grassic Gibbon'. *Scottish Educational Journal* 2 April 1954, pp. 222-3.

Thomaneck, J.K.A., '*A Scots Quair* in East Germany'. *Scottish Literary Journal* 3:1, July 1976, pp. 62-66.

Thomson, Mary, 'My Friend Lewis Grassic Gibbon'. *Scots Magazine* 131:6, September 1989, pp. 602-7.

Trengrove, Graham, 'Who is You? Grammar and Grassic Gibbon'. *Scottish Literary Journal* 2:2, December 1975, pp. 47-61.

Valentine, Mark, 'Lewis Grassic Gibbon'. *Book and Magazine Collector* 203, February 2001, pp. 40-50.

Vettese, Raymond, 'Lewis Grassic Gibbon and Diffusionism'. *Epoch* 9, December 1996, pp. 15-17.

Wagner, Geoffrey, '"The Greatest Since Galt": Lewis Grassic Gibbon'. *Essays in Criticism* 2:3, July 1952, pp. 295-310.

Wagner, Geoffrey, 'Lewis Grassic Gibbon'. *Aberdeen University Review* 34:107, Autumn 1952, pp. 326-37.

Wagner, Geoffrey, 'The Other Grassic Gibbon'. *Saltire Review* 2:5, Autumn 1955, pp. 33-41.

Webster, Jack, 'Literary Journeys: Back to Blaewearie'. *Scottish Review* 24, Christmas 2000, pp. 20-29.

Welfare, Humphrey, 'Standing Stones in Kinraddie: The Archaeology of *A Scots Quair*'. *Northern Archaeology* 17-18, 1999, pp. 187-90.

Whittington, Graeme, 'The Regionalisation of Lewis Grassic Gibbon'. *Scottish Geographical Magazine* 90, 1974, pp. 75-84.

Wilson, Patricia, 'Freedom and God: Some Implications of the Key Speech in *A Scots Quair*'. *Scottish Literary Journal* 7:2, December 1980, pp.55-79.
Young, Douglas, 'A Major Novelist'. *Library Review* 20:7, Autumn 1966, pp.502-5.
Young, Douglas F., 'Lewis Grassic Gibbon'. *Scottish Review* 14, May 1979, pp.34-40.
Young, Douglas F., 'Lewis Grassic Gibbon's *Sunset Song*: a commentary with readings'. Glasgow: Jordanhill College, 1982. (sound cassette)
Young, Douglas F., 'Nine back from the unknown'. *The Speak of the Place* 2:3, Autumn 2000, pp.2-3.
Zagratzki, Uwe, 'Lewis Grassic Gibbon's Free Narratives: A Homage to the Free Spirit'. *Études Écossaises* 3, 1996, pp.149-58.
Zagratzki, Uwe, '"Mitchellizing/Gibbonizing" – Political Correctness Revisited'. *The Speak of the Place* 2:1, Autumn 1999, p.2.

F: BIBLIOGRAPHY

F1   Geoffrey Wagner, 'James Leslie Mitchell/Lewis Grassic Gibbon'. *The Bibliotheck* 1:1, 1956, pp.3-21.
F2   W.R. Aitken, 'Further Notes on the Bibliography of James Leslie Mitchell/Lewis Grassic Gibbon'. *The Bibliotheck* 1:2, 1957, pp.34-35.
F3   Douglas F. Young, 'James Leslie Mitchell/Lewis Grassic Gibbon: A Chronological Checklist: Additions I'. *The Bibliotheck* 5:5, 1969, pp.169-73.
F4   James Kidd, 'James Leslie Mitchell/Lewis Grassic Gibbon: A Chronological Checklist: Additions II'. *The Bibliotheck* 5:5, 1969, pp.174-7.
F5   William K. Malcolm, 'James Leslie Mitchell/Lewis Grassic Gibbon Checklist: Additions III'. *The Bibliotheck* 11:6, 1983, pp.149-56.
F6   William K. Malcolm, 'Bibliography' in his *A Blasphemer and Reformer* (Aberdeen: Aberdeen University Press, 1984), pp.200-3.
F7   Ian Campbell, 'Lewis Grassic Gibbon Correspondence: A Background and Checklist'. *The Bibliotheck* 12:1, 1984, pp.46-57.
F8   William K. Malcolm, 'Critical Works on James Leslie Mitchell/Lewis Grassic Gibbon: A Bibliography'. Database at Grassic Gibbon Centre, Arbuthnott. Created August 2000 and updated regularly. **www.grassicgibbon.com**

Contributors

Valentina Bold is Senior Lecturer in Scottish Studies at the University of Glasgow Crichton Campus, Dumfries, and is the editor of *Smeddum: A Lewis Grassic Gibbon Anthology*, published in the Canongate Classics series in 2001. She is currently editing James Hogg's *The Brownie of Bodsbeck* for the Stirling/South Carolina Hogg edition and working on a book on Hogg and the autodidactic tradition in Scottish Poetry.

David Borthwick was born in Ardersier, Inverness-shire. He is currently completing his doctoral thesis at the University of Aberdeen. The title of his thesis is 'Searching for Voices: Maintaining the Self in the Contemporary Scottish Novel'. Previous research includes a dissertation on the short fiction of George Mackay Brown.

Ian Campbell was born in Lausanne and awarded his doctorate at the University of Edinburgh. His father was minister of the parish next to Kinraddie and he was introduced to the work of Lewis Grassic Gibbon as a schoolboy in Stonehaven, the beginning of an interest which has continued to the present day. His *Lewis Grassic Gibbon* was published by Scottish Academic Press in 1985 and he is currently preparing a re-issue of Gibbon/Mitchell's fiction (apart from the *Quair*) for Birlinn Books, a project begun with Polygon. As a friend of the Mitchell family, he has worked to bring Mitchell's archive to the National Library of Scotland and to support the Centre in Arbuthnott.

Gerard Carruthers lectures in the Department of Scottish Literature at the University of Glasgow. He is co-editor of *English Romanticism and the Celtic World* (Cambridge University Press, 2003) and has written over thirty essays on a range of eighteenth- and twentieth-century topics.

John Corbett is a Senior Lecturer in English Language at the University of Glasgow. He is the author of *Language and Scottish Literature* (1997) and *Written in the Language of the Scottish Nation* (1999). With J. Derrick McClure and Jane Stuart-Smith, he co-edited *The Edinburgh Companion to Scots* (2003).

Keith Dixon is Professor of Anglophone Studies at Lumière University, Lyons, and editor of *Études Écossaises* (published by Université Stendhal, Grenoble). He is also Series Editor of La Bibliothèque Écossaise (Éditions Anne-Marie Métailié in Paris). He has been writing about modern Scottish culture and politics for the last twenty-five years.

Sarah M. Dunnigan is Lecturer in English Literature at the University of Edinburgh. She is the author of *Eros and Poetry at the Courts of Mary Queen of Scots and James VI* (Palgrave, 2002), and of articles on medieval and Renaissance Scottish literature, Renaissance women's writing, and twentieth-century Scottish writing. She is a co-editor of *Scottish Literature* (2002) and of the forthcoming collection, *Woman and the Feminine in Medieval and Early Modern Scottish Writing*.

Catriona M. Low was born and brought up in Aberdeenshire. She graduated from the University of Aberdeen in 1995 with an MA in English and Scottish Literature and currently works in administration.

Alison Lumsden was appointed as Lecturer in the School of English and Film Studies at the University of Aberdeen after working for many years as research fellow for The Edinburgh Edition of the Waverley Novels. She is co-editor of Walter Scott's *The Pirate* and *The Heart of Mid-Lothian* and is currently editing *Peveril of the Peak*. She is also interested in Scottish women's writing; she has published on Nan Shepherd and is co-editor of *Contemporary Scottish Women's Writing* (2001).

William K. Malcolm has spent twenty-five years engaged in research on James Leslie Mitchell. His doctoral thesis from the University of Aberdeen was published in 1984 as *A Blasphemer & Reformer: A Study of James Leslie Mitchell/Lewis Grassic Gibbon*. A director of The Grassic Gibbon Centre at Arbuthnott, he edits the Centre's newsletter, *The Speak of the Place*. He has recently finished editing a miscellany of Mitchell's uncollected writings, including correspondence, notebooks, essays and manuscripts.

Margery Palmer McCulloch is a graduate of the Universities of London and Glasgow. She has published widely on twentieth-century Scottish Literature, including critical studies of Edwin Muir and Neil M. Gunn, and is currently working on a revaluation of the literature and criticism of the interwar 'Scottish Renaissance' period. She has contributed many articles on writing by women to books and journals and her study guide to Liz

Lochhead's *Mary Queen of Scots Got Her Head Chopped Off* was published in 2000. She teaches Scottish Literature at the University of Glasgow.

Isobel Murray is Professor in Modern Scottish Literature at the University of Aberdeen. In 1984 she published *Ten Modern Scottish Novels* with her husband Bob Tait and with him began the series of in-depth interviews with Scottish writers, *Scottish Writers Talking*. She has produced editions of Naomi Mitchison, Robin Jenkins and Jessie Kesson, and her biography of Kesson, *Jessie Kesson: Writing Her Life* was published in 2000. She is an Associate Editor of the *New Dictionary of National Biography* and a Vice-President of the Association for Scottish Literary Studies.

Hamish Whyte is a poet, editor, translator and former librarian. He has compiled bibliographies of Edwin Morgan and Liz Lochhead and is currently an Honorary Research Fellow in the Department of Scottish Literature, University of Glasgow. Among the books he has edited are *Noise and Smoky Breath: An Illustrated Anthology of Glasgow Poems 1900-1983*, *Mungo's Tongues: Glasgow Poems 1630-1990* and *An Arran Anthology*. He also runs Mariscat Press, publishing contemporary poetry.

Isabella Williamson is Manager of the Grassic Gibbon Centre at Arbuthnott and was one of a small group of people who were instrumental in setting up the Centre, the aim of which is to promote the life and work of Lewis Grassic Gibbon and to create local employment. She was born in Nairn and brought up in Lossiemouth, but has now lived for nearly thirty years in Arbuthnott, where she is married to a farmer. In addition to running the Grassic Gibbon Centre, she has found time to study for an MBA with the Open University Business School.

Index

Labour movement, *see* politics
language
  Braid Scots, 89, 91, 102
  equality of dialogue, 16
  foreignising strategies, 24, 50, 90,
    in *Sunset Song*, 93-94
    in *Spartacus*, 94-96
  linguistic and poetic strategies in
    A Scots Quair, 10, 16, 23-24, 43,
    50-51
  see also under Lewis Grassic
    Gibbon, *A Scots Quair*
  literary Scots, 23, 91
  orality, 24, 29, 49, 91-92
  prose style and sexual violence, 21,
    100-01
  prose style of *Sunset Song*, 89, 90-94
  prose style of *Spartacus*, 94-98
  radical writing, 43, 49
  and disruptive strategies, 49, 50
  rhythm in prose, 24, 29, 49, 91,
    92, 93-94, 97-99
  self-referring 'you', 73, 91-92
  synthetic Scots, 91
  urban dialect, 36, 102
  examples of, 64-74 *passim*
  writers from 'Scotshire', 18
Lawrence, D.H., 15, 116
Left Review, 80, 88
Lenin, Vladimir Illitch, 38, 119, 140
Liebknecht, Karl and Rosa
  Luxembourg, 83, 119
Linklater, Eric, 19, 144
Listener, for Edwin Muir on *Cloud
  Howe*, 32, 39
littérature engagée, 22, 79-81, 87, 88
London Burns Club, 17
Low, J.T. on *Sunset Song*, 138

Macafee, Caroline, on use of Scots in
  Sunset Song, 93, 102, 103
MacAulay, Ronald, on urban dialect,
  102
MacColla, Fionn, prose style of, 90

MacDiarmid, Hugh (C.M. Grieve),
  9, 10, 15, 16, 17, 18, 19, 80, 88,
  102, 118, 121, 123, 126, 143,
  144, 146, 147
  A Drunk Man Looks at the Thistle,
    17, 34
  'Ballad of the General Strike', 34
  and Caledonian Antisyzygy, 139
  Contemporary Scottish Studies, 26
  'First Hymn to Lenin', 38
  'The Innumerable Christ', 95, 118
  'Lourd on my Hert', 139, 147
  misrepresentation of Gibbon's
    politics, 138
  and Scots language, 10, 89, 91
  Scottish Scene, 9, 12, 139, 146
  'Second Hymn to Lenin', 17
MacDonald, Ramsay,
  use of language, 90,
  politics of, 140-41
Mackenzie, Compton, 15, 18, 25,
  127, 144
McLean, Duncan, on Lewis Grassic
  Gibbon, 9, 11
McQueen, John, Caledonian
  Antisyzygy and the Scottish
  Enlightenment, 131, 135
Macpherson, James and *Ossian* texts,
  23, 130, 131

Malcolm, William, 12, 88, 111, 114
March, Cristie L., *Rewriting Scotland*,
  12
Marx, Karl and historical process, 31
  see also politics
Mary Queen of Scots, 76, 125
Massingham, H.G., and prose style,
  89, 99
Maxton, James, 127
Mayan civilisation, 80
Mearns Leader, Gibbon's letter to,
  136, 146
medieval makars, 76, 78, 87
Millar, Hugh, 128

Proust, Marcel, 28
Pushkin, A.S., 137

Religion and its representation, 33,
    34, 35,142
    biblical references, 31, 34, 76
    Christ and Christianity, 84-85,
    118, 119, 120, 133
    Christian socialism, 32, 33, 38
Rig-Veda, 76
Roman Empire, 83
romanticism, 15

Sassi, Carla, on Scottishness in
    Grassic Gibbon's Fiction, 49, 52
Schiller, Friedrich and Mary Stuart, 125
Scott, Sir Walter, 125, 131
Scott, William Robert, on Francis
    Hutcheson, 135
Scottish ballads, 116
Scottish Enlightenment, 124-33 *passim*
    and Adam Ferguson, 125
    and David Hume, 125
    Francis Hutcheson and Gibbon's
    'Religion', 133, 135
    and Jacobitism, 125, 126
    and Lewis Grassic Gibbon, 20, 23,
    124-33, 134-35
    and Thomas Reid, 131
    and William Robertson, 125, 134
    Adam Smith, *Theory of Moral
    Sentiments*, 125-26, 128, 129, 134
    and William Tytler, 125
Scottish Farmer, 138
Scottish PEN, 19
Scottish Renaissance, 32, 49, 124
    and Lewis Grassic Gibbon, 15-19,
    32-33, 143, 144
    self-education in Gibbon,
    MacDiarmid and Muir, 16
Shepherd, Nan, 17, 21
    The Quarry Wood, 55, 56-57, 59-60
Smith, Grafton Elliot, and
    Diffusionism, 145

Smith, G. Gregory, 139, 147, *see also*
    Caledonian Antisyzygy
Smith, William Robertson, 128
Soutar, William, 116
Spartacus and his representation, 83,
    84, 85, 120
    see also Spartacus
Spartacists in Germany, 83
Spence, Lewis, 19
Spengler, Oswald, 31
Stevenson, Robert Louis, 116, 122
Stuart, Muriel, 19

Thomson, George Malcolm, 17, 25, 144
Trengrove, Graham, on grammar and
    Grassic Gibbon, 74, 102, 113
Tulloch, Graham, on language of
    Sunset Song, 94, 102, 103
Tweed, Dorothy, on *Spartacus*, 82

Victorian age, 15
Voltaire, François-Marie, 83

Wallace, William, 140
Wells, H.G., 32
Welsh, Irvine, and Lewis Grassic
    Gibbon, 21, 23, 64-74
    'A Smart Cunt', 70
    The Acid House, 75
    Marabou Stork Nightmares, 66-67,
    69-70, 75
    Trainspotting, 69, 70, 72-73, 75
Whalsay, 17, 19
White, Gilbert, and prose style, 89, 99
Whitfield, Peter, *Grassic Gibbon and
    his World*, 20
Wood, Wendy, 127
Woolf, Virginia, 28
World War One, 15-16, 32, 82, 118,
    138

Young, Douglas, 12, 62

Zagratzki, Uwe, 12